Management for Professionals

The Springer series *Management for Professionals* comprises high-level business and management books for executives. The authors are experienced business professionals and renowned professors who combine scientific background, best practice, and entrepreneurial vision to provide powerful insights into how to achieve business excellence.

Georg Michalik

Co-Creation Mindset

Eight Steps towards the Future of Work

Springer

Georg Michalik
cocreation.com
Greater Zurich Area, Switzerland

ISSN 2192-8096 ISSN 2192-810X (electronic)
Management for Professionals
ISBN 978-3-031-21190-4 ISBN 978-3-031-21191-1 (eBook)
https://doi.org/10.1007/978-3-031-21191-1

This Springer imprint is published by the registered company Springer Nature Switzerland AG
The registered company address is: Gewerbestrasse 11, 6330 Cham, Switzerland

Preface

The department was divided. Alliances had formed between team leaders, and there was open conflict. The head of department had his favourites and others he could not get along with. The assignment was to get to the root of the conflict together with the head of department. The coach started with one-on-one discussions. In the process, he observed that each of the people involved had a credible version of events, but that the different versions did not fit together. How could that be?

If you have ever mediated a dispute yourself, you will probably have experienced something similar. The reason for this is that people construct their own reality. In doing so, they condense the story and arrive at different conclusions. However, an amicable solution is only possible if the parties involved recognise the same reality, are open to other points of view and allow themselves to be convinced.

The more complex the situation, the greater the likelihood that people will construct their own reality and the more difficult it will be to agree on solutions. The VUCA world (Volatile, Uncertain, Complex, Ambiguous) poses this challenge to companies and other organizations. They face a growing gap between an ever-increasing number of options and the need for faster, consensus-based solutions.

Co-creation aims to bridge the gap between possibilities and sustainable solutions. In co-creation, people connect to recognise their shared reality, to set a common goal and, from this, to arrive at actions that are binding for everyone. The idea of co-creation is obvious, and more and more people are of the opinion that only in this way is real problem-solving possible.

Co-creation shows us how to uncover our hidden potentials. Together we can achieve things that would not be possible alone. But this is not always so easy. The book shows how the co-creation mindset and the eight steps of the co-creation process make it possible for people to overcome their single-minded ideas, connect with each other and together make the impossible possible.

The book is full of practical examples of how this has been successfully applied in business. It gives managers, HR professionals and consultants a wealth of ideas on how to awaken the dormant potential of their teams and organizations.

The goal of this book is to clarify what is meant by co-creation and how it is applied. It details an eight-step implementation process and describes how a whole organization can develop a culture and practice of co-creation. The reader will be shown how co-creation differs from other forms of collaboration. Co-creation is more than just a new buzzword. It's a different way of looking at how people work together.

Who is this book addressed to?

This book is addressed to people who are thinking about how they can perceive, decide and act together more effectively and efficiently. This usually happens when they repeatedly come up against limits in their perceptions, decisions and actions.

It is aimed at managers, technical managers and those who are functionally involved in the development of their organization: human resources, corporate development and continuous improvement.

It is also addressed to experts who help guide companies and organizations in their development. For them, it is a storehouse of insights, methods, experiences and proven procedures.

The book is also intended to provide an impetus for all the members of an organization to explore different ways of collaborating and to shape their future together. Teams that work with the Co-Creation Mindset are happier, more creative, faster and more committed in execution.

Q & A

I am often asked to describe co-creation in a sentence: what it is, what it is not, how it works, when to make use of it and so on. This Q & A right at the beginning of the book is intended to answer your basic questions and to pique your curiosity.

What is co-creation?

- Co-creation is a way of jointly shaping the future in organizations.
- Co-creation builds on human connection: knowing yourself, connecting with others and being bound together by a common purpose.
- Co-creation is an attitude: only in openness, trust and transparency is it possible to find sustainable solutions to complex problems.
- Co-creation is a process that leads people to consistent cooperation in eight steps.
- Co-creation can change corporate cultures, leading them out of the old world and into a new one.

When should it be used?

- When organizations are looking for a future-oriented form of value creation.

(continued)

- When a major goal or a vision needs to be defined or implemented.
- When people are no longer working well together.

When should it not be used?

- When the will to share responsibility is not there.
- If there is not enough decision-making authority.

When is co-creation recommended instead of other methods of collaboration?

- Co-creation instead of agile methods: if the relevant structures, processes and attitudes have not yet been clarified, then co-creation is a progressive way to reach that point.
- Co-creation instead of team development: when the development of a team should be linked to a concrete goal.
- Co-creation instead of continuous improvement, lean, kaizen, etc.: when the gap between "is" and "ought" has become so large that it can no longer be bridged by mere corrections.

When are other methods of collaboration recommended instead of co-creation?

- Project management: when it is clear why, how and what is to be done, then it is a matter of implementing this through projects.
- Process management: when the projects have been implemented and it is a matter of integrating them into daily processes.
- Meetings: when co-creation is too exhausting, and you want to switch off for a bit.

How can success be measured?

- An initial measurement is carried out through the Potentialum organizational diagnosis. How successful the measures were can be determined by follow-up measurements.

What does it cost?

- A better question would be: "What is it worth to us if our organization is successful and the people in it are committed?"

(continued)

How long does it take?

- The co-creation kick-off workshop lasts a day and a half. A lot can come out of it.

I hope that you enjoy this book and that it leads you to many insights.

Greater Zurich Area, Switzerland
June 2020

Georg Michalik

Contents

List of Figures

List of Tables

1 Introduction

What exactly is "co-creation"? What lies behind it? Is it just a trend? Is it just an old idea in a new package? How can we use it in our organizations?

Co-creation is more than a trend, more than a method and more than new packaging for received wisdom. Co-creation stands for a change in the way people think, feel and act. It grows out of a feeling of increasing helplessness in the face of problems. Even knowledge and innovation are not always helpful. It often seems that problem-solving is becoming more complicated by the day, not in spite of technological progress, but because of it. Innovation begets innovation, so that the number of options available to us grows exponentially. Technological progress can help us when the appropriate solutions can be found and applied, but keeping track of these and choosing the right ones is becoming increasingly challenging (Harari, 2015). On their own, individuals find this task overwhelming. It takes people who know how to communicate in an appropriate way to find the right paths forward.

How do we manage to figure out what these paths are in our organizations? The external environment is changing faster than ever, and companies have to react just as quickly.

What if we were to succeed in developing corporate cultures in which it was possible to foresee future developments? This would require an understanding of how openness, transparency and permeability can represent a competitive advantage. Companies need to understand that they are harming themselves if they promote a culture in which people work against each other instead of with each other.

This happens, for example, when successes are achieved in one division at the expense of other divisions within the company. It also happens when particularly talented employees are kept in their own division instead of being shown opportunities for development throughout the whole company, or when developers advance their own solutions without coordinating with product development in other divisions. A special term has become established to refer to these phenomena, which mostly emerge at interfaces within companies. In these cases, we speak of "silo thinking". If you are affected by this, you might be asking yourself: "How can

G. Michalik, *Co-Creation Mindset*, Management for Professionals,
https://doi.org/10.1007/978-3-031-21191-1_1

this be? We're all in the same boat! If only everyone else thought and acted for the sake of the whole company, then everything would be better".

This point is obvious and has often occurred to people. But if it is so obvious, why don't we do it? The answer seems quite simple in principle, because on the cognitive level we know what to do. On the emotional level, however, we find social behaviour outside the framework of our existing personal relationships incomparably more difficult. With our friends, families, neighbours and colleagues, as well as at sports clubs and everywhere where we are already connected to people, we willingly engage in social behaviour. With strangers, however, we do not feel connected in the same way, especially if there are many of them, if they are from somewhere else or even if they just look different.

1.1 Being Connected with Each Other

Perhaps some readers will object that this picture is exaggerated and simplistic. Human beings are much more diverse. Of course, this is true. However, a very specific aspect should be emphasised: we tend to view people who have less in common with us with more distance than people with whom we have more in common. The better we know our fellow human beings, the greater our emotional closeness.

Take the following example:

"Malaysia Airlines has recently been in the global media spotlight, due to the loss of contact with Flight MH370 and the search for the missing aircraft. The scheduled flight from Kuala Lumpur to Beijing disappeared from air traffic control surveillance at Subang Airport at 01:21 local time on 8 March 2014. Since then, the Boeing 777 with 227 passengers and twelve crew members [sic] on board has been missing. Despite the most extensive search operation in the history of aviation, neither the flight recorder nor debris have been found so far." (www.welt.de) (n.d.).

I can still remember how I felt, when I first heard the news in 2014: "Hopefully the plane will turn up. Maybe it's just a mistake". Days later, when still no trace of it had been found, it was clear that a major accident had occurred. My thoughts at the time were: "That's terrible. Those poor people and their relatives". However, I must admit that I went back to business as usual after that.

Can you remember what your thoughts and feelings were? How do you feel today about the fact that MH370 is still missing?

Now imagine how you would have been affected by the disaster if some of the basic conditions had been different. How would you have felt, for example, if you had spent your last holiday in Malaysia? How would you have grieved if your best friend or partner had been Malay? Or if there had been a tour group with 20 people from your country on board? Or if it had been a plane belonging to your country's national airline that had disappeared over the Atlantic?

In none of the cases would anything have changed for you personally. Nevertheless, most people would be more deeply affected under these circumstances. That would be true for me, at least. People feel more or less connected to each other depending on how much they have in common. A personal connection is a prerequisite for taking the interests of others seriously.

Of course, there are many individuals who have realised for themselves that it is important to connect with others, without reservation or discrimination. They engage in volunteer work, pursue a socially oriented profession or simply reach out to others, whether they know them or not. Acting in this way is mostly the result of a personal learning experience. Our socialisation in our family and environment also contributes to this learning experience. People need to experience for themselves why it is worthwhile to act socially. Without this experience, we primarily perceive the differences between us, rather than what unites us. Perhaps we were lucky and have been treated well by strangers or perceive others positively ourselves. In this way, we can learn what happens when we respect what unites people. If you feel this way, then you have probably had positive experiences of connection yourself. In doing so, you have been able to recognise the benefits of thinking and acting together with others and made it part of your attitude towards other people.

What does this mean for working together in companies or even beyond system boundaries? How well do we know all our colleagues and what positive experiences have we had with them? According to the view presented above, alienation ought to be greater in large organizations. Employees no longer know each other personally. They see strangers in their own company. If this is the case, then the obvious solution could be to create situationally based emotional closeness, and thus to make cross-departmental thinking, feeling and acting possible.

This is exactly where co-creation comes in. It seeks to enable people to have this positive experience of connecting with others.

When people connect with each other to create something new together, when they use their collective potential to confront complex problems, when they overcome their fears and realise that their fellow human beings are not a threat, then co-creation can take place. For it is together with our fellow human beings—whether we know them or not—that we must overcome the great challenges that face us. Only then can the new, the necessary, come into being in our companies and in the world more generally.

1.2 Finding Solutions Together

Aren't these thoughts also at the foundation of cooperation? You may be asking yourself what distinguishes co-creation from cooperation.

As the neuroscientist Gerald Hüther says: "When people connect, when they develop their potentials together, then something emerges that is more than cooperation. Then we can speak of co-creation" (Hüther, 2016).

The term cooperation is defined in very different ways depending on the context. The Oxford English Dictionary defines it succinctly as: "The action of working together towards the same end, purpose, or effect" (Oxford English Dictionary). The *Gabler Wirtschaftslexikon* refers primarily to cooperation between companies: "Cooperation of varying intensity, duration and purpose between legally independent companies. Cooperation partners can be both competitors, i.e. companies at the same economic level, as well as companies at a different economic level" (Weerth & Mecke, 2018). For cooperation in psychology, the *Spektrum Lexikon der Psychologie* states: "Cooperation has been studied within psychology primarily by social psychology, with the prisoner's dilemma being a frequently studied experimental game situation, the central research paradigm. The prisoner's dilemma is also considered a prototype of a social dilemma in which short-term self-interests are placed above long-term general interests. The influence of social orientation on behaviour was shown in these numerous experiments. The classical approach considers cooperation as a social relationship that exists between the goals of the actors in a particular social situation. A distinction is made between cooperative and competitive situations. In the cooperative situation, the goals of the actors are positively related to each other, whereas in the competitive situation they are negatively related to each other" (Spektrum, 2000).

In cooperation, the focus is thus on the congruence of goals and the balancing of interests. In this process, the actors keep to themselves. In co-creation, the actors come together as a unit and create something in common. This makes co-creation very different from cooperation. Co-creation can be defined as follows: "Co-creation is connecting people and their goals to jointly create solutions".

Let us return to the phenomenon of silo thinking. You may now be wondering whether overcoming silo thinking is not, in essence, simply about working better together within organizations. If we pursue this line of thinking, then co-creation would help to overcome silo thinking in companies.

Imagine a silo: in most cases, it is a long storage container. It is intentionally designed such that there is no interaction with the environment. Silos are sealed, only being opened for filling and emptying. Wikipedia describes this situation in unintentionally metaphorical terms: "Silos are basically filled from the top and emptied from the bottom" (Wikipedia). We are also familiar with this arrangement from corporate silos (Fig. 1.1).

Decision-making processes in corporate silos also run from the top to the bottom, while the execution message runs from the bottom to the top. Thus, in the silo, we have a strong vertical orientation when it comes to communication. One might say that people do not look to the left or right, but rather up and down. However, companies do not get very far by orienting themselves on this vertical axis. They can increase vertical integration and can learn to work more efficiently, but they can only effectively enter into exchange with other divisions, customers, stakeholders, etc., along the horizontal axis.

Effectiveness requires horizontal perception, thinking and action. Some companies have recognised this and developed horizontal processes. They call these "end-to-end business processes". Here, the process is considered to extend all the way from the customer enquiry through to the company's performance. The divisions involved can include marketing, order processing, production, shipping, service and many more. On the horizontal axis, interfaces arise that require different control and escalation mechanisms than on the vertical axis. In a standardised linear process, like end-to-end processes, these interfaces are known and can be managed.

Fig. 1.1 Working in silos

Fig. 1.2 Surfing the wave

There are either specific people responsible for this or cross-departmental control and coordination groups.

The situation is different, however, when it comes to the non-linear, complex processes described at the beginning. If we were to chart them, we might assume that they are chaotic: they skip process steps and move freely within hierarchies. They are iterative, sometimes incredibly fast and occasionally bring everything to a standstill. If a company does not learn to deal with them, they can turn into a serious challenge. However, if a company learns to skilfully manage them, then it creates the opportunity for major leaps forward in development. In this case, the company learns not only to create waves itself, but also to surf on them (Fig. 1.2).

The basic prerequisite for dealing with complex problems is "relational thinking" (Franzen, 2018). This form of thinking is contrasted with feature-oriented thinking, which suffices for solving linear complicated problems. Feature-oriented thinking compares the features inherent in different things and chooses those that seem more useful. By contrast, relational thinking sets things in relation to each other, establishing relationships and attempting to recognise their shape within the whole of things.

Relational thinking is demanding, because it requires calmness, patience, presence and space. Under pressure to meet deadlines and to succeed, we tend to prefer simple, repeatable formulas. Once when discussing coffee capsules with an expert, I stated that if you were to find the right type of capsule, you would get excellent coffee, but that I myself preferred the hand-ground coffee from my portafilter because it tastes a little different every day. He replied that he could understand where I was coming from. They had done research, and there were indeed customers like me. However, they only made up 5% of coffee drinkers, while the other 95% preferred to have exactly the same taste every time.

Co-creation not only seeks to generate solutions through relational thinking, but to do so by cultivating relationships to and collaboration with others. What would we be able to achieve, if co-creation were to apply relational thinking to collaborative work in organizations?

That is the claim advanced in this book. It aims to show how shared relational perception, thinking, feeling and decision-making can make co-creation possible. Co-creation should fulfil one central condition: it should suit the tastes of 100% of the people involved, not merely 5%. We believe that this is possible, as long as we have the right mindset and methods.

The following chapters will describe how to create spaces of shared relational thinking, how to produce waves in these spaces and ride them together, how companies can use this approach to address non-linear complex challenges and how a culture of fearlessness and mutual respect can emerge in the process.

1.3 Being Connected: Finding Solutions Together

If people enjoy working together, they will work together.

To arrive at really good solutions, it helps when people find a way to connect fully with each other, such that they are able to draw on their shared potential. This is possible with just two people, but such a process can also involve several people who join together as a team. In joining together in a process of co-creation, the individuals should still retain their individuality, so that their personalities and experiences can enrich the team. It would be great to be 100% a team, while recognising oneself and feeling recognised as an individual within it (Fig. 1.3).

Cooperation and collaboration have become important buzzwords in companies in recent years. Yet it is not always quite clear what the difference between them is supposed to be. Do we really need another term to describe a particular way of working together?

As you read this book, you will learn that co-creation builds on a fundamentally different premise than previous approaches to working together. It is therefore advisable to introduce a new term to describe this particular approach: co-creation.

Fig. 1.3 Being able to be the whole team—and within it the "I" for individual

In Chaps. 4 and 5, we will look at the Potentialum organizational model. There, we distinguish cooperation from co-creation, in that cooperation is a team's knowledge of the rules of cooperation, while co-creation is the application of this knowledge to value creation.

People in organizations need to know how they want to and should work together. These rules define how responsibilities, roles, tasks, communication, interfaces, etc., are handled. However, on its own, this knowledge does not make a company really efficient. For this, it needs to connect people who have complete mastery of their specialisation to form a "performance community" that makes it possible to create something new.

New things come into being from connection; they "emerge". Aristotle described this emergence as follows: "That which is composed of components in such a way that it forms a unified whole—not in the manner of a heap, but like a syllable—is obviously more than the mere sum of its parts" (Aristotle). One might say that when masters of various subjects unite come together in pursuit of a single goal, when they have a shared understanding of an object, they have the power to change things. Such a result can only come from a conscious connection between experts. This too is co-creation.

Moments like this are often not planned, but somehow simply happen. A situation of this type arose when I was taking the train to the airport with two business partners after days of intensive work. The journey took an hour. For 2 days, we had been working on a concrete project and, at the same time, had kept talking about an idea that we only sensed on some level. Exhausted, we drifted off, started philosophising. All of a sudden, a new idea emerged from the unity and diversity of our thoughts. The three of us still talk about what happened that day, laughing about how one of us took a nap and suddenly everything was as clear as day.

We had not been actively looking for this situation; it simply happened. It was not entirely by chance, since we had had deep conversations with each other again and again, but it emerged coincidentally at that moment and under those circumstances.

Are these "aha" moments between people that create great things, that bring about real innovation and change, merely the product of random chance? Or can they also be brought about consciously? Can we create spaces of time, experience and connection in which co-creation can occur again and again in very different constellations? We have been working on this problem and believe that this question can be answered in the affirmative. These moments can be deliberately brought about. It is always very specific things that we do, moments that we create, spaces that we need in order for this to become possible.

Imagine what it would be like if you could consciously create great moments like the one on the train. If they were no longer left to chance, and thus rather rare? If we could do this, then it would be a big step forward for our organizations. We would be able to connect our brains ever more comprehensively into goal-oriented, and yet inspirationally open thinking spaces—creating a shared consciousness that is more than mere computing power. For humans possess what computers do not: wisdom, deliberation, experience and values. They can incorporate purposeful action, and thus make use of what makes us human at our core: uniqueness, creativity, unpredictability and sometimes surprising irrationality from which something new can emerge.

We call these moments "co-creation"—that is, a human connection aimed at creating continuous value. Co-creation is not left to chance, but is consciously brought about, in order to be exploited and learned from. Through it, we learn about ourselves and what we want to achieve.

Through co-creation, we create a "collective consciousness" from those involved in the process. In this collective consciousness, people connect with each other, as well as with the matter at hand, understanding together what their role is in the process and experiencing themselves as no longer separate from each other. In this moment, the individuals are connected to each other in what is happening. They see themselves and the others as an essential part of the perception, evaluation and shaping of the whole. This is where co-creation takes a distinctive path from other problem-solving or workshop methods. If we reach this high level of connection with others and the common connection with a goal, then we can synchronise our thinking going forward. In synchronisation, cognitive abilities and sensations are joined together in a network, opening up new mental capacities for coping with complexity.

We see: In cooperation, people seek the common denominator. They keep to themselves and contribute their interests, and the result is negotiated. This common denominator is the compromise. In itself, a compromise is not a bad thing, but it is also always less than what could be possible. Because as long as they are in a negotiation situation, people are under stress. And under stress, our creativity is limited.

Cooperation also only takes place as long as our interests overlap. When this is no longer the case, cooperation breaks down. Co-creation is looking for an alternative way. In essence, this book describes this alternative path: people in the co-creation all press the "reset button" and start all over again, together. With this, they have nothing to lose, but only to win. This is also the reason why those involved in co-creation can approach each other without stress.

However, this requires strong personalities who are willing to trust the result of the group more than the result they have defined for themselves. To do this, they need to know their strengths and the strengths of others in order to trust themselves and the others.

When people manage to overcome their fears and anxieties, only then do they unleash their full potential.

We have to learn all this anew. Because our entire socialisation revolves around our individual performance: school, university, profession: with few exceptions, it is often about being the best ourselves. This limits us in solving our global problems. We have to learn again to be creative with each other.

1.4 Structure and Overview

This section explains the structure of the book and gives an idea its contents. This should enable the reader to get an overall impression of the argument. The individual topics will be discussed in detail in the following chapters.

Chapters 2 and 3: Co-Creation

The second chapter will start with the "co-creation mindset". Co-creation is about shaping the future and changing the present. Co-creation and dealing with change are closely linked. In management theory, the Kübler-Ross change curve (Kübler-Ross, 1972) is often used to explain how people react to change.

Collective intelligence approaches take a different path. One of the masterminds of this field is Otto Scharmer of the Sloan School at MIT in Boston.

The co-creation methodology presented later in the book strives to integrate these approaches, thus proposing a simple, less dogmatic approach to working together. It allows organizations to open themselves to the transformation ushering in the new world of work. Co-creation thus takes a different approach, in that it claims to connect people at the core, in order to then arrive at solutions together. In this way, it differs from many other approaches that first seek a solution and only then establish a deeper connection through the result.

The different levels of connection in co-creation are presented: person-to-person connection, connection through a common goal and connection through the shared experience of a process.

During this process, participants experience different emotional states. By illustrating the emotional journey of the participants in a co-creation workshop, it is possible to capture what people experience in co-creation and how cohesion and commitment emerge from it.

Chapter 3: This approach to working together makes certain demands on those involved. It is necessary for them to share a mindset, values and principles. These are described in the section "Basic Assumptions of Co-Creation".

The explanation of these basic assumptions then leads us to an understanding of how the mechanisms of co-creation work and what psychological processes it is built on.

Chapters 4 and 5: The Potentialum Organizational Model

The fourth chapter takes a look at the new world of work: what is changing around us, how the economy is reshaping itself and what consequences this has for how we work together. What does this mean for the individual? We are at the beginning of the fourth industrial revolution, and these questions are on everyone's mind. People want to understand what is changing.

Chapter 5 presents the development of the Potentialum organizational model. It was designed to meet the requirements of our business environment. The Potentialum organizational model makes it possible to see quickly and comprehensibly how the different areas of a company are interconnected. The model identifies domains where there is a need for development and describes how it can be used to find a distinctive path into the future.

The Potentialum organizational model also serves as a tool for organizational diagnosis. If this diagnosis is carried out before co-creation, the results can show us what actions the organization as a whole needs to take.

In the second and third chapters, co-creation is derived from and justified in relation to the individual's perspective, social interactions, organization and economic environment. This lays the foundation for a detailed presentation of the co-creation process in the sixth and seventh chapters. The sixth chapter illustrates the co-creation process itself, while the seventh chapter shows how the organizational transformation towards co-creation can happen.

Chapters 6 and 7: The Co-Creation Process

The sixth chapter describes the eight steps of the co-creation process. Each of the eight steps has a distinctive name. An overview of this process will be given at this point, as a basic understanding is already needed before the detailed presentation in Chaps. 6 and 7 (Fig. 1.4).

Connection is the alpha and the omega of co-creation. In the first step, "Connect", it is a question of connection. This connection is the basis for everything that follows. The first issue is the goal and the "why" question. Does the shared idea answer the question of meaningfulness or "purpose"? What benefit or incentive do people see in this goal? What binds them collectively to this idea? Finally, what connects them, as a group of people who want to work together, on the level of their existence, their basic motivations and their values? Differences are okay, as long as they can be presented openly and transparently. However, unresolved issues must not be ignored. "Connecting" requires a lot of attention and determines the subsequent success of the co-creation process. Therefore, there should be a broad consensus at the end of the first step that it has been handled correctly. If doubts remain, it is advisable not to proceed until they have been resolved.

"Discover": Discovering the facts

After the connection necessary for the common project has been established in the first step, the second step is to understand more precisely how the "current situation" is perceived. This involves a pure exercise in taking stock. It is not a matter of evaluating the past or present situation, but only of collecting data. The term "Discover" covers two different approaches:

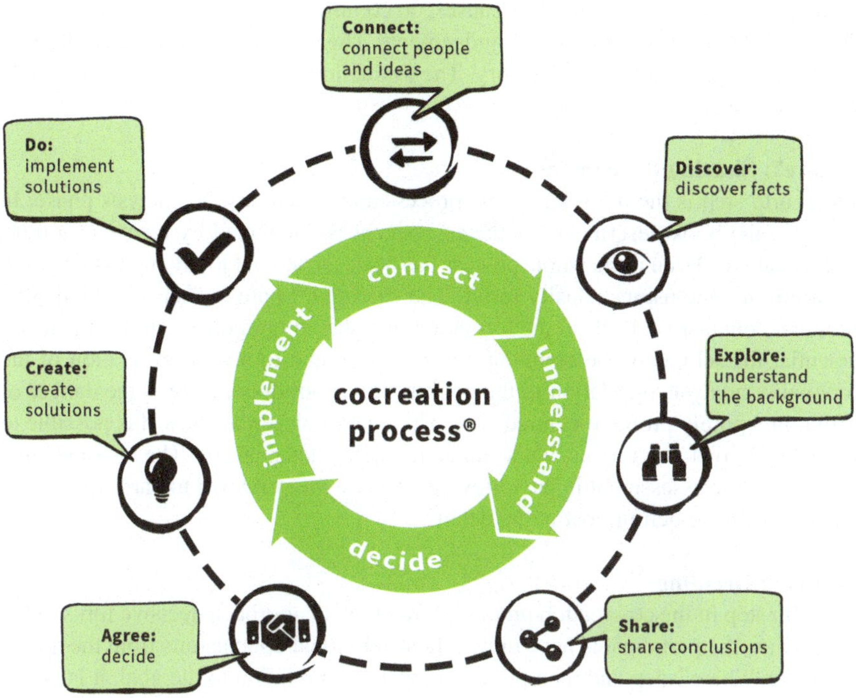

Fig. 1.4 The co-creation process

1. Taking stock during the workshop: If the actual situation is described in the co-creation workshop itself, it is initially a question of one's own perception. This is followed by a joint analysis and the identification of those factors that are considered essential by everyone.
2. Taking stock in preparation for the co-creation workshop: Especially at the beginning of a co-creation journey, it can be useful to get a holistic picture, in the sense of a view of the whole company or organization. This is what Potentialum is for. With Potentialum you get an overall picture of the organization, as well as of its self-image. After an online survey of all the organization's members and the presentation of the results, the latter are jointly evaluated and analysed during "Discover". The Chaps. 4 and 5 describe the Potentialum model and this procedure in detail.

"Explore": Understanding the background

The third step of the co-creation process "Explore" involves understanding the current situation in more detail. In "Discover", we looked at the situation of the organization or company. The next step is to give meaning to the current situation. This section identifies how the situation captured in the analysis might have come about. To do this, a joint investigation into the causes is undertaken. Different methods are described that enable this to be done with different numbers of participants. By diving into the causes, a common awareness of past patterns emerges. The third step also avoids judgements. The team abides fully in a collective openness towards their shared history. The evaluation of the causes takes place only in the next step.

"Share": Sharing the conclusions

The fourth step is the midpoint of the process and concludes the analysis phase. In this part, the book describes how the assessment is conducted by means of a root-cause analysis. Even if the whole process has been carried out jointly up to this point, a variety of conclusions usually result. The sharing ("Share") of each participant's personal conclusions leads to the formation of a shared opinion about what is really essential for achieving the common goals. It is crucial to set the evaluation of the root-cause analysis in relation to the goal. If this is not done, there is the danger of acting in a purely problem-centred way. This section describes how it is possible to keep the big picture in focus, while engaging in detailed analysis. The measures that result from the assessment in the following step are thus oriented towards the shared vision instead of getting lost in the details.

"Agree": Deciding

The fifth step in the co-creation process shows how to approach decisive forks in the road. Once the participants have drawn their individual conclusions from the analysis in the "Share" step and then put them together in relation to the goal, it is now a matter of plotting the basic course for the next steps. The participants decide on the necessary fields of action that need to be worked on so that the goal can be achieved.

This section describes what is meant by fields of action and how they differ from concrete actions or measures. Concrete measures are only defined in the following step on the basis of these fields of action. During "Agree", the participants take direct responsibility for further action. If the process so far was more perceptive and analytical, the participants now feel that everything they decide will have consequences. On the one hand, this feels good, because they are finally allowed to take action; on the other hand, they now realise that it is a question of shaping the future and that this will have consequences for them and others.

"Create": Creating solutions

The sixth step of co-creation, "Create", involves the development of solutions based on the analysis and the fields of action identified in the earlier steps. The aim here is to use our entire creative potential and to fill the fields of action with possible solutions. During the process so far, many ideas have already matured, which now only need to be compiled. Later, it will have to be decided together which of these ideas should be implemented. At this point, the group has already matured to the point that the phenomenon described earlier is now seen to be true: "When people unite with each other in view of a single goal, when they understand one thing together, then they have the power to change things". This is exactly the effect we have experienced again and again in the workshops. At this stage, the actual solution is no longer a problem and is obvious to everyone involved. The solutions "only" have to be collected and their implementation prioritised.

"Do": Implementing solutions

After deciding in the sixth process step which solutions are to be pursued further, it is now a matter of organising their implementation. This section describes this step, in which responsibilities are clarified, potential milestones with time horizons are set and team members are named. This is often the first phase of the implementation project.

"Connect": Reviewing collaboration

The co-creation session concludes, as it began, with "Connect", as an eighth step. At this point, the book describes how the co-creation workshop can be evaluated. Looking back on the collaboration and drawing conclusions together about what went well or what could be done better provides the basis for further collaboration in the project and should not be neglected.

Chapter 8: Transformation of the Organization

After explicating the co-creation process in terms of the eight steps listed above, in Chap. 8 the book deals with the transformation of the organization. At the beginning of the chapter, the different models of transformation are examined. This refers to the application-oriented aspects of co-creation, which mainly revolve around the space, the available time and the possible forms of co-creation.

In the space of co-creation, a place is created where something new can come into the world. What is new, an idea, always needs a place where it can emerge. It consists neither of the people themselves nor of the place nor of the process. Rather, it is the combination of these elements that makes it possible to materialise the space between people and their ideas and conceptions, to make this space part of the emergence of something new. Otto Scharmer speaks in Theory U of "presencing", which is a composite of "presence" and "sensing" (Scharmer, C. O., 2009). This is where situations arise that do not involve the pursuit of individual special interests. We create situations in which we realise that we come from a common origin and that we are basically pursuing the same interests. This realisation enables us to free ourselves from our individual limitations and to see ourselves as part of a greater whole. When we occupy a shared space, are in sync with each other through our engagement in the process and are transparent in our feeling and thinking, amazing things can happen. Together with the company PLAYROOM, based in Vienna, we have created "CREATE" for this purpose, a representation of the co-creation process standing in space. In Sect. 8.1 the importance of space for co-creation is described.

The co-creation process can be implemented in very different situations, formats and time budgets. The chapter goes on to identify these situations, to describe the formats that can be used and to share our own experiences.

Basically, the co-creation process can be used in the following situations:

- Organizational co-creation
- Daily co-creation
- Virtual co-creation
- Coaching co-creation
- Leadership co-creation

Organizational co-creation The co-creation process can support organizations in implementing key issues across different levels and divisions, such that those affected become participants and solutions have broad support. This sub-chapter describes a 1- or 2-day workshop format involving any number of participants.

Daily co-creation The co-creation process can help teams to realise a solution that involves everyone collectively, and thus creates a real team understanding in the collaboration. The book describes a 1-h workshop format called CC60.

Virtual co-creation The co-creation process can help people and teams who are not in the same place to find multi-perspective answers to their challenges. This section looks at the extent to which co-creation can also be implemented when the participants are not in the same place.

Coaching co-creation The co-creation process can help individuals to find resource-oriented solutions to individual challenges with the help of a coach. The role of the coach naturally changes, as he or she then has to take on the role of the "co-creator" at times. This section also looks at how such coaching can be conducted and which factors make co-creation coaching successful.

Leadership co-creation The co-creation process can be applied in leadership situations. The manager guides the employee through a mental process and helps him or her to make conscious decisions based on reflections about the past and the desired goal.

Transformation of the entire organization The individuals belonging to the organization take on specific roles in the transformation. If the transformation is viewed as a project, then responsibilities can be assigned to these roles. The management, as the client, the HR department, as the project leader, and the managers, employees and internal and external experts, as project collaborators, are jointly responsible for making the co-creation transformation possible.

The new culture must be anchored at the level of the employees, because the employees represent by far the largest group in the company.

Chapter 9: Co-Creation and the Role of Leadership

The management level is responsible for introducing the process of co-creation in the company and ensuring that it is applied in a sustainable way. First of all, there is the manager, with his or her personal commitments, values and skills. However, in order for the transformation to succeed, "co-creation" should go beyond this to become a joint initiative of the management.

The management is supported by the human resources department. The corresponding section describes the role human resources should take in the transformation. Leadership development, as part of what HR offers, is examined in the following section. How can it itself become an ambassador of change through the way in which it is delivered?

The penultimate section of Chap. 9 explains the actual process of organizational development in the direction of a co-creation culture. It begins with some observations on the relationship between the developmental stage of the organization and co-creation. The conclusion is reached that more or less all forms of organization relevant today still function according to the hierarchical organizational principle and that a top-down organizational development process is therefore needed.

Chapter 10: Co-Creation and the Organizational Development
One of the best-known models for a gradual approach to organizational change is John P. Kotter's eight-step model described in Leading Change (Kotter, 2011). Our experience in organizational development has shown that we follow a similar process. This section, therefore, describes organizational development through co-creation in line with Kotter's model.

Chapter 11: The Co-Creation Coach and Process Facilitator
Chapter 11 explores the role and key challenges of the coach in process facilitation. The co-creation coach is the professional facilitator of the co-creation process. He or she either works as an external service provider or is a member of the organization itself.

Co-creation coaches accompany both micro- and macro-level processes: at the micro level, they lead co-creation workshops; at the macro level, they help guide the organization towards a co-creation culture.

Chapter 12: Summary and Outlook
The concluding 12th chapter summarises the potential "aha moments" found in the book, and thus provides an overview. Furthermore, I venture to give my own personal perspective.

2 Co-creation

Abstract

The co-creation mindset is explained coming from change management theory. It is made clear that there are very different views in change management: In one world people are involved in the change, in the other world they are changed from the outside. Co-creation seeks the involvement of those involved. When the participants enter the co-creation space for the first time and are confronted with the layout of the space, their attention is absorbed by the various stimuli, and they need some time to get used to the setting. Co-creation aims to let the shaping of the future happen through the people involved, to give them the confidence, the resources and the know-how to engage in co-creation. The more heterogeneous the group is and the more pronounced the individual aspects are, the greater the potential of the whole.

Keywords

Change management · Collaboration · Diversity · Future

The chapter basically explains what is meant by co-creation. It illustrates where we could use co-creation in collaboration.

The co-creation mindset is explained coming from change management theory. It is made clear that there are very different views in change management: In one world people are involved in the change, in the other world they are changed from the outside. Co-creation seeks the involvement of those involved.

It is important that the people in the process connect with each other and with the common goal.

It is described in detail which emotional phases people go through in the different steps of co-creation.

G. Michalik, *Co-Creation Mindset*, Management for Professionals,
https://doi.org/10.1007/978-3-031-21191-1_2

2.1 Co-creation Versus Collaboration

A client asked me the following question: "We are successfully introducing co-creation in our company, and yet we still find it difficult to explain to the staff what it actually is. How would you describe co-creation in three sentences?" Together, we considered what the tangible components of co-creation are for people in her organisation and came up with the following points:

- It's about how people work together.
- It's about openness, about what we have in common and about recognising shared interests.
- It's about results that are endorsed and shared by all.

This gave us an explanation that is good for everyday use: "Co-creation is how we work together. It's about connecting with each other first, so that everyone is involved. In doing so, we arrive at better solutions, high levels of engagement and a shared sense of responsibility".

What does co-creation strive for and how does it differ from many other forms of collaboration? Co-creation seeks to connect the participants at the level of their consciousness. In this way, the unity of people in the process is sought, since they realise that they are pursuing a common goal and that their individual needs are better met through the process than if they tried to go it alone. "Alone" also means "alone in the group". It is often the case with participants in a workshop pursuing a goal that each person is individually concerned to ensure that their personal interests are not neglected in the process. This leads to the analysis and search for a solution taking on the character of a negotiation: "I give in a little here; you give in a little there". However, this puts people in exactly the dilemma they are familiar with from everyday life and which they want to resolve through the workshop: restraint and caution instead of joint creativity.

The following example is intended to describe the difference between these two worlds of problem-solving and creativity. A company that manufactures production components for industry and is one of the market leaders in its sector started with a single product when it was founded. Over the years, other products were added. The products fulfil the same purpose, but differ with respect to their materials, areas of application, processes and functions. This, in turn, led to the development of quasi-independent divisions, each with their own product development, production, locations and administration. They are marketed under a common brand. This decentralised form of organisation has led to the rapid growth of the divisions, and thus of the company as a whole.

In recent years, customers' needs have changed. They want integrated solutions, as expressed by the keyword "Industry 4.0". The company could also be very good at this, as it offers a wide range of products and all solutions come from the same source. To achieve this, it would be necessary for the product-development units, which are located in the corresponding company divisions, to work closely together. The coordination of product development was important in the past as well, since the

Table 2.1 The typical agenda

January meeting	• List of topics • Discussion • Solution finding • Decision • Voting in the respective "houses"
March meeting	• List of topics • Feedback on the vote from the respective "houses" • Renegotiation • Solution finding • Decision • Voting in the respective "houses"
May meeting	• Feedback on the vote from the respective "houses", etc.

products should look similar and the software should be easy to use. For many years, the development managers had been meeting every other month to coordinate and promote joint developments, see Table 2.1. The meetings were chaired by the overarching software department, as it was their job to ensure that the interfaces between the products run smoothly. The coordination and decision-making logic was as follows:

It is clear from the decision-making and coordination process that joint problem-solving only partially helps to find a solution. Another element is the negotiation of interests. The development leaders were mentally constrained in the meetings. They knew that whatever they worked out in the inter-group meeting still had to be "sold" in their own plants before it could be accepted.

Now we can ask ourselves whether this is an extreme case that does not match what we see in other circumstances or whether it is not to some extent the case in everyday life. Even if the participants in a meeting are not explicitly attending as delegates of their unit, they always represent certain interests. People come with their own ideas and needs, in order to coordinate and solve an interface problem. The question is then: Do they manage to integrate these interests into a common perspective?

Only when the integration of specific needs and ideas succeeds are people free to engage fully in the process and actually strive for the best-possible solution, in both absolute and individual terms. Prior to that, people are absorbed in advancing their own interests. They will ask themselves: What is the "best possible"? This cannot be answered before the end of the process. But it is enough if those involved are sure that this is what everyone is striving for: the best-possible outcome for each individual and for the collective as a whole. This often leads to new and surprising paths that deviate from what is normal and predictable. The result that emerges has the quality of uniting the interests of those involved, much more than a predictable result would have, because it involves going off the beaten path.

How did the story of the product developers in the example described above continue? After many years of coordination meetings, the dilemma facing those involved became increasingly clear. The demands made by their "houses" to network and integrate the products with each other were constantly increasing. As a result, the development managers had to move closer together, leading to increased friction in their factories. As a result, the number of "back-and-forth" loops increased and decision-making processes took even longer. This unsustainable situation led the development managers to question their collaboration within the framework of the decision-making body.

In the course of a specially arranged 2-day workshop, they developed an understanding of their collaboration, a common goal and clarity about how their individual objectives are reflected in it. This meant thinking, acting and deciding with reference to their common, overarching interest. For the interface management in their parent companies, they were thus equipped with a strong commitment, which now enabled them to argue much more consistently and find a common solution in fewer rounds.

From this example, one of the principles of co-creation becomes clear: "In co-creation, people join together in a common consciousness to let the future emerge".

Connection with each other, the clarification of the common goal and the transparent integration of individual needs must stand at the beginning of the process.

2.2 The Co-creation Mindset

What has been written about co-creation so far shows that co-creation adheres to a very specific idea. Lying behind it is a vision of people working together. What is the particular mindset of co-creation and how can it be explained?

Co-creation is all about shaping the future so that we do things differently. When something new emerges, what is old changes. People deal with change differently. Management specialists have proposed numerous explanatory models for how people experience change. This is not only due to our individual personality, but also due to how people are involved in change. What can we learn for co-creation from dealing with change? Is there perhaps a golden road of change?

2.2.1 Dealing with Change

Two of the best-known theories of change are Elisabeth Kübler-Ross's change curve (Kübler-Ross, 1972) and Otto Scharmer's Theory U (Scharmer, C. O., 2009). Both represent the experience of the participants in the form of a curve. In the following, these two graphs will be compared. The differences between them give an indication of the images we have of people experiencing change. This should provide the basis for deducing how co-creation can bring about a positive experience of change in those involved.

Elisabeth Kübler-Ross was a Swiss American psychiatrist. She was concerned with death and how we deal with dying, grief and mourning. She is one of the founders of modern death research (Wikipedia). The model of change she advocates

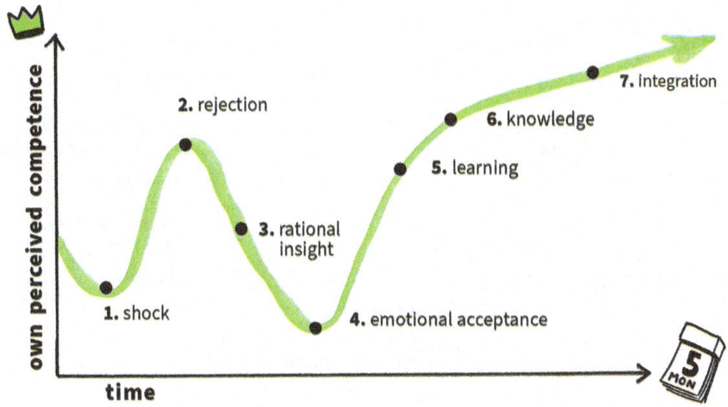

Fig. 2.1 Change curve according to Kübler-Ross (1972)

(Kübler-Ross, 1972) involves the transfer of the five phases of dying to change processes (Fig. 2.1).

The horizontal axis is the time axis, along which the change is experienced. The vertical axis shows one's own perceived competence. The y-axis thus describes the emotional experience of the person "affected" by the change.

In shock (phase 1), one's own perceived competence decreases first. Then, in phase 2 (rejection), a form of negation takes place. In this phase, one's own perceived competence increases strongly again, rising above the original level. "Rational insight" and the "emotional acceptance" lead to a complete breakdown of perceived competence. In the following three phases, there is an initially erratic and then solidifying build-up of one's own effectiveness, even far beyond the original level as the illustration suggests.

The two core statements expressed in the so-called change curve are the following. First, change is primarily negative for people. They initially react with shock, uncertainty and sadness. Second, people do not accept the change, but after the shock, they react with denial until insight begins to take hold. In the end, they manage to integrate the changed circumstances into their reality and their own perceived competence increases.

Another representation of the experience of change is Otto Scharmer's U-curve from his book Theory U: Leading from the Future (Scharmer, 2009).

Unlike Kübler-Ross' model, Scharmer describes a condition as it is when those affected are made participants and given the space to process change. To begin with, people experiencing change need to have the opportunity to become aware of their old patterns of behaviour. He calls this "downloading" (Scharmer, 2009). In German, we say: "You have to vent first". If it is OK to vent and to remain like that, then the person becomes aware of their own thoughts and feelings. This is the basis for a re-evaluation of the situation; then people can see things with different eyes. If they transfer their realisation to the situation, this can bring about a "letting go" of what exists. This also makes them aware of what needs to be worked on. Now we reach

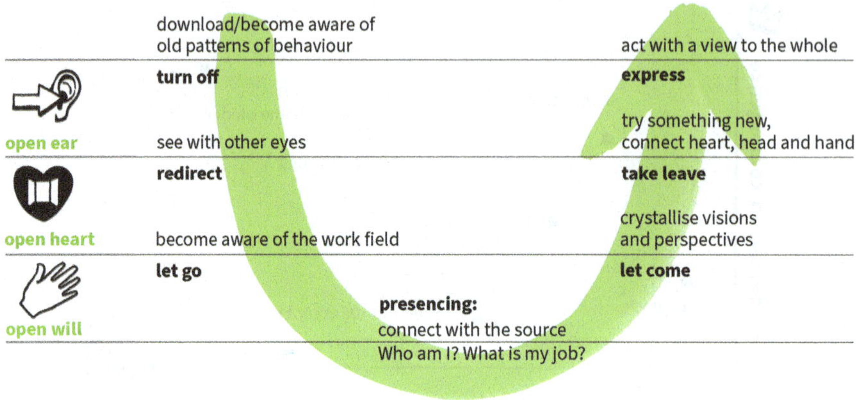

Fig. 2.2 Theory U according to Otto Scharmer (2009)

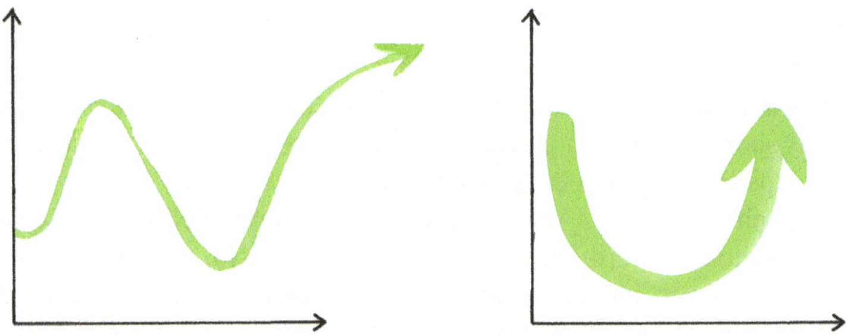

Fig. 2.3 Comparison of the Kübler-Ross and Scharmer curves

the point of reversal, the "presencing" in which presence happens. In a suitably designed setting, the person makes a decision on the basis of their own realisation: "Who am I? And what am I supposed to do?" If the person can answer this question clearly and with determination, then a lasting change in their thinking has taken place. The following three stages are then almost inevitable processes: emerging, "crystallise visions and intentions"; integrating, "try something new, connect head, heart and hand"; and communicating, "act with a view to the whole" (Fig. 2.2).

Scharmer thus describes how decision-makers can begin a journey that connects them with the environment beyond their own perspective. To do this, they must be given the opportunity to become aware of their old ways of behaving. This is the prerequisite for seeing things in a different light. Only then is it possible to let go of what already exists. At this point, the actual insight happens. This takes place in "presencing". From this realisation, the new has the possibility to emerge and find its way into the world.

We now have two different perspectives on how people experience change (Fig. 2.3). If we put the two curves side by side, we see the following:

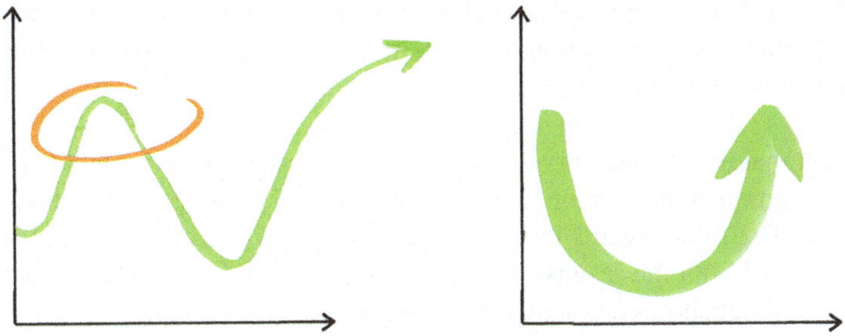

Fig. 2.4 Difference between the Kübler-Ross and the Scharmer curve

If you compare these grossly simplified representations (Fig. 2.4), what difference do you notice between the two curves?

The answer is obvious. There is a hump in the change curve that does not exist in Scharmer's U-curve. Doesn't this existing or missing hump say more about the image that management theory has of change than about how people actually experience change? What can we deduce from this about how people engage in decision-making processes today and how they should be engaged in decision-making processes in the future?

Kübler-Ross did not set out to produce a general curve to chart the human experience with change. In end-of-life care, she observed certain characteristic behaviours. Later, this was transferred by others to dealing with situations of change in general. Kübler-Ross calls the first phase "denial" (Kübler-Ross, 1972). In this situation, the patient learns of his or her terminal illness. Patients often do not want to accept this message. They believe that everything is not so bad, that it is just an unpleasant dream from which they will soon wake up and everything will be fine again.

Management theory has taken up this passage from the Kübler-Ross model to explain resistance in change processes, interpreting it as follows:

"The first reaction to change is usually shock. This initial shock [...] can result in a temporary slowdown and loss of productivity. Performance tends to dip sharply, individuals who are normally clear and decisive seek more guidance and reassurance, and agreed deadlines can be missed. The shock is often due to:

- lack of information,
- fear of the unknown,
- fear of looking stupid or doing something wrong.

After the initial shock has passed, it is common for individuals to experience denial. At this point focus tends to remain in the past". (University of Exeter, 2019).

This description from the University of Exeter clearly shows the idea of change as it is represented in management theory, which assumes that change comes over people like a fatal disease, as Elisabeth Kübler-Ross describes it. Those affected receive little information—much is unknown to them and the future seems uncertain.

At this point, we have to ask ourselves how management theory understands the process of change in organisations. Does it involve limited information, little clarity, little stakeholder involvement and considerable fear of the future and the consequences?

The fact that the change curve is still the most common representation of change processes casts a dim light on our understanding of how change is managed in companies. The future seems to be planned at a strategic level, and employees are then confronted with the results, without being involved from the beginning.

Otto Scharmer shows a completely different way of involving people in change:

How can we better perceive and connect with a future possibility that is about to emerge? I called this way of working out of the emerging future as it is emerging, presencing. [...] Presencing means to sense one's own highest future potential, to allow oneself to be drawn into it and then to act from that place—i.e. becoming present in the sense of our highest future possibilities (Scharmer, 2009).

In Scharmer's work, people are not affected parties, but participants whose experience, knowledge and feelings are needed to realise the best possibilities.

The difference between the two theories is clear: while the classical approach assumes that change is decided somewhere and those affected remain affected and react accordingly, Scharmer calls for change to happen transparently through those involved, to involve them and indeed to let something new emerge through them. If people can shape change themselves from the beginning, if they are part of the journey, then there is no denial, no fundamental resistance and no fear of looking bad.

In other words, shock and denial are unnecessary. The future can be shaped in such a way that people experience change as enrichment, that they are not afraid of it. A healthy respect may be appropriate, but people must not be made afraid of being thrown into the unknown.

But why is the change curve so popular? Management training and change management seminars teach that change—or more precisely, the people experiencing change—can be "managed". The change manager must be prepared for the fact that employees will not necessarily embrace the change measures joyfully. At the same time, they learn that it is only a matter of time until the employees get over it. Moreover, motivation and willingness to perform even go up afterwards. Doesn't that sound a bit too simplistic and transparent?

This theory ignores the fact that, in shock and denial, things develop differently than expected. The plan may never be implemented or frustration at the change process may be so great that the costs far exceed the benefits.

Let's look again at Scharmer's U-curve. What is fundamentally different here? As noted above, the cusp that stands for rejection and its concomitants "shock", "rational insight" and "emotional acceptance" is missing. In Scharmer's case, "switching off", "redirecting" and "letting go" take place instead. A process that takes people's needs seriously must give them the opportunity to say goodbye to their old ways of thinking with dignity.

If employees are the given the opportunity to reflect on what has gone before in peace and with mutual respect, and to orient themselves together towards what is new, then there is no need for a hump of denial.

Against this background, what does the Co-Creation Mindset look like?

Co-creation aims to let the shaping of the future happen through the people involved, to give them the confidence, the resources and the know-how to engage in co-creation. If these basic conditions are met and the employees realise that they are supported by knowledge, processes and tools in travelling this path in the most energy-efficient way possible, then the probability is high that the people in companies will become enthusiastic co-creators.

The Co-Creation Mindset is based on the hopes and fears people have when change is in the offing. Whether they are involved or confronted with it evokes different feelings. Whether change is successful depends on the experience of those involved. We have seen that change that is imposed and that creates consternation, rather than participation, produces less predictable results than an approach that integrates people into the process of change from the beginning.

Co-creation is an attitude that builds on the involvement of employees. It goes a step further. It is not only a question of acceptance and the co-creation of change. Co-creation builds on the fact that employee involvement is a necessary condition for shaping the future. Only by connecting the minds, hearts and wills of people in organisations will it be possible to identify forward-looking solutions.

2.2.2 Connection as a Prerequisite

People and their interests are connected in co-creation before they engage in content analysis and solution finding. This is different from many other approaches to collaborative future creation. Co-creation relies on the fusion of personalities into a common team personality.

Co-creation requires connection and works to maintain it throughout the process. It does this on three levels:

1. Direct connection via the recognition of similarities and differences at the level of personality.
2. Connection through a common goal. The participants recognise the common interest and understand what hopes are connected to it for each individual.
3. Connection via the co-creation process. The co-creation process turns the intuitive inner process into a joint process.

2.2.2.1 The Direct Connection from Person to Person

At the beginning of co-creation stands the direct connection between people. When people meet, they first ask themselves the question: Who are the others? Can I trust them?

It is difficult for people to engage with the content before they have formed a picture of the other people involved. Most facilitators know this, which is why rounds of introduction are now standard.

Co-creation takes advantage of the initial situation and transforms the uncertainty in the encounter into emotional security and connection. The participants get to know each other on the level of their emotional preferences. This step can be implemented relatively easily by means of a personality inventory.

One could question whether people are ready to open up to strangers in this way, because we are at our most uncertain when we are getting to know each other. The group is coming together for the first time in this particular composition or way. Experience has shown that people are very willing to engage, if they understand and accept the reason for it. How this is done will be explained in more detail in the section on the "Connect" process.

2.2.2.2 Connection Through a Common Goal

In addition to the direct human connection, the existence of a common goal creates cohesion among those involved. Only when it is clear that the goal is something that everyone wants to work for can the situation be analysed and solutions found. This also includes everyone knowing what everyone else's individual interest is. The individual needs may and will be different, but they should all be reflected in the common goal.

Experienced facilitators may, at this point, ask themselves how this differs from their way of doing things today: "Isn't it clear in all workshops that there needs to be a common goal?" The difference lies in the meaning and depth given to the connection. In 1-day co-creation workshops, it can happen that intensive discussions lasting until the lunch break are necessary for clarity and a real connection to be created. After that, things move all the faster. If the process of finding a common goal drags on, then occasionally the suggestion is made: "Let's just start with this goal and then we'll see what comes out of it. We can always adjust it". In this case we would speak of a "working goal", a provisional goal so that the "actual process" can get going.

Isn't it usually the case that traditional workshops use working goals, instead of genuine connection goals that everyone stands behind unconditionally? This is probably the case and is hardly ever questioned. How is it then possible that in non-co-creation workshops, results are nevertheless achieved with which the participants agree?

While co-creation seeks to establish connection between the participants and the goals right at the beginning, making it a prerequisite of the process, traditional workshops take a different approach. They usually start with a working goal, and the connection takes place at the end via the result achieved: "Great that we achieved that today. Now we have a plan for how to proceed". All the participants are happy that there is a result and that they can now return to their tasks. Hence, the result itself is the success, regardless of how the participants find their own goals and ideas reflected in it. This has consequences for the commitment to implementation.

If the goals are purely working goals, the participants will only be half-heartedly engaged during the analysis and solution finding. They are aware that the working goal may not be exactly what is important to them as individuals. Moreover, they have not collectively committed to it as a group, meaning that it has a much more non-committal character. Only at the end is the relevance check done by each individual participant, mostly in silence. If the result coincides with their personal wishes, the person will do everything to make it happen. If the opposite is true, however, then they will not engage or even actively undermine it.

2.2.2.3 Connection Through the Common Process

In addition to the human and goal-oriented connection, cohesion is also created through the process that the participants go through together. On the level of relationships and goals, the participants grow closer right at the beginning of the co-creation session. Process-driven cohesion is reached by the participants over the course of the whole workshop. Ordinary processes achieve this simply in virtue of the team members doing the same thing together. However, the co-creation process goes a step further. The four phases of co-creation correspond to the logical process of how people find solutions for themselves. In this way, they recognise themselves in the process.

The eight steps of co-creation, as already briefly presented in the section "Structure and Overview", differentiate the four phases. People intuitively go through these steps on their own when they are looking for a solution to an issue. While people rarely do this consciously, they do recognise the corresponding steps in the co-creation process. They are familiar with them from their own deliberations. For the participants, this means that they are familiar with the process from their own experiences with problem-solving in the past.

In the co-creation workshop, the participant realises that his or her inner process is the basis of the joint process. The co-creation process externalises the inner processes of the participants. People therefore perceive the process as completely natural. It does not seem forced, and no one has to contort themselves to fit the process. This creates a connection for everyone in the team, because intuitively they would all proceed in the same way. At no point in the process is there any disagreement about how to proceed. The participants can directly observe the externalisation of their inner processes. This gives them the basis to move through the stages of the workshop like a consciousness.

The co-creation mindset (Fig. 2.5) brings together the following three elements and connects them in the co-creation process:

- The personality of each of the participants: the "I"
- The team personality of all participants: The "We"
- The shared conception of the future: The "Goal"

In essence, it involves people connecting with each other such that they can develop a common consciousness, in order to let the future emerge from it. The expression "let emerge" only inadequately expresses what is meant. When people

Fig. 2.5 The co-creation mindset

connect in this way, the future is not planned or created because individuals assert their interests, but rather the future emerges from the collective consciousness.

We could say: "In co-creation people connect on the cognitive, motivational and emotional level, in order to go through a process in a synchronised fashion, as individual aspects of a common consciousness, through which they allow something new to come into the world".

This definition of co-creation makes clear that people can connect on very different levels. Hence, it is about more than a technical connection on the cognitive level. Thinking is more than a purely cognitive act. It also includes intuitive, experience-driven processes. Co-creation aims to bring about a multi-layered connection between the participants, so that solutions to complex challenges become possible. First and foremost, this includes people's motives and personality traits. These cannot possibly be seen as separate from the matter at hand. And, of course, emotions—which are always in play—become stronger the more involved the participants get, the more important they consider the issue and the greater their commitment.

In theory, it is possible to describe the goal of co-creation and the attitude behind it. The participants' experience can also be described. However, words reach their limits when it comes to describing the intangible energy between people that can arise in the co-creation process. It is this group energy that gives the confidence necessary to forge a new path and to break out of old thinking. Thus it is not just an idea that comes into the world, but an idea borne by the group. This type of idea has more power than one that is the product of some creative technique and lacks human connection.

The following example is intended to illustrate how mindset can create the basis for sustainable change:

EXAMPLE

The management of a company had set itself the goal of becoming stronger in the domain of Corporate Social Responsibility (CSR). CSR had existed as a department in the company for more than 10 years. Against the background of increasing ecological and social awareness among the general population, it was decided to increase the importance of CSR and to implement measures to revitalise it. A whole day of co-creation was planned for this. The participants were the board members whose business areas were closely related to CSR issues, as well as the division manager responsible for CSR.

The first hour was invested in connecting the participants on the personal level. Everyone had filled out a personality questionnaire and introduced themselves to each other based on the results. This broke the ice and sparked interest in the other people in the group. We then explored similarities and differences between the individual preferences in the group: What is particularly important to you that is less pronounced in me and vice versa? What should we pay attention to in the collaboration ahead so that we each use our potential to the fullest? Where do we have our common "blind spots" and what should we remind each other of in order to achieve a good result?

The connection that was thus created between the participants represented a solid foundation for an open and transparent search for an effective and unifying goal.

The search for the goal began with the CSR manager presenting her area and her CSR method. She also described the challenges she faced when CSR was integrated into many processes, thus operationalising the issue at the expense of real engagement. Her goal was to create fresh momentum and engagement. In doing so, she took a bold step forward, saying that things were not going the way she wanted them to. Afterwards, the division heads described how they perceived the company in relation to CSR and how it affects their divisions. It became clear that the benefits of CSR were not being felt by the business units that were particularly affected. The division heads also described how difficult it had become for them to act credibly and to gain acceptance from employees and customers, when social and environmental issues were not adequately addressed. These accounts were presented in an atmosphere of mutual trust, openness and self-criticism. At no point were others made responsible for the issues.

(continued)

If you transfer this situation to Otto Scharmer's U-curve, the moment of presencing was reached at this point: the old patterns of behaviour were exposed and made clear to everyone. The change of perspective gave the participants a different view of CSR. Finally, it became clear to everyone that something had to be done, even if it was unclear what exactly that should be. In that moment, everyone was fully present and ready to let something new emerge in the form of a common goal.

The first proposals for goals were then put forward. It was clear that these ideas were more or less the same kind of goals that already existed in other forms. Therefore, no one had to be convinced to look for others instead. The group was now all on the same page, and everyone had the same feeling. They had a vision of the future that they simply couldn't express yet. The group was still too bogged down in old ways of thinking and was becoming increasingly dissatisfied with itself, because the proposals made did not express what they all felt.

Then the following short dialogue took place:

Person 1: "Listening to ourselves, I can't shake the feeling that we can do whatever we want, but that we're not going to convince anyone, because we're already doing this in some form. More of the same isn't going to get anyone's attention".

Group: *thoughtful silence*

Person 2: "What you're saying is interesting. I think you're absolutely right. We're thinking in the wrong direction".

Group: *murmurs of agreement*

Person 1: "OK, if that's the case, then why don't we just accept that our picture of certain issues is the way it is and do something completely different?"

Person 3: "Exactly: The existing situation will change in some way or not. We don't have much influence on that. But we could set ourselves a completely different goal. Something that has nothing to do with the shortcomings of the past. Instead, we can create a new approach in a completely different field... I have an idea: What if we set ourselves the goal of...".

Person 2: "That's brilliant. If we get involved here, we can still really make a difference".

Group: *agitation and supportive comments*

Person 3: "I propose the following. We take as our goal that we... and we formulate it like this...".

By this moment, at the latest, the mood had tipped towards boldness and joy. Now it was just a matter of finding a catchy phrase that expressed what everyone was feeling.

What is clear from this example is that the co-creation team saw itself as a unit. It was not a question of pushing through individual interests. Thanks to their connection that would have been unthinkable for those involved. It would have been a breach of trust—without this trust and commitment ever having been demanded. The participants shared their personalities, values and aspirations with each other. In doing so, they bonded to form a unity. There is no room for egoism in unity. Everyone is aware of this without anyone having to say it.

In co-creation, the participants merge into a whole for a certain period of time. This creates a connection between hearts, wills and thoughts, so that a new whole is created that is much stronger, even more powerful and wiser than an individual could ever be. This is only possible if individual thoughts, goals and feelings can be drawn on at the same time. Therefore, co-creation creates a field in which people discover that they are individual aspects of a collective consciousness. Co-creation thus has a different understanding of the role of people in shaping the future. It seeks to overcome the egocentric, and instead to seek purity of thought, purpose and feeling.

Co-creation is, so to speak, about "being the whole together with others". This involves three key aspects:

1. *"Together with others"*: Co-creation lives from the connection with other people. In extreme cases, this can be only one person undergoing coaching. But it can also be a numerous people at a large group event.
2. *"Self"*: Even if it is about the whole, it is always the individual aspects and experiences that contribute to the whole. The more heterogeneous the group is and the more pronounced the individual aspects are, the greater the potential of the whole.
3. *"Whole"*: "achieving wholeness" combines two perspectives: it takes more than one person to become the whole and the result represents a holistic view.

The co-creation mindset is present throughout the whole period of co-creation. It starts beforehand, with a view to co-creation, it is fundamental during co-creation and it resonates after the current co-creation session is over. The connection between the participants is paramount during this period and is protected by the coach. It is challenging for the participants, as they have little opportunity to act as individuals during this time. The group should remain stable throughout the process, and it is preferable not to have individuals checking in or out. Since a separate group personality forms, so to speak, during co-creation, a careful start but also a careful and appreciative letting go and conclusion of the co-creation session is needed.

In sum, it can be said that co-creation first seeks to establish a direct connection between people through their personality traits. They then recognise what they have in common through their individual goals and their connection in relation to a shared goal before they engage in analysis and solution finding. This connection is then maintained by working through an intuitively shared problem-solving and solution-finding process together. As a consequence, co-creation differs from other concepts of teamwork, in that it privileges connection over outcomes. Traditional workshops often start with working goals and leave it to the individuals afterwards to identify their common share in the result achieved.

2.2.3 Emotional Experience

Co-creation aims to create an emotional bond between the participants. It aims to make the group feel like a unit, while enabling individual aspects to be distinguished, i.e. diversity is possible in unity. Shared emotional experiences strengthen this connection. Understanding them gives the coach the possibility to better encourage the group dynamics.

During the co-creation process, the individuals involved pass through different emotional states (Fig. 2.6). What does the emotional journey of the participants in a co-creation workshop look like? The following section will describe the typical emotional phases of the co-creation process, as we experience them in our co-creation workshops.

Of course, emotional sensibility cannot be generalised. People experience different feelings as they move through the co-creation process. The descriptions of the emotional states occurring during the four phases and at each individual step represent a general mood, rather than the emotional state of each participant. There are always some people who are already a step ahead and others who need a little more time.

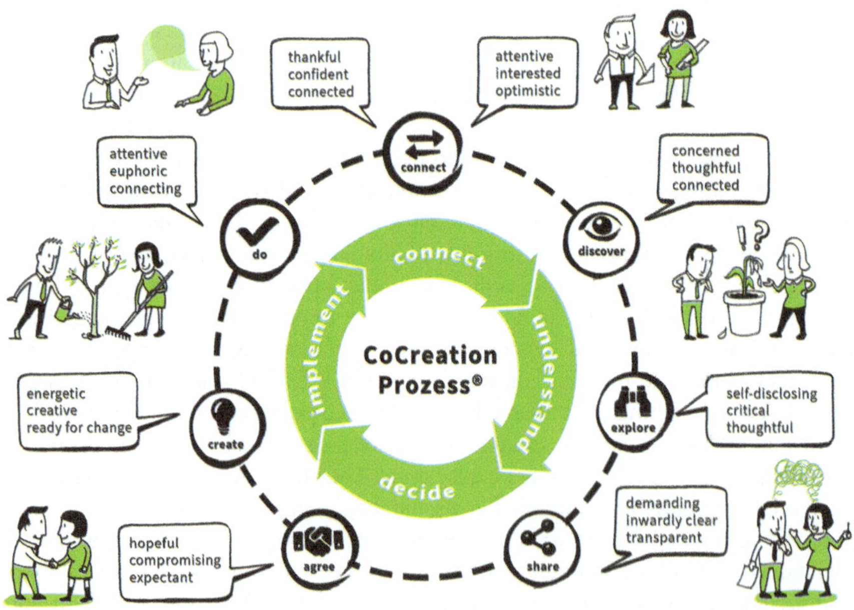

Fig. 2.6 Emotional experience during the various steps of the Co-Creation process

The co-creation process begins with "Connect". At the beginning, the group is still waiting. When the participants enter the co-creation space for the first time and are confronted with the layout of the space, their attention is absorbed by the various stimuli, and they need some time to get used to the setting (see Sect. 8.1 "Space"). Next, the process of getting to know each other begins: "Who will I spend the day with? Who do I already know? Who do I like? Who haven't I met before?" are probably the typical thoughts that go through the participants' minds at the beginning. Then their attention turns to the coach or coaches in the room and the scan begins again: "What kind of people are they? Are they nice? Do they know what they're doing?" The mental state of the participants at this stage shifts between "waiting" and "curious". Since the coaches know what is happening, they can sense the mood and thus break the ice.

In the "Connect" step, the participants first determine their personality type and introduce themselves to each other based on their findings. After that, there is a discussion about how cooperation should best be organised with this mix of types. People are now connected, and their attention can thus turn to the "second most-important issue": "What do we want to achieve?". This questions places one of the bigger milestones before the group: defining the common goal. Once this goal has been successfully determined, you can feel the group start to relax and to confidently look forward to the rest of the day. Now everyone is fully present and ready to dive into the topic at hand.

The next phase, "Understanding", requires analytical clarity, transparency and trust in the group. Thanks to the "Connect" step, the team is ready for this. Critical issues can be addressed openly. Once all the critical issues have been identified in the "Discover" step by means of the "situation analysis", something like collective concern and honesty emerges: "Now it's time to put everything on the table, and not only what's working. We shouldn't shy away from talking about the things that aren't so good". Through this work and the grouping together of the results, the participants now feel even more connected to each other. If root-cause analysis is then used in the "Explore" step, the depth of trust and transparency increases further: "Now we really have to call a spade a spade". This is the time of the deepest connection between the participants. They are now "self-revealing, critical and reflective". They thus create the basis for collectively assessing the situation in the "Share" step: "If this is the cause, then we see that...". At this stage, the participants are connected to each other in their judgement—differentiated, diverse and balanced.

The halfway point has now been reached. The participants have completed the analysis. With this, they can also leave behind a certain state: a reflective, inward-looking analytical state. This phase was mentally and emotionally exhausting, and the participants now need a longer break. Ideally, the understanding phase ends at lunch time.

The next two phases, which involve deciding and planning the implementation, are carried out with momentum and verve; now all the repressed energies are released. Since it is now clear what the situation is, definite statements are needed about the fields of action in which the group wants to become active. At the same time, the group becomes aware of its responsibility. Its members realise that it is not just a matter of making big plans, but that they themselves will later take responsibility for these plans. The "Agree" step is emotionally demanding, because the decision can only be made as a whole group. It is no use if one person says, "I'll do it". Everyone has to say "yes" together. There needs to be clarity in the decision. In this way, the team creates expectations of its own ability to act and creates hopes with respect to its impact.

The next step, "Create", is a "deep emotional breath". At this point, solutions can be thought up and written down without any worries. This exercise is fun and gives the group energy. "Create" gives the team breathing space before the "grand finale": the "Do" step. In the "Do" step, responsibilities are clarified. Who will take responsibility for implementing the best ideas? At this point, things become very concrete, and the participants commit themselves not only as a team, but also as individuals. They realise that the timeout given to them by "co-creation" is coming to an end and that they still have a lot of other work to do, as well as a private life to take care of. Against this background, they are now supposed to say "yes" to additional work. What strengthens the participants in this situation is to learn from each other that they are all willing to do it: "Yes, I will take on this project, even though I still have no idea how I will fit it in with my workload. But I will do it and I will keep the promise I made to you". If this spirit is palpable, then everyone will be ready to make and keep their pledge.

Finally, the group explicitly connects again in the "Connect" phase. They look back on the co-creation together and are grateful for what they have experienced, feeling connected with the group and confident about the next steps. Depending on culture and personality, someone might say: "I think we have set ourselves a lot of goals, I don't know if we can do it. But I hope we will achieve it, because it would be amazing for us".

This is how we experience the typical emotional journey of the participants in co-creation. As we have seen, there are also highs and lows here, but these always take place along with a feeling of being supported by the team.

The emotional dynamics described connect the participants and fuse them together. Such an experience presupposes a demand for attitudes, values, principles, processes and tools. These demands manifest themselves in the basic assumptions of co-creation. Whenever co-creation is mentioned, it must be measured by whether it can meet these demands.

3 The Basic Assumptions of Co-creation

Abstract

The basic assumptions underlying co-creation are its mindset, the values of co-creation and its principles. Mindset, values and principles create the common denominator of how co-creation should be lived. They can be referred to and thus create clarity as to what belongs to co-creation and what does not. They also create an understanding of the spirit of co-creation. It can be the north star to question repeatedly whether one is on the right path.

Keywords

Mindset · Culture · Principles · North star · Lean

This chapter describes the basic assumptions underlying co-creation. This is its mindset, the values of co-creation and its principles. Mindset, values and principles create the common denominator of how co-creation should be lived. They can be referred to and thus create clarity as to what belongs to co-creation and what does not. The chapter also creates an understanding of the spirit of co-creation. It can be our north star to question us repeatedly whether we are on the right path.

3.1 Co-creation Dimensions

In order to give an overview of the basic assumptions of co-creation, in what follows the central levels of co-creation are shown and their components identified (Fig. 3.1):

Co-creation Mindset Co-creation is more than a method. It represents a mindset concerning how people can best face their shared challenges together. A short definition would be: in co-creation, people connect to a shared consciousness, in order to make the future visible.

G. Michalik, *Co-Creation Mindset*, Management for Professionals,
https://doi.org/10.1007/978-3-031-21191-1_3

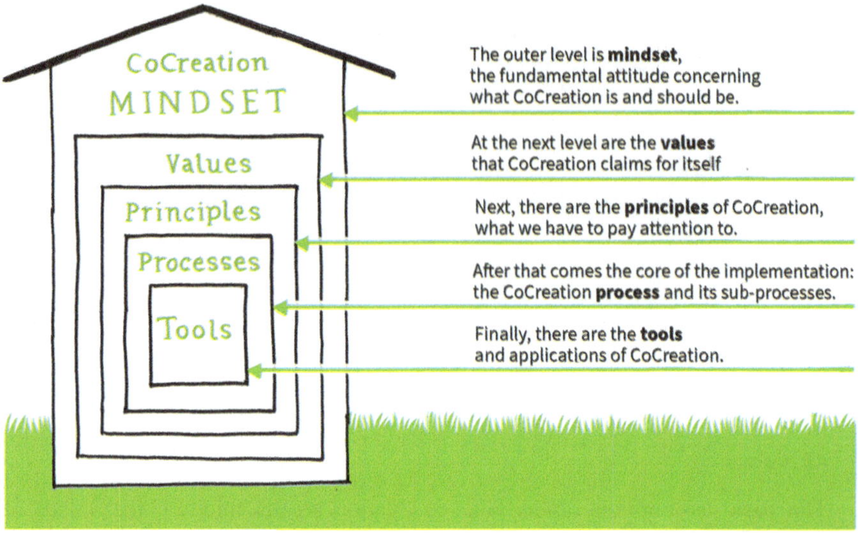

Fig. 3.1 Levels of co-creation

Co-creation Values The three most important values of co-creation are: connection, commitment and trust. These embody and promote the attitude of co-creation. Connection, commitment and trust are not independent of each other. One can start with each value to make the other two possible. All three are fundamental to the success of co-creation.

Co-creation Principles The principles are practical experiences gained in co-creation that ensure that the application of the mindset and values occurs as successfully as possible. The principles are not rigid, but evolving. They themselves require constant questioning and adaptation by the co-creation coaches.

Processes The co-creation process, with its eight steps and sub-processes, is the theoretical foundation for the practical implementation of co-creation. The participants are guided step by step through all the necessary phases by means of which perceiving, feeling, thinking and deciding as a whole become possible.

Tools By tools, we mean all the concrete aids and framework conditions that make an effective co-creation process possible. Here we have to mention the spatial layout: How should the space in which co-creation takes place be designed and set up? Also worth mentioning are the psychometric methods that can be used to better understand ourselves and others, as well as providing a basis for connection. Potentialum makes an important contribution to the overall understanding of the actual situation of the organization. Other tools include the creative methods employed in solution space and retrospective reflection about the intermediate phases, to name only the most important ones.

In the following section, the first three levels—mindset, values and principles—are explained in more detail. Each of these three levels makes a claim about what co-creation should be and about the people who work with co-creation. The levels of processes and tools are described in Chaps. 6 and 7.

3.1.1 The Co-creation Mindset

The co-creation mindset is the fundamental attitude behind co-creation. It describes how people best make plans together. Co-creation thus claims to be more than a method. People who adopt this mindset support each other in co-creating the future. The co-creation mindset has been described in Sect. 2.1.

3.1.2 Values of Co-creation

The function of values for co-creation is to have a set of values that serve as a basic orientation for the participants as to what is desirable in co-creation. Values are the cornerstones of the co-creation mindset. They describe what the co-creation mindset fundamentally strives for. This enables a common orientation in co-creation.

The values should ensure that the definition of co-creation is expressed in the following mindset: "In co-creation, people connect on the cognitive, motivational and emotional levels in order to go through a process in a synchronised fashion, as individual aspects of a common consciousness, through which they allow something new to come into the world".

The values should serve as a guiding star, so that this attitude can actually be achieved.

The three most important values advocated for and by co-creation are:

- Connection: connecting people on different levels
- Trust: protection of participants/individuals
- Commitment: innovation—creating and implementing something new

These values refer to cooperation in the joint shaping of the future. They describe what can be expected from each other, in order for this togetherness to succeed. They are therefore values that shape relationships, since the relationship, the connection between people, stands at the centre.

Connection In co-creation, the "co-" is taken literally. The task is to create as much "co-" as possible and reasonable under the given circumstances. "Co-" is also a prefix in the words cooperation and collaboration. There, too, it has its justification. However, it has a different meaning than in co-creation. The conventional understanding is that several people do, work or create something together. However, doing something together does not mean doing it as a unit. Cooperation, as described at the beginning, is at best a "social relationship", where each person keeps to himself, represents his interests, keeps a certain distance and is careful to keep a safe distance. Co-creation seeks to overcome this separation of people. It seeks to connect people for a certain period of time, so that they then think, feel, evaluate and act on the basis of this unity.

Commitment The question that business leaders and the HR department often ask themselves is: How do we create commitment in the organization? Commitment also translates into "engagement" and "dedication". The overlap between the terms shows that engagement is needed to live commitment. If something leaves me cold or unconvinced, then I am also less conscientious in fulfilling my promises or the expectations placed in me. The reverse is also true: lived commitment creates engagement. Commitment that is not lived and promises that are not kept are demotivating and do not contribute to engagement. Companies are eager to have committed employees, because this has a direct impact on costs. Non-commitment leads to procrastination, repetition and inefficiencies. In co-creation, commitment is important because people are fully engaged and committed to the shared process. They will only do this regularly if they have the experience that everyone is sticking to agreements. If this is not the case, it becomes more difficult with each round to get people to engage in co-creation.

Trust When I ask in workshops or leadership programmes what the most-important element in cooperation is, "trust" usually takes first place. However, unlike connection and commitment, trust cannot be directly influenced by the actor. This makes it more challenging to introduce trust. It cannot be planned. However, people can actively connect with others and behave in a reliable way. Then others give that person their trust. It is not wrong to say that "trust is given". Being given trust is therefore a consequence of one's own actions, and can thus only be influenced indirectly, for example, by connecting with others and behaving in a reliable way. In co-creation, trust is the soil in which cooperation can grow. The most fundamental part of co-creation is the beginning and the end of the collaboration, the part we call "Connect". It is in connection that the trust necessary for co-creation is established. Everything else builds on this.

Connection, commitment and trust are directly interdependent in a reciprocal cause–effect relationship (Fig. 3.2):

Initially, the actors connect with themselves, with the goal, with the other actors and, finally, with each other in relation to the goal. Everything falls under the theme of "connection" at the beginning. This sometimes goes faster, while at other times, it goes slower. In a co-creation workshop, you take an unusually large amount of time for this. Once, we started the evening before and were unable to finish this phase until 11 am the following day. It was amazing that the rest of the co-creation process could then be completed in only 3 h. The moment the "Connect" phase was successfully completed, it was like a spell was broken. It was fascinating to watch: the participants came out of hiding. What had seemed laborious and like a tactical manoeuvre suddenly became fun and easy.

Fig. 3.2 The foundation of trust

By creating connection, trust is worked on directly. This provides the necessary basis for further work in the co-creation session. In the period between the end of the co-creation session and the next meeting, commitment is very important. Therefore, at the end of the co-creation session, the responsibilities for the intermediate phase or the follow-up are clarified in detail. That way, at the start of the next co-creation session, the "Connect" stage can be kept much shorter. Now, honouring commitment builds trust for the next steps. When everyone sees that they have implemented their promises, existing trust is refreshed, and the group is once again equipped with sufficient confidence for the upcoming co-creation.

Mindset and values are what make co-creation what it is: an attitude that can be applied independently of structures and processes. Seen in this light, co-creation is not a new method, it is more fundamental. The co-creation process and the tools it uses build on this.

Are the mindset and values of co-creation also able to enrich other known methods and to make them even more effective? This would require existing structures, processes and methods to be carried out using the co-creation mindset and values.

In this case, one could ask what value the attitude of being connected and the values of connection, trust and commitment would have for agile methods like design thinking or scrum? The same question can, of course, be asked about other, more traditional methods. However, it is precisely agile methods that represent the new forms of working together.

The example of design thinking will now be used to briefly explain how co-creation as a mindset and value system can enrich other approaches.

Design thinking is one of the most widely used agile methods. Its effectiveness is undisputed: "Design thinking is based on the assumption that problems can be solved better when people from different disciplines work together in an environment that promotes creativity, develop a problem together, take people's needs and motivations into account, and then develop concepts that are tested multiple times" (Wikipedia).

The basic idea of design thinking is to start acting as quickly as possible. In acting, a prototype is created, and this is presented to an expert in order to quickly receive initial feedback. In this respect, design thinking differs fundamentally from co-creation in its approach. Or rather, design thinking is primarily about efficiently generating solutions that satisfy customer needs. This takes place primarily in phases 3 and 4 of the co-creation process, i.e. "Deciding" and "Implementing".

Design thinking thrives on a high level of dynamism and short cycles of prototyping and further development. According to its definition, it involves "people from different disciplines working together in an environment that promotes creativity". Diversity among the participants is an essential factor for the development of new ideas. Like other methods, design thinking assumes that when people come together in a certain environment, they will automatically connect with each other through the task at hand.

One of the basic assumptions of co-creation is that we should not only connect through the task and the end result, but explicitly use time, space and a methodical approach to create a shared consciousness. It doesn't matter whether this is the co-creation process or another process. It could also be the design thinking process. If the mindset and values of co-creation underpinned the application of the design thinking method, would the efficiency of design thinking improve?

The result of this could be to maintain the strong dynamics and customer orientation of design thinking, while benefiting from the collaborative consciousness of a diverse group.

As the example of design thinking shows, it is worthwhile for different methodological approaches to check whether co-creation mindset and its values might not help enrich them.

Design thinking follows different principles of implementation than co-creation does. The next section will look at the principles involved in applying co-creation.

3.1.3 The Principles of Co-creation

The principles of co-creation give advice on what to look for in the implementation and realisation of co-creation. They are the result of practical experience gained in co-creation. Being aware of them can help to ensure that the application of the mindset and values happens successfully. The principles create the framework within which co-creation can take place under the best-possible conditions. This collection of principles is not exhaustive and is constantly evolving, just as the co-creators' wealth of experience is constantly evolving.

Essential principles are listed and briefly explained below.

The Group Needs Take Precedence over Individual Needs

During co-creation, the needs of the group take precedence over those of the individuals involved. This principle serves to protect the whole, which is delicate, fragile and needs to manage its energy. To this end, it should be remembered once again that the co-creation group itself should be its own collective consciousness. It is fed and enriched by the individual perspectives of its members. The interventions of the individuals should concern the functioning of the group, rather than satisfying individual interests. What is at issue in each case is difficult to explain on the theoretical level. It helps to sensitise the collective consciousness to disruptive factors, and thus enable the group itself to deal appropriately with disruptions.

Individuals Must Have Their Space and Be Taken Seriously

Just as important as protecting the group is giving the individuals their space and taking them seriously. It is precisely the diversity and the difference in positions and experiences that lead to the enrichment of the group. It is usually innovative leaps that take the whole team the furthest. Innovative leaps are often caused by insights that arise in individual participants. In order for these to emerge, to be expressed and to be integrated benevolently into the collective consciousness, an atmosphere of mindfulness and mutual appreciation is needed.

Another reason makes this second point significant. The participants as individuals bring themselves fully into the collective consciousness for co-creation. This is only possible if they let go of their individual interests for this time. They should find and create an atmosphere characterised by permeability and openness. In order to do so, they have to make their own "firewall" more permeable to a certain extent. If they are a little less concerned about their own protection, it is of the utmost importance that an environment is created in which they can open up without danger.

Who is responsible for ensuring that this happens and that the co-creation process meets this high standard on an on-going basis? First and foremost, the co-creation coach. His task is to make sure that the corresponding mindset, values and principles are adhered to. It is important that the rules that the group has given itself in the "Connect" stage are also adhered to. If he acts wisely, he will above all try to enable the group to check and demand compliance with the standards themselves.

Co-creation Has a Beginning and an End

In order to uphold the principle of individual protection, people need to find conditions that make it easy for them to get involved. To this end, it is helpful if the participants explicitly check in to the co-creation and check out again at the end. The co-creation process includes the "Connect" stage for this purpose. It is both the first and the last step of the process. It is structured in such a way that the participants are led into the co-creation and also back out of it again, without this having to be explicitly stated. The state of collective consciousness emerges at the same time and is dissolved at the same time. This procedure not only serves to protect the participants, but also protects the collective consciousness itself. This can be seen as an independent temporary identity that should itself be protected. It is precious because it has emerged from the individual perspectives of the people involved, and it is thus the bearer of numerous hopes and expectations.

The Group Starts and Finishes the Co-creation Process Together

The collective consciousness of the co-creation group cannot simply be switched on and off. It emerges together with the inclusion of all the individual perspectives, and it ends together. It follows inevitably that the co-creation exists as long as it is agreed and as long as all the participants are in the room. If an individual leaves the room, the co-creation process also pauses. From the experience of numerous co-creation workshops, it has been shown that if a participant even briefly leaves the room, it can lead to a break in the process. It is therefore advisable to schedule breaks rather frequently and to refrain from having individuals take time-outs on their own. It goes without saying that not only the physical presence, but also undivided attention of the participants is a condition for success. To this end, all computers and mobile phones should be switched off and packed away. This signals to the participants that they are ready to start.

The co-creation process ends at the agreed time and after the check-out has taken place. Now it happens again and again that a participant has to go to the airport early or otherwise has an event that cannot be postponed. In order to be able to deal with this, it is advisable to agree on common rules at the beginning. In addition, the schedule should be jointly reviewed and agreed upon at the start. Workshops usually last as long as the majority of those present have time. From my own experience, however, it seems better to set the end time of the co-creation process for when the first participant has to leave. This takes some getting used to for participants at the beginning, but soon leads to participants scheduling a later rather than an earlier flight.

Solutions Require Understanding

Moderators are often told that they should be solution-oriented instead of problem-oriented: "The discussion about suitable counselling strategies is sometimes very polarising. In the language of some coaches, 'problem-oriented' sounds like a swear word that stands for 'ruminating on problems' and 'not finding a solution'. Solution-oriented approaches are often dismissed by their critics as superficial, because solutions without an explanation of the causes are patchwork, or [...] 'workarounds', which merely eliminate symptoms and provide superficial answers". (Behnsen).

Co-Creation is a solution-oriented mindset which allows the solution to emerge jointly from an understanding of what is not going well—or not yet going well—and what is going well. Analysis and understanding occupy an essential space and position. At each step, it is always important to reflect on the common goal, so that the team does not get lost in problem considerations.

Hence, we can also say that the co-creation process is an iterative process of solving and understanding. The results of the different stages of problem analysis are repeatedly evaluated in terms of their importance for the goal. Problems that are important, but have little relation to the goal set for co-creation are given less consideration than causes that have a direct relation to the goal.

Now it becomes even easier to understand why goal setting at the beginning of co-creation is of such paramount importance. Not only does it serve to form the collective consciousness, but the goal provides a point of orientation, so that both an evaluation of the root cause analysis and the finding of solutions are possible.

Basically, when we look back at the causes, it should be with a forgiving and healing gaze, not a judgemental one.

Decision Matrix: Value × Influence

The co-creation process takes place in eight steps, whereby "Connect" is both step one and step eight. In the first three steps of the process, which are part of the analysis phase ("Discover", "Explore" and "Share"), more information is generated than can be processed in the next step. In each case, there is an opening followed by a subsequent compression. The same thing happens in the following two phases of decision-making and implementation, with the process steps "Agree", "Create" and "Do". After each step, the co-creation team must decide once again which information that has been acquired should be taken as the basis for the following step. This means that the team has to sort out again and again which information is less important and which information and insights are absolutely essential.

How does the group reach a decision which serves as the basis for the next round? In order to do so, decision parameters are required: "Each alternative course of action leads to a result depending on the possible environmental states. In order to choose between the alternatives, each environmental state must be evaluated according to the decision-maker's objectives". (Wirtschaftslexikon 24).

One of the two decision parameters used in co-creation is the value of the alternative. This value is high when the chosen alternative has a direct impact on the desired goal. It is clear to all participants that "if we take this or if we do this, then we are working very directly towards our common goal".

The other decision parameter is the capacity of the participants to change the current state. The two classic factors that belong here are money and time. Often both are directly connected with the goal and thus have a high value, but the group may only have a limited influence on them.

These two decision parameters result in the decision matrix Value × Influence (Fig. 3.3):

In order to visualise the decision, it has proven useful to draw the matrix of Value × Influence, to write the alternatives on post-its and to stick them in the matrix. This makes visible which alternatives are most likely to be pursued.

Open and Compress

The co-creation process moves along the eight process steps. Each process step reveals new aspects and information:

- "Connect": the goal
- "Discover": the facts
- "Explore": the background
- "Share": the conclusions
- "Agree": the fields of action

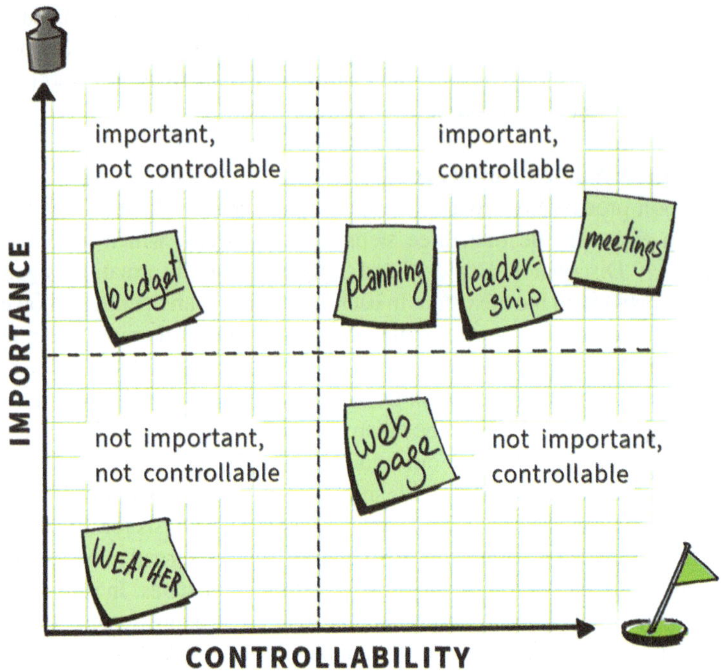

Fig. 3.3 The decision matrix

- "Create": the solutions
- "Do": the actions

This means that each step of the process has a result at the end. Incidentally, this also makes it easier for participants to stay on the ball. This is because partial successes are achieved throughout the process and progress is thus visible.

One of the principles of co-creation is how the results of each process step are achieved. This always follows the principle of a diverging "opening up" and a converging "compression" (Fig. 3.4):

During the "opening", space is opened up: spaces of understanding, spaces of possibility and spaces for decisions. Through this opening, the space for collective consciousness is freed up. If little space were created here, no collective consciousness would come about, and the benefits of co-creation would not be available.

At the same time, it is necessary to condense the results into a few keywords at the end of each step. Otherwise, these spaces will expand exponentially, and the level of complexity will no longer be manageable after the second step. In addition, "condensing" has a second important function. It forces the group to regularly decide: "What is important to us? What is really our focus?" Making determinations gives direction and clarity to the collective consciousness. Decisions bring about an alignment of the collective thinking and feeling and only thereby give it direction (Fig. 3.5):

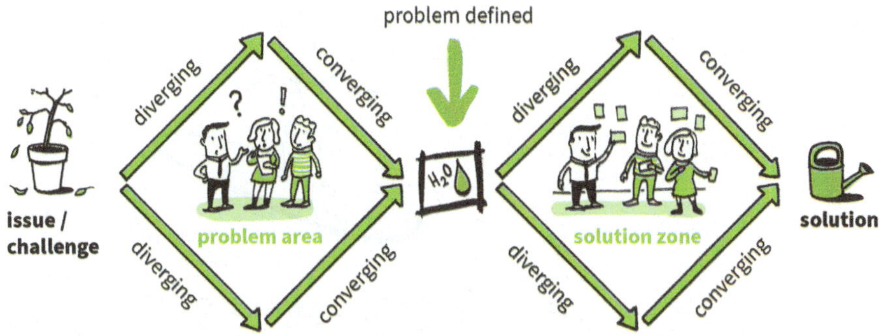

Fig. 3.4 Process of diverging and converging

	opening	closing = result
connect	target space, possible goals	the one common goal
discover	situations and phenomena	the max. 5 essential causal fields
explore	causal fields for every essential situation	the max. 5 most essential causal fields
share	fields of action for the 5 causes	the max. 5 most important fields of action
agree	alternative solutions for each field of action	the max. 5 most important fields of action
create	alternative solutions for each field of action	the preferred solution for each field of action
do	who could take responsibility	who is responsible

Fig. 3.5 Opening and compressing

Fig. 3.6 Co-create, eat, sleep, repeat

Co-create, Eat, Sleep, Repeat

Perhaps you are familiar with the T-shirt or bumper sticker that reads: "Surf, Eat, Sleep, Repeat". It expresses the idea of doing the same thing over and over again, in order to become absorbed in it and find fulfilment—the ideal of persistent development. This slogan is well suited to co-creation, since, on the one hand, various process steps are used in the search for the best-possible solution, while, on the other hand, the time required for this must be kept in mind (Fig. 3.6).

For example, if only 1 h is available for co-creation, this requires a correspondingly pragmatic approach. When a company starts to use co-creation, the idea is often to hold a workshop where the most important issues are put on the table and new insights are gained and then implemented. Once that is done, everything else continues as before—or so the idea goes. However, co-creation is anything but a one-off event. Co-creation is first and foremost an attitude, a mindset that changes "how" members of the company deal with their challenges.

It cannot be a one-time event. It is rather a process of common awareness: in the process, the realisation should develop that people, as part of a system, can develop—and should nurture—a shared consciousness. Co-creation is a developmental journey for the whole staff. It could be called a CAP (Continuous Awareness Process) with reference to CIP (Continuous Improvement Process). Whatever people do together will change the system, which in turn will have an effect on them. If they do this collectively and reflectively, they become aware of the collective change they have undergone. Achieving this result requires the members of an organization to regularly re-evaluate, to implement the results, to gain experience and then to come together again for the next co-creation session, learning together by reflecting on the experience and then adopting actions on this basis for the next implementation phase.

The second and third chapter described the basics of co-creation. In later chapters, the co-creation process is presented in detail. Before that, a framework model of the organization will be presented in Chaps. 4 and 5. Co-creation improves cooperation in organizations, and for this reason, it is necessary that people understand what the relevant factors in the organization are that they have such a major influence on cooperation.

4 The Potentialum Organizational Model

Abstract

Co-creation takes place in organizations and companies. What moves organizations today? What are the factors that determine success and failure? The picture that participants have of their company determines what conclusions they draw and which measures they arrive at in workshops. Co-creation without such a common picture would be random and arbitrary. In order to successfully develop forward-looking results, a common understanding of what the organization stands for, what is important to it and where it is on the path to the goal is needed.

Keywords

Organizational development · Change · Measures · KPIs · Management

In this chapter, we take a step back from the immediacy of co-creation and look at the overall system of the organization. Co-creation takes place in organizations and companies. What moves organizations today? What are the factors that determine success and failure? The picture that participants have of their company determines what conclusions they draw and which measures they arrive at in workshops. Co-creation without such a common picture would be random and arbitrary. In order to successfully develop forward-looking results, a common understanding of what the organization stands for, what is important to it and where it is on the path to the goal is needed.

G. Michalik, *Co-Creation Mindset*, Management for Professionals,
https://doi.org/10.1007/978-3-031-21191-1_4

4.1 The Levels and Self-Image of the Organization

Most readers will have encountered the following situation. An organizational unit has decided to make a difference in a company. They want to become better and achieve ambitious goals. They set out to attain high levels of commitment, engagement and on-time delivery. Workshops are held with the relevant departments and teams. Processes are optimised and the readiness of all participants is high.

Back in the fabric of the whole company, the employees begin to implement the agreements. This works quite well among themselves. However, at the numerous interfaces with the rest of the organization, things go on as before. Commitment is not quite as strong and deadlines are not always met. Sooner or later, this also has an effect on one's own department. As a result of the dependency on the rest of the company, good intentions cannot be maintained.

Blame is apportioned and the goals that have been worked out begin to crumble. Since everyone in the department is more or less in the same situation, no one is really interested in making this an issue. During coffee breaks you hear statements like: "We would do that, but in the other department everyone does what they want".

What can be done in such a situation? An idealistic boss might say: "We just have to lead by example long enough and the whole company will change". A realistic divisional manager would either recognise that this is tilting at windmills and look for the next challenge outside the company, or he would call for a sustainable change to the whole organization in a board meeting.

If the whole company then decides to take the path towards more commitment, engagement and conscientiousness about deadlines, the following realisation is probably at the root of it:

"If we want to improve, this can only come about if the underlying patterns are recognised, addressed and resolved throughout the company. Changes at the micro level, which depend on the macro level, can only succeed if the framework conditions are fundamentally sound".

Awareness involves the different levels of the organization. These are interdependent. Accordingly, it is difficult for a given division to sustainably implement the resolutions. Sociology works with three analytical levels: the macro, the meso and the micro level.

- Macro level: phenomena such as society, culture and civilisation
- Meso level: intermediary entities such as organizations, institutions and social networks
- Micro level: the actions of individuals in interaction with others (groups)

According to this account, organizations are socially located at the meso level. They mediate between the actions of individuals and social structures.

The same system can be found in organizations themselves, which can also be divided into these three levels (Luhmann, 2000).

Organizational theory has developed a number of patterns. The transfer of the sociological approach to organizations is one of these. The division of organizations into micro, meso and macro levels distinguishes the level of aggregation of the consideration of an organization. The micro level is the individual, the meso level groups and the macro level the whole company and other institutions (Peffer, 1982).

Most micro-level processes are dependent on macro-level processes. If this dependency does not exist, change can be successfully implemented at the micro level. In all other cases, the big picture needs to be recognised and worked on. Even if this processing has not yet been completed at the macro level, it helps to know the connections at the level of deeper processes and to take them into account in their design.

How can we imagine this in practice? In the example given, the company's board would get a picture of the organization. To do this, he should ideally involve all the company's employees. No one knows the company better than the employees as a group: they can provide a sober, unbiased view of the company's situation. In addition to the underlying model, Potentialum also provides a diagnostic tool that can be used to develop a self-image of the company. It is like a map on which the strengths and weaknesses can be recognised at a glance.[1]

With the help of these results, the board can then hold a co-creation workshop and decide on initial measures. Co-creation workshops would then be carried out in other divisions of the company, and the measures would be broken down as goals for the next level.

Measures of change often manifest themselves in altered structures and processes. These have an impact on all other related structures and processes. It is like an "organizational mobile". If a thread is pulled in one part, another part begins to wobble.

However, the division head who brought the topic up to the board would not have to wait until the initiative starts in his division. If he wants to develop his division further, he can already start doing so. With the results of the organizational diagnosis, his department knows exactly what to look out for. It knows which structures and processes are being worked on. The measures that are decided in co-creation workshops in his division would—with the big picture in mind—be aligned accordingly and thus promote the development of both the division and organization as a whole.

Co-creation can thus take place at all levels simultaneously. The more global the scale on which the company starts, the more likely it is to act at the macro level. As more iterations are gone through, the fields of action relate to partial aspects of the organizations, areas, specific functions, services or products. This is where the micro-level of the organization is located. All the levels are interdependent. However, work at the micro level must never disregard the global issues at the macro level. This applies above all to structures and processes that ensure networking at the overall company level.

[1] Potentialum is a stand-alone online analysis with an advisory process: www.potentialum.ch

It is immediately obvious that there are dependencies between the levels of the company. What other dependencies need to be taken into account?

Processes and structures are also interdependent in terms of content. If, for example, an organization's understanding of leadership changes, this has a direct influence on HR processes. It follows that work on specific issues can only be successful if it has an integrated perspective and takes interactions into account. Therefore, it is imperative to always have an overall picture of the organization on the radar.

These requirements will be discussed further in Chap. 10 on co-creation and organizational development. At this stage, however, it is important to understand that an organizational model and associated diagnostic tool is needed to align individual co-creation outcomes. There needs to be a big map that can be used to classify individual co-creation workshops. Otherwise, co-creation workshops that are not oriented towards the overall development of the organization would represent isolated measures that could not contribute to the sustainable development of the organization.

The question now arises as to what an organizational model would look like which, on the one hand, would be able to represent the complexity of organizations in a simple way and, on the other hand, would take the essential aspects into account.

The following section begins by discussing the framework conditions of such a model. In the following section, the factors are then derived from the framework conditions and the model is created.

4.2 Framework Conditions for an Organizational Model

In the previous section, it was explained that companies are located at the meso level. They are located between society (the macro level) and the social action of individuals (the micro level). Donges (2008) calls the interface between the organization and society the "macro-meso level" (which includes "the organization in society") and the interface between the organization and individuals the "micro-meso level" (which includes individuals in organizations.)

Donges states in the same passage: "The meso level of organizations is thus not simply the middle of the three classical levels of social science theory, it represents a 'way of looking at things that is pushed between the macro and micro levels and mediates between them' [...]. Donges calls this the mediating character of the meso level. The mediating character of the meso level is rooted in the 'hermaphroditic existence' of organizations. Organizations are both (corporate) actors that act vis-à-vis other corporate actors in society and structures in which individual actors act [...]. Exaggeratedly formulated: an organization is always both micro and macro".

This makes clear that organizations are the melting pot of global economic and social individual trends. Many things meet here and must be integrated: on the global level, megatrends such as digitalisation, globalisation, climate change and so on; on the individual level, megatrends such as the generational question, individualisation and changing values.

An up-to-date organizational model should take this into account. It should be able to map the micro and macro levels so that it can integrate the megatrends on both levels.

4.2.1 Influence of the Macro Level

How does the macro level currently impact companies? We are at the beginning of the Fourth Industrial Revolution: "The so-called Fourth Industrial Revolution is characterised by individualisation or hybridisation of products and the integration of customers and business partners into business processes". (Bendel, 2019). To be able to do this, companies must change the way in which they deliver economic services. This necessarily means that the form and functioning of organizations must also adapt. What are the key factors that make a company fit for the future today? What are the areas that a company must pay attention to, if it wants to manage the transformation into this new world?

Industry 4.0 describes how the industry of the future is changing. Does this designation assume that we are still in the industrial age? In the past, industry has been understood to mean significant continuity and predictability. In Industry 4.0, however, individualisation and the integration of customers and business partners are particularly important. In other words, the clear opposite of continuity and plannability. The model of the Taylor tub aptly illustrates the development.

The Taylor tub (Fig. 4.1) was named after Frederick Winslow Taylor. Taylor was an American engineer and is considered one of the founders of labour science. His name is representative of the transition from the manufacturing age to the industrial age. His approach was called "scientific management".

It was based on the following principles (Wikipedia):

1. The external (e.g. suppliers) and internal (e.g. workflows) processes of a company can be calculated and mastered.
2. The work can be separated into executive and planning work.
3. The workers and machines only perform individual functions (specialisation) that can be centrally planned and controlled (centralisation).
4. Using scientific methods, it is possible to determine the best way to carry out a work step.
5. The work processes necessary to manufacture a product consist of a specific and definable sequence of execution functions.
6. People only work to earn money.

Continuity and predictability were a phenomenon of the industrial age with little dynamism, an era that is just now coming to an end. In the period before that, there were high levels of dynamism and individualisation in local markets. Today, in the information and knowledge age, we have high levels of dynamism and

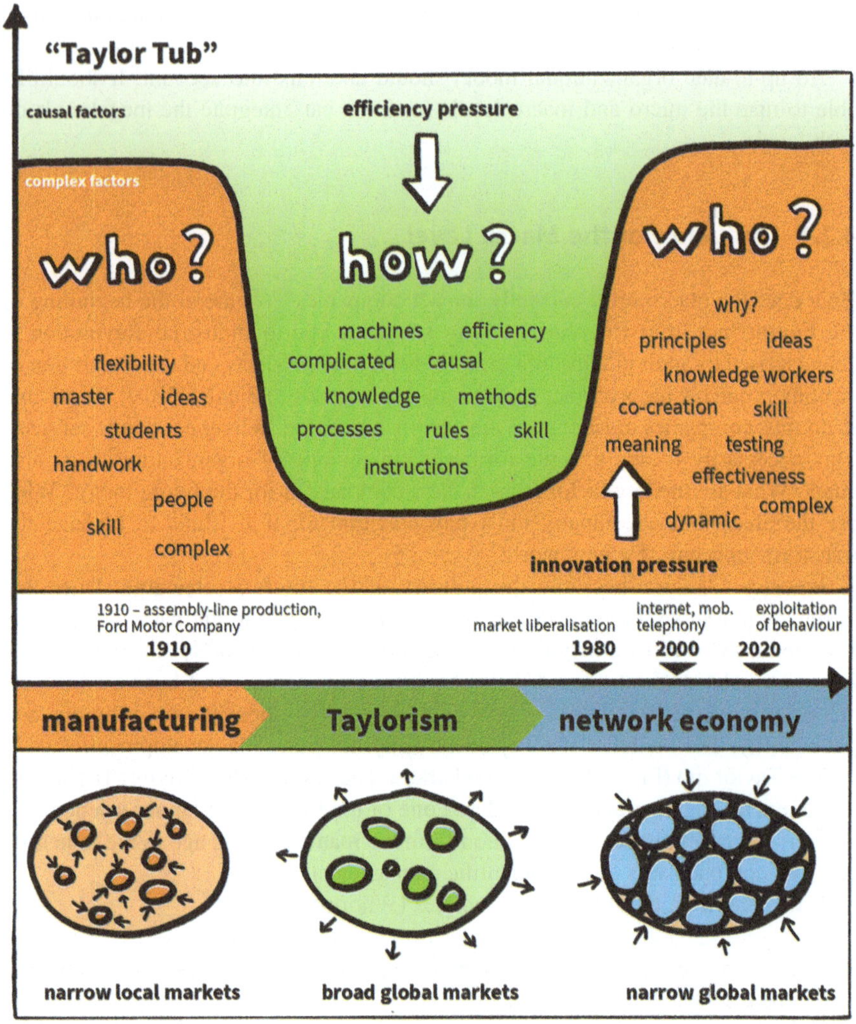

Fig. 4.1 Taylor tub (following Oestereich, 2019)

individualisation once again, only now in global and narrow markets. So it is clear that our understanding of industry has to change. Today, we have increased complexity and volatility. It makes organizational forms necessary that are much more agile than in the decades before.

4.2.2 Influence of the Micro Level

It is not only the global economic environment that is undergoing fundamental change, but also people's expectations of how they can shape their work. These changes can be felt everywhere. Unlike in the past, our working lives are changing so fast that most workers are aware of this change. The speed of development is greater than our threshold of perception. This means that we have not yet come to take previous trends for granted before the next trend is already noticeable. This makes the change perceptible to working people and present in their consciousness.

At present, there are essentially three megatrends which, at the micro level of organizations, make their further development inevitable.

1. *Work-Life Flow:*

During a cosy get-together on a Sunday evening, our neighbour casually said: "Look, thirteen emails in my business inbox, and that's on a Sunday". In public transport everywhere, people are reading or answering emails, making business calls and jotting down ideas. There are few companies that have not yet dealt with whether or not they want to allow their employees to work from home, what scope the scope of this might be and whose responsibility it is. The pioneer in Germany is Microsoft:

"Work-life flow instead of work-life balance. Increasing complexity of work, the growing importance of knowledge, diverse skills and teamwork—in the course of their digital transformation, companies are creating more and more open platforms for employees and interdisciplinary teams to drive innovation. [...] With the idea of 'work-life flow', Microsoft orients itself towards the reality of its employees' lives and allows them more flexibility in organising the daily lives of them and their families. The work-life flow replaces the concept of work-life balance. Here, the self-determined organization of everyday life with flowing transitions takes the place of a rigid distribution of work and private life, which can hardly be represented in everyday life" (Richter, 2016).

2. *Future of Work:*

The Future of Work mindset addresses the redesign of the world of work. It concerns attitudes towards work among people, organizations and society as a whole. Future of Work represents a counterbalance to work-life flow, where the boundaries between professional and private life are beginning to dissolve, the new-work movement takes care to ensure that the new working world is motivating and flexible to the extent that the private sphere also has its place. Unlike in the past, however, it is more in line with the needs of today's employees.

This model includes self-determined working hours, individual employment contracts and strong co-determination: "The central values of new work: autonomy, freedom of action, self-realisation and participation in the community" (Evsan) (n.d.).

In terms of cooperation, new work is characterised by flat hierarchies and mixed teams. This requires a different understanding of leadership. Leadership is no longer line management. Rather, the focus is on the function of leadership as support in the orientation towards the common goal. Leadership can then also occur through teams, through roles and in self-leadership.

3. *Work 4.0:*

Megatrend number three in the world of work is the "Work 4.0" model: "With increasing digitalisation, people's work is also changing in general, regardless of the sector. This affects the design of the workplace itself. New tools and communication possibilities are creating completely new ways of working (together). Whether co-working spaces, home offices or mobile working—they all enable people to have very individual working models. Virtual teams can be put together and departments linked, regardless of location". (denk-neu.com, 2019).

The megatrends at the micro and macro level in our world and societies require many companies to adapt their business model. They must evolve in order to remain adaptable. Change itself becomes a constant companion.

4.2.3 Developing Organizations

Companies still see the situation in very different ways. Some companies are fully aware of the change. They are considering what they can do to prepare their organization for the future. Other companies don't seem to let these insights get to them. They attend events on Industry 4.0 and they see the developments, but at the same time, they seem to be in denial, as if they're thinking: "This Industry 4.0 thing is a trend that doesn't affect us".

Is the reason for this that the challenge of adapting to the "network economy" seems too overwhelming? The image of the three monkeys involuntarily comes to mind (Fig. 4.2):

However, closing one's eyes, not listening and not speaking out won't help. It would be more helpful for companies to openly face the challenge. This is the case when those in charge realise that they are quite capable of making the shift to the new era.

If a manager reads up on modern organizational forms today, he will find impressive examples. Reinventing Organizations by Frederic Laloux (2015) is full of case studies on self-organising, agile companies. It is easy for business leaders to forget that these companies were in very different places when they started. They see

Fig. 4.2 The three monkeys

the impressive examples, compare them to their own reality and see the difference with their company. Then they may realise that they would have to do things very differently. This can seem like a huge challenge, one that is too big to overcome. Perhaps it is also too risky: "After all, at the moment our business is still doing alright. Should we really risk it when we don't know if we will even manage the journey?" This can lead to them possibly giving up before they have even started the process of change.

If you look at the long rows of books on the shelves of management literature, you sometimes get the impression that they are case studies that have been successful in the specific company. But are they necessarily patent recipes that invite imitation?

What decision-makers need is less the shining example and more a systematic approach that allows the company to write its own individual story. This path cannot be prescribed from the outside. Every company has to find it itself. In every company, the path will look different. Every organization is unique, just as the people in the organization are unique.

The decision-makers need a map that is tailored to their company. It has to be unique and show the way forward for this organization in specific. Furthermore, it would be helpful if the map was not fixed for all times, but continuously adapted to current needs. In other words, the organization needs to draw its own map and keep adapting it to the changing landscape. Potentialum provides companies with the framework and tools to create their own map.

When it comes to change, we think of change management. Is Potentialum a form of change management? What distinguishes Potentialum from classic change management?

The traditional understanding of change management is that one static state is transformed into another static state through the expenditure of considerable resources: "Change management encompasses all projects, activities, measures and tasks that are intended to bring about a far-reaching change in an organization. Mostly it is about pursuing new strategies, changing developed structures, renewing technical and organizational systems, improving processes and procedures or influencing and changing the behaviours of employees in the organization". (Fleig, 2019).

This conception of change management works with a project management methodology. It follows the three-phase model developed by Kurt Lewin (1947) from the first half of the last century (Fig. 4.3):

However, such fundamental change projects now only occur in exceptional situations, e.g. a company takeover, a strategic change of direction or when overcoming a major crisis. Fundamentally, the Potentialum approach tries to avoid such change necessities by seeing change as adaptation and as part of working together on a daily basis.

The very fact that such major change projects are necessary can be a sign that the organization has ossified. An organization that functions like an organism is constantly renewing itself. In an organism, the cells are constantly renewing themselves, so that major deficits cannot arise in the first place.

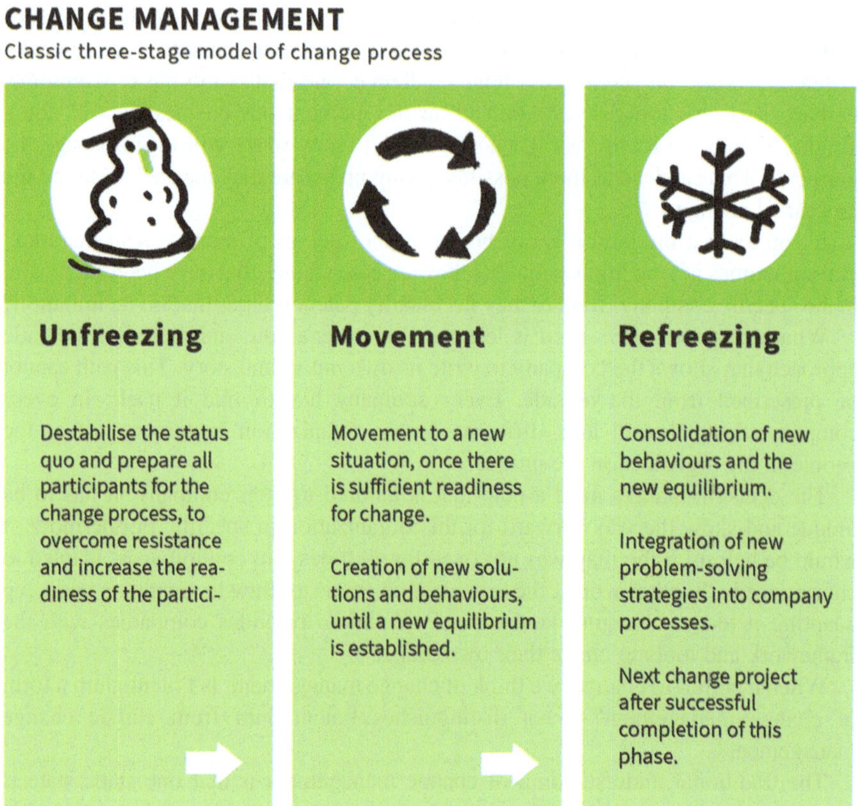

Fig. 4.3 The three-phase model of change management according to Lewin (1947)

Nassim Nicolas Taleb goes one step further and speaks of antifragility (Taleb, 2014). "Antifragility is more than resilience or robustness. What is resilient or resistant withstands shocks and stays the same; the antifragile gets better" (Taleb, 2014). Antifragility is only achieved through repeated failure. Change management in Lewin's sense means waiting to change until there is no other way. This includes the risk of having waited too long. Antifragility, on the other hand, means trying things out again and again and learning from them. As Seth Godin puts it: "Fail fast and cheap. Fail often. Fail in a way that doesn't kill you" (Godin, 2005).

How can this insight into the nature of change be reconciled with the integrative task of the meso level of organizations?

On a global level, the changes represented by the Taylor tub are becoming faster, more complex and more dynamic. We speak of the "VUCA world". VUCA is an acronym for the terms volatility, uncertainty, complexity and ambiguity. It describes difficult framework conditions for corporate management (Wikipedia).

When the global environment changes so rapidly and unpredictably, organizations need management tools that are sufficiently flexible. A 5-year plan may suggest plannability, but it cannot possibly ensure it, given the circumstances. Instead, other forms are developing that combine entrepreneurial vision with planning flexibility.

Objectives and key results ("OKR" for short) is an approach to corporate management that follows this logic (Grove, 1983).

OKR is a thinking and goal-setting framework that helps companies to align their goals. At the same time, OKR ensures that work is actually done on the important goals. OKR follows a simple process of setting and aligning corporate, team and personal goals (objectives) and linking each objective to 3–5 measurable outcomes (key results), in order to measure progress. Measurement is done on a regular basis. In this way, the team always knows where it stands.

OKR thus combines a major objective with the on-going measurements of concrete results (key results). After each measurement, it is possible to correct the actions to see if their implementation has brought the team closer to the big goal. From the measurement, adjustments can be made to the actions in order to then vigorously work on their implementation until the next measurement.

Potentialum considers the key results of the development of the whole company. This makes it possible to align objectives and key results—which are pursued and achieved more at the micro level—with the overall development of the company.

Objectives, measures and results (key results) must therefore be continuously aligned with each other in order to move through the VUCA world in a targeted and simultaneously agile manner.

This provides the basis for the connection between Potentialum and co-creation. Co-creation is a central part of the Potentialum model and the organization's understanding of Potentialum should be an essential part of co-creation. Co-creation and Potentialum are closely linked and complement each other. However, both approaches can also be used independently.

In co-creation, the project goal and the measures are defined, and the success of the implementation is reviewed retrospectively. At the same time, Potentialum sets the objective and reviews the key results of the development of the whole company.

This ensures on-going alignment between the micro and macro levels of the organization.

Allowing one's own antifragile enterprise model to emerge through experience is Potentialum. Co-creation is an essential part of this. The following section explains the structure of the Potentialum model and its process methodology. It also explains how co-creation can contribute to the development of a self-developing organization.

Structure of the Potentialum Model

5

Abstract

The Potentialum model and the Potentialum analysis are intended as a tool enabling companies to better understand their organization. The model provides an easily understandable mental framework so that everyone involved can talk about the same thing. The analysis gives an up-to-date picture of the company. At a glance, everyone can see where its strengths and weaknesses are.

Potentialum is an organizational model that provides a shared perspective on the company. In using it, actors quickly come to speak a common language about their company. As an analytical tool, it can help an organization to hold up a mirror to itself. The results can be used to reach an agreement on the way forward. In the process of co-creation, the map is an important orientation tool for choosing and implementing fields of action.

Keywords

Analysis · Organizational development · Organizational model · Perspective

The Potentialum model and the Potentialum analysis are intended as a tool enabling companies to better understand their organization. The model provides an easily understandable mental framework so that everyone involved can talk about the same thing. The analysis gives an up-to-date picture of the company. At a glance, everyone can see where its strengths and weaknesses are.

Potentialum is an organizational model that provides a shared perspective on the company. In using it, actors quickly come to speak a common language about their company. As an analytical tool, it can help an organization to hold up a mirror to itself. The results can be used to reach an agreement on the way forward. In the process of co-creation, the map is an important orientation tool for choosing and implementing fields of action.

G. Michalik, *Co-Creation Mindset*, Management for Professionals,
https://doi.org/10.1007/978-3-031-21191-1_5

5.1 Constituents of the Potentialum Model

Could this analysis not just rely on the key figures from controlling? Turnover development, employee satisfaction, throughput times, etc. are important indicators. However, one should also be aware of their limitations:

1. Key figures often come with a time delay. Thus, problems may already be extremely advanced by the time the company becomes aware of them.
2. Key figures may not be meaningful and lead to wrong conclusions. A stable order intake may say nothing about how stable the business will be in the future. Without knowing it, the company may be building on a cash cow whose end is near. Customers are still buying because they have the old system. If they switch to the new system, turnover collapses overnight.
3. Key figures are more or less "dead matter". They need to be interpreted by an experienced controller, CEO or CFO. This is exactly where the danger lies, because the assessments made by individuals become relevant for the orientation of the entire company.

This is not meant to be a fundamental criticism of indicators. The key figures that have already been determined are important indicators. They contribute to the overall picture and can strengthen or weaken our impression. However, they arrive relatively late and with many concomitant factors that call for caution, if options for action are to be derived from them alone.

First and foremost, the company needs a mirror to hold up to itself, a full-body mirror in which the essential cornerstones become visible in their interaction. Mirroring also means that the protagonists themselves create the mirror image. The perspective of an external consultancy can provide an additional indicator, just like the key figures, but the self-image must be generated by those who are already on board.

If a company has such a tool, then its employees can decide on measures together, implement them and get a picture of the effectiveness of the measures together. They can exchange ideas with each other and agree on the next steps via co-creation. They can check their results, evaluate them together and plan ahead using co-creation. In this way, the company will continue to develop in a self-directed way, on the foundation of a broad knowledge base.

This can be seen as a planned trial-and-error process. Together, the organization finds out how best to achieve a desired result or a correct solution. It achieves this by trying one or more ways or means and by identifying and eliminating errors or causes of errors.

This approach has already become established in many areas. We then speak of kaizen, continuous improvement, lean management and so on. But these methods are hardly ever applied to the targeted development of the organization as a whole. This often takes place in sub-areas, in projects or in product development. Moreover, often it is only the relevant experts who are involved in the process.

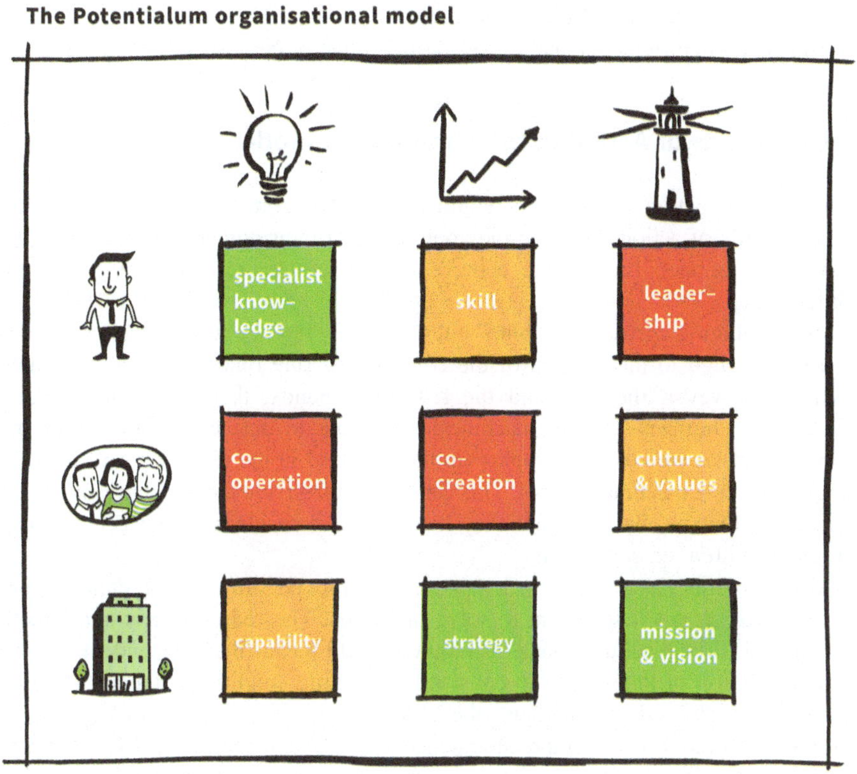

Fig. 5.1 The Potentialum organizational model (Michalik, 2020)

Potentialum facilitates the process of iterative organizational development for the whole company. All the employees are experts who make assessments, contribute their experiences and observations, and propose ideas for the next step—because all the employees are experts about their organization.

The Potentialum organizational model is as follows (Fig. 5.1):

The Potentialum organizational model takes the form of a matrix. The columns represent "fields of action", while the rows represent "actors". This results in nine "impact factors" at the interfaces. A tenth impact factor is the framework surrounding the model.

In the following sections, the components and the overall model are explained in more detail. First, the fields of action are explained, then the actors and finally the resulting impact factors.

The development of Potentialum is derived from four models of organizational theory:

- Douglas McGregor: The Human Side of Enterprise (McGregor, 2006)
- Niels Pfläging: Organization for Complexity (Pfläging, 2015)

- Simon Sinek: Golden Circle (Sinek, 2009)
- Kaplan and Norton: Balanced Scorecard (Kaplan & Norton, 2008)

5.1.1 Fields of Action in the Potentialum Model

The fields of action in the Potentialum model—the columns of the matrix—are called "fields of action" because the application of their components produces the company's impact. In order to achieve impact, companies have very different philosophies.

Niels Pfläging speaks of a "blue" culture and a "red" culture: "Machine intelligence is limited to the domain of the complicated (the blue). In work and value creation, however, the blue and the red shake hands: there, both are present. Fortunately, humans—unlike machines!—are able to act in the domain of the complicated, as well as the complex (in the blue and in the red). Humans can deal with surprises—machines cannot. This can be seen from the fact that humans can do something that no machine can: they have ideas. And ideas are needed to solve problems with a red component".

Both cultures place different demands on employees. In the blue culture, pure "knowledge" is often sufficient to solve problems. The red culture is much more demanding. In this culture, "skill" is required. Skill means the independent transfer and application of knowledge to constantly changing conditions. To cite Pfläging once again: "In today's markets, the ability to solve red problems is crucial. Companies today need machine intelligence to compete for efficiency. The Achilles heel of today's companies is not, however, their lack of ability to use machine intelligence, processes, rules or standards. It is their inability to make use of existing human intelligence. This inability creates suffering in organizations and at work. This affliction is a legacy of the industrial age, whose sluggish, large mass markets made the ability to master blue problems decisive for competition. That age is over: in tight and dynamic global markets with strong competition, solving red problems is becoming the dominant competitive advantage. Tayloristic structures, instruction and control, however, stand in the way of the ability to solve these problems". (Pfläging, 2016).

Pfläging shows how pure data becomes "skill". This is done by linking data to information. The selection of relevant information creates knowledge. Learning then leads to the application of knowledge and becomes "skill". Thus, "learning" becomes "performing". Data and information are "dead" until we give them meaning. Knowledge is different and needs to be absorbed and processed by people. Skill is then the value-creating element. Only people are capable of this. They can combine knowledge content to solve new, previously unknown problems (Oestereich, 2019), (Figs. 5.2 and 5.3).

Knowledge and skill are two of three fields that move people. The third field is the direction of action. It arises from the desire to achieve a certain goal. Besides knowledge and skill, it is "wanting" that moves us to act. "Wanting" refers to the

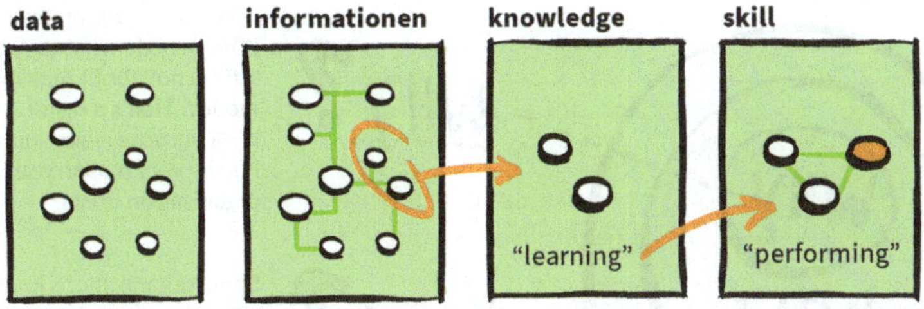

Fig. 5.2 Data, information, knowledge, skills (Oestereich, 2019)

Fig. 5.3 How skill is created

meaning and significance of the goal. For people in organizations, the question is: Whose responsibility is it to answer the question of meaning?

Basically, one would say that each person is responsible for giving meaning to his or her actions. This is also the case in classical hierarchical organizations. But this would be extremely difficult for employees if they did not know what the overall meaning of their actions should be. For individual meaning derives from the meaning of the organization.

In hierarchical organizations, this task is assumed by the leadership. It should provide orientation so that competent, responsible and coordinated employees can act together. The amount of leadership needed for this is determined by various factors:

- Level of knowledge and staff skills
- Clarity of the company's mission, vision and strategy
- Knowledge and understanding of the mission, vision and strategy
- Staff buy-in to the mission, vision and strategy
- Degree of freedom in implementation

Employees with a high level of knowledge and skill and who are aware of the common mission and vision will make up their own minds about the meaning of their actions. They will be able to decide for themselves how to act. Depending on the level of maturity and development of the organization, different forms of

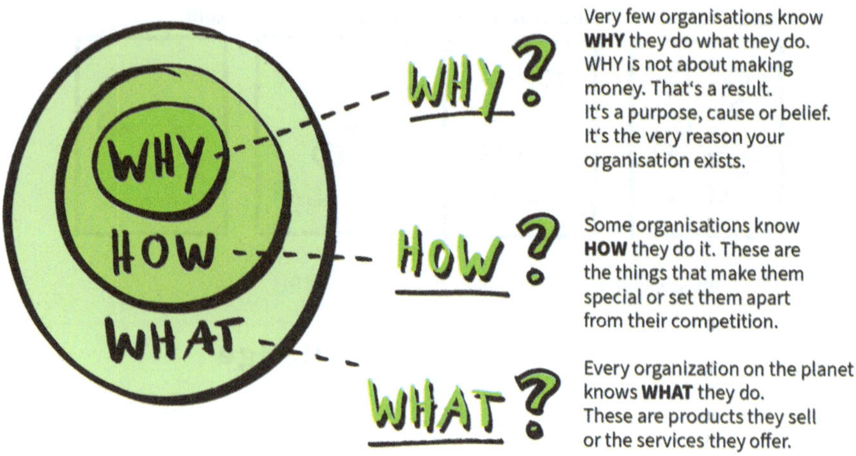

Fig. 5.4 Golden circle (Sinek, 2009)

leadership are needed. In a well-developed, mature organization, it is the culture and values that set the direction. In organizations that are on their way to becoming mature organizations, other proxies for the vision, mission, culture and values are needed. These include, for example, management, decision-making bodies, rules and so on.

In order to determine the impact factors of the Potentialum model, the three fields of knowledge, skill and willingness emerge. In hierarchical organizations, the latter is represented by the leadership. Before the impact factors are determined, the models of Sinek and Kaplan & Norton will be considered in the next sections.

The approach adopted by Simon Sinek asks "why" people want something. By means of the "Golden Circle", he describes three levels of action (Fig. 5.4). At the centre is the "why". The "why" describes the motivation, the actions that result from it and the effect that is produced. On the basis of the "why", the "how" is derived. It determines strategies and processes for successfully implementing the "why". Finally, the "what" is the level that deals with the company's products and services.

Sinek points out that many companies have clarified the "what". They offer a service or a product. Next, they think about how they did this, the "how". Finally, they may think about why they are doing it at all. If they develop their communication and marketing strategy on this basis, it is not very convincing. It is much more convincing if they answer the question of why they intend to do something right at the beginning. This puts the focus on the mission, on the question of meaning and purpose.

In co-creation, this question stands at the very beginning of every journey. This is because the discussion about it creates clarity among those involved. This inevitably leads to the next steps. In full-day co-creation workshops I have often had the experience that answering the question of the actual goal, the "why", took until the lunch break. This is no cause for alarm. The clearer the participants are about

	Pfläging	Sinek	Meaning
level 1	will	Why?	Why do we do what we do?
level 2	skill	How?	How can we implement our goals?
level 3	knowledge	What?	What should we do concretely?

Fig. 5.5 Comparison between Pflaeging and Sinek

what the goal, reason and purpose of their project is, the faster and clearer the subsequent steps will be.

If we now place Pfläeging's three levels next to Sinek's factors, the following picture emerges (Fig. 5.5):

Pfläeging's three levels match Sinek's three questions. The first level is concerned with clarifying the fundamental goal. The question arises: Why do we do what we do? The answer to this is the prerequisite for being motivated to do something.

The second level then concerns implementation: How do we want to proceed? The question of the approach is a question about our skills. Are we or am I able to do what is necessary to achieve the goal?

Level three is the foundation of skill. The knowledge of what needs to be done. If the necessary knowledge is not present in the actors, then it is impossible to start acting. This is true even if the goal is clear.

From Pfläeging's and Sinek's models it becomes clear what the fields of action in an organizational model must focus on:

1. Learned knowledge, theoretical competence, learned skills, decision-making power
2. Competence in action, implementation ability, experiential knowledge, mastery
3. Motivation, direction, leadership, meaning and purpose

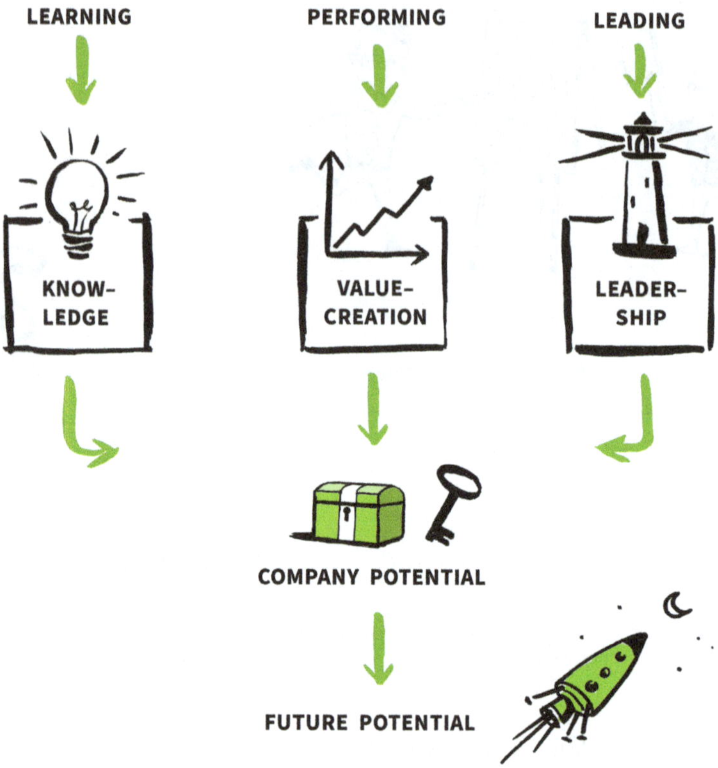

Fig. 5.6 Fields of action in Potentialum

The fields of action in the Potentialum model (Fig. 5.6) summarise the contents of these three dimensions as follows:

4. Knowledge: knowing the essential information
5. Value creation: transforming knowledge into performance
6. Leadership: wanting, making sense, alignment

The potential of a company derives from these. This is where the as yet unexploited opportunities lie dormant. But this is also the source of what makes the company what it is today. Knowledge of the company's potential is what makes planning for the future possible in the first place. Future viability emerges when the company knows the possibilities for its "path to the future". With the knowledge that everyone in the company is aware of these opportunities, future-oriented co-creation can begin. It is not crucial whether the organization is already taking advantage of the opportunities. It is much more important to know them and to set out together to exploit them.

How can this knowledge of potential be used concretely? What function do knowledge, value creation and leadership have for shaping the future?

	KNOWLEDGE	VALUE CREATION	LEADERSHIP
asks about:	what	how	why/goal
does	learning = grasping	performing = applying	leading = giving direction
meaning for the organisation	foundation for value creation	performance and economic efficiency	orientation towards a common goal
area	further education and improvement processes	functions	self-management and line management

Fig. 5.7 Functions of knowledge, value creation and leadership

The function of knowledge, value creation and leadership can be described as follows, depending on one's perspective (Fig. 5.7):

The function of knowledge is to create the foundations of value creation. In organizations, this happens through learning. Learning can be organised formally, usually through a dedicated department. However, continuous learning at work is becoming increasingly important. There are a number of models that support learning on the job:

- 70/20/10: on the job learning
- Action learning
- Continuous improvement process (CIP)
- Lean management (LM)
- Kaizen

The function of value creation is to create value for the customers and the company. This is done by applying knowledge to concrete challenges. These can be products or services. Added value is created for the customers, as well as turnover for the company. The relevant departments and entities are responsible for this.

The task of leadership is to give value creation a common direction. It seeks to bring about targeted action aiming at value creation. Only in this way is it possible to achieve strategic goals and exploit synergies. In this context, it is not mandatory to understand leadership as line management. It can also be exercised by teams and through self-responsibility. This is called self-management.

5.1.2 Actors in the Potentialum Model

The actors are those who execute the fields of action. In other words, they are responsible for knowledge, value creation and leadership. But who are the actors in the company? Are they not simply the employees?

It was already explained at the beginning of this chapter that the division into micro, meso and macro levels allows for different levels of aggregation when looking at an organization. The micro level can refer to the individual, the meso level to groups/teams and the macro level to the whole company (Peffer, 1982).

The actors are first and foremost the employees. These are grouped together at different levels: teams, departments, divisions, the company as a whole. The most basic distinction results in three levels of actors (Fig. 5.8):

- Micro level—employees: the individuals in the organization; the level of the individual human being; how he or she is part of the whole; what is important for the individual, how he or she can contribute and how he or she is rewarded for it.
- Meso level—teams: grouping of employees at different levels; teams, departments, project teams, divisions, main divisions, etc.; hierarchies are also spoken of in this context.
- Macro level—company: the totality of all individuals and teams; the company is an organ and has its own personality; this is, on the one hand, the "legal person" and, on the other hand, everything that makes up the company as a whole, its history, its culture, the brand, etc.

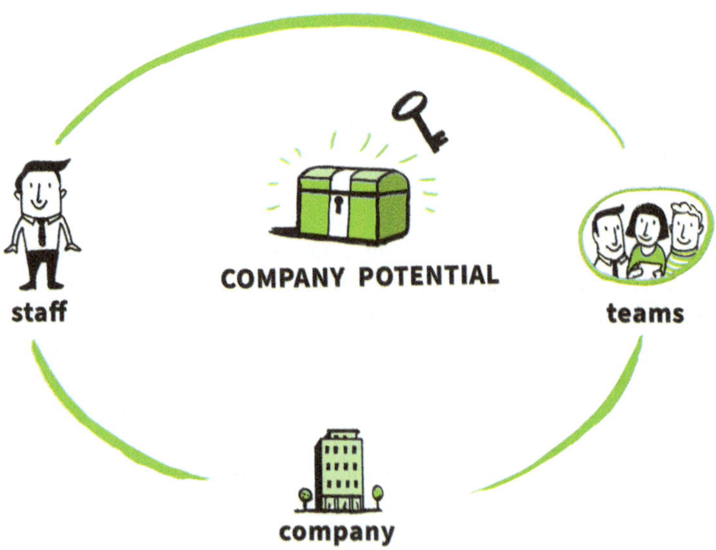

Fig. 5.8 The three levels of actors: employees, teams, company

On the first level, we find the person acting on their own, i.e. the person as an individual. The second level is the team. The team is a manageable group of people. They work together on projects, in structures or even across structures. Finally, on the third level, the top level, we find the organization as a whole, with its own identity and culture. Taken together, these levels constitute the company's potential. They make use of their knowledge, their capacity to create value and their common leadership orientation.

5.1.3 Impact Factors in the Potentialum Model

If we now combine the three fields of action (knowledge, skills and leadership) with the three actors (employees, teams and company), the result is the Potentialum organizational model (Fig. 5.9).

The Potentialum model results from the intersection of two dimensions.

On the x-axis, the fields of action (Fig. 5.10):

On the y-axis, the actors (Fig. 5.11):

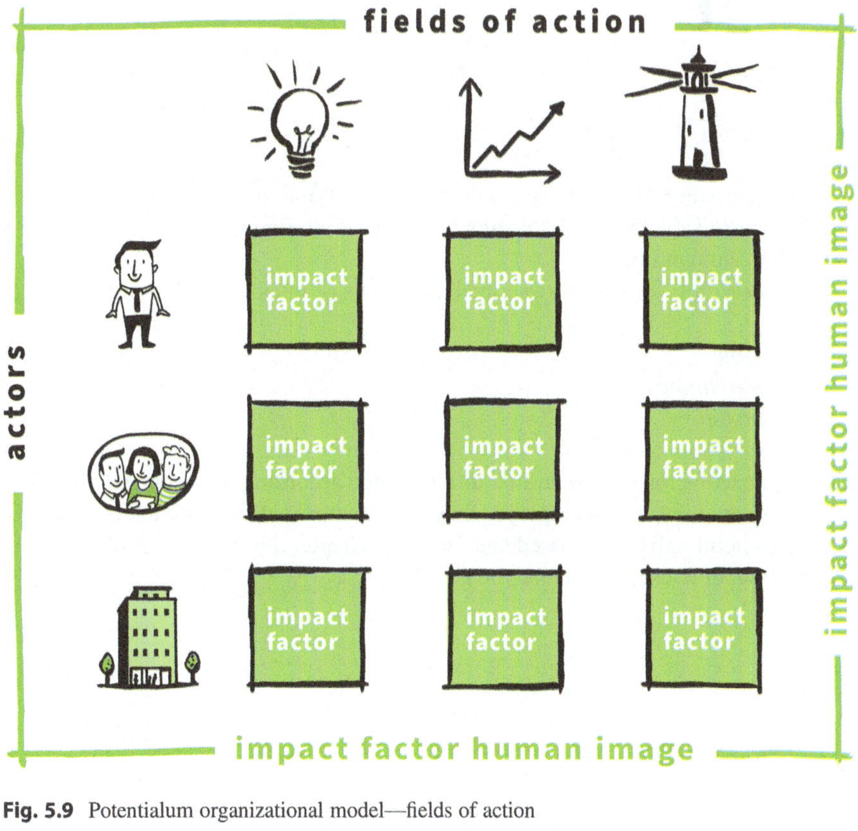

Fig. 5.9 Potentialum organizational model—fields of action

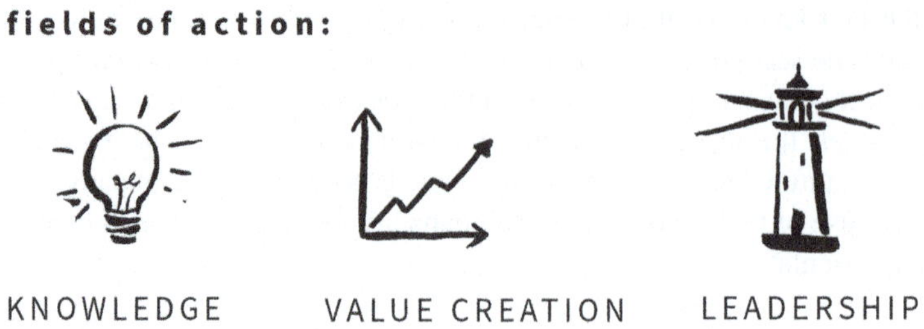

Fig. 5.10 Fields of action

Fig. 5.11 Actors

At the interface between each field of action and actor (Fig. 5.12), there is an impact factor (Table 5.1). This results in a total of nine impact factors, plus a tenth factor: the “human image”.

Impact factors 1–9 can be described as follows (Tables 5.2, 5.3, and 5.4):

1. *Knowledge*
2. *Value creation*
3. *Leadership*

The impact factors can be further differentiated according to the perspective from which they are viewed. An employee may see a company differently than a customer does. This point will be discussed later on in the chapter. First, it is helpful to explain how the model is used as an analytical tool.

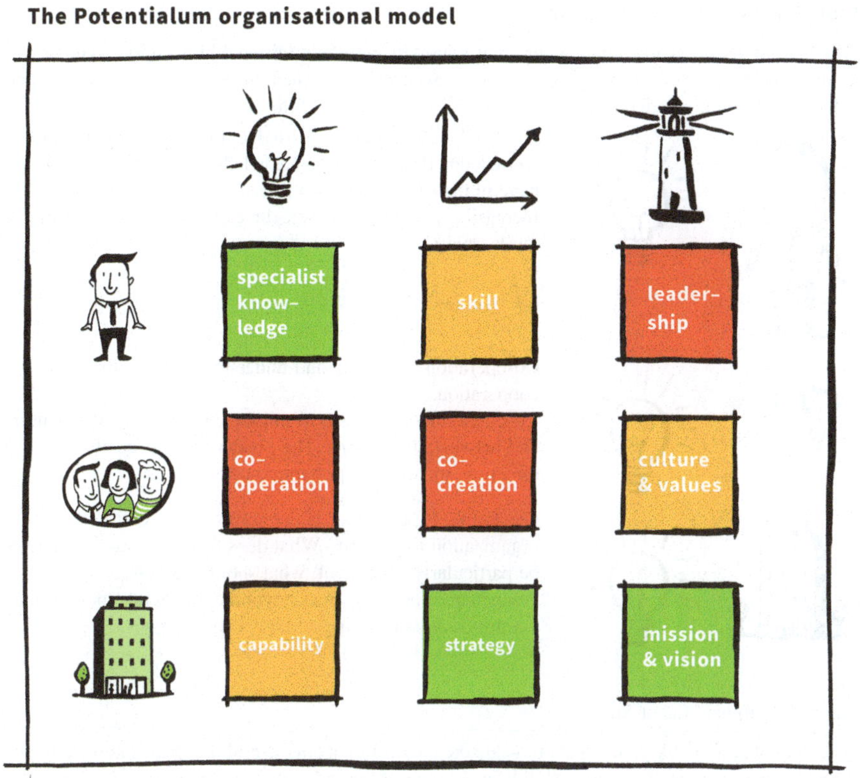

Fig. 5.12 The Potentialum organizational model

Table 5.1 The impact factors

1.	Knowledge × employees =	individual knowledge/specialist knowledge/expert knowledge
2.	Knowledge × team =	co-operation
3.	Knowledge × company =	capability/"organizational capability"
4.	Value added × employees =	skill/implementation/mastery
5.	Value added × team =	co-creation
6.	Value added × company =	strategy
7.	Leadership × employees =	leadership/self-leadership
8.	Leadership × team =	culture & values
9.	Leadership × company =	mission & vision
10.	Human image =	theory XY: how employees are viewed

Table 5.2 Impact factor Knowledge

The field of action "knowledge" is of great importance in the traditional blue culture. The best-known field there is the classic field of human resource development in Box 1: training and further education. But knowledge also provides the basis for the red cultures.

		Knowledge: individual knowledge, the foundation of skill. Knowledge describes what knowledge individuals should have in their role. This also includes competence models. Increasingly important is self-directed learning and on-the-job learning.
		Co-operation: Knowing and understanding the rules of cooperation. Co-operation describes how employees work together within and between their teams. The greater the degree of self-direction, the more important co-operation is.
		Capability: "Capability" is the ability of the entire organization to perform. What does the organization want to be particularly capable of, what should its core competences be? This goes beyond competence models and yet provides their basis.

Table 5.3 Impact factor Skill

The field of action "Skill" is all about value creation. Skill is only useful if it brings knowledge to bear in a way that creates value. Skill is at the core of the red culture. Proximity to the customer and a focus on value creation are central.

		Skill: individual ability to apply knowledge in a value-adding way. The highest form of skill is mastery. The master has broad knowledge and can creatively combine the elements at his disposal into new solutions.
		Co-creation: value-added teamwork. In the process of co-creation, masters of their trade come together to achieve the greatest added value for the customer.
		Strategy: describes how value creation should happen. The strategy sets the direction of value creation. It serves as orientation for the co-creation, determining the areas in which it should be active to create value.

Table 5.4 Impact factor Leadership

The field of action "Leadership" should ensure that individual and collective action are oriented in the same direction across all three levels. This is important in both blue and red cultures. In this way, forces can be bundled together and directed towards a higher common goal. In contrast to the first two columns, there is an interface at each of the three levels: The vision is the basis of the mission. The mission is the basis of the strategy. Values are defined by the organization. What is then done with them is determined by the culture. Culture and values are reflective surfaces for individual sense-making and self-leadership.		
		Finding meaning and self-leadership: people with a high level of knowledge and skill, who are familiar with the common mission and vision, make up their own minds about what the meaning of their actions is and how they should behave. Leadership through culture and values: a reflective surface to guide actions and members of the organization.
		Values: principles of interaction with all stakeholders. The values provide guidance about the form in which the organization wishes to pursue its purpose. Culture: shared norms, values and beliefs. Culture is like a shadow that shows you how the organization behaves. You cannot change it directly, but it is the result of actions.
		Vision: the organization's lighthouse, providing orientation and direction. The vision defines the purpose and the desired future space in which the organization wants to move. All actions should be guided by this vision. Mission: in the mission, future actions are written down and shared with each other. This then represents the foundation for the strategy.

5.1.4 Potentialum Analysis

At the beginning of this chapter, we saw how Potentialum enables a distinctive business model to emerge through experience.[1]

This section explains how the model can be used in an analysis of a company. The result of the analysis is a "company map" that shows where the greatest potential lies. From this, the need for action in the near future can be determined. In the coming months and years, the success of the implementation can be checked by means of follow-up measurements.

How Is this "Map" Created?

The map is created by means of a self-assessment of the company by its employees. They create a picture of where the strengths and weaknesses of the organization are. The survey assumes that the perspective of an outside expert is not the best source of

[1] Potentialum is a stand-alone online analysis with an advisory process: www.potentialum.ch

Fig. 5.13 Colour code Potentialum model

information. Rather, the perception of the company's actors—its employees—is the essential criterion for future viability.

This can be explained using an example. Let us assume that the impact factor "co-operation" was rated low by the employees from the "customer" perspective. This means that the employees have stated that from their point of view, customers could be of the opinion that they, the employees, do not work together closely enough.

In principle, this realisation is more important than the question of whether the customers actually think that the employees do not cooperate much with each other. This is because the actors have to improve the situation, not the customer. Therefore, the insight that the customer might think that they do not work well together is already part of the future intervention.

In order to produce the map, the employees assess the company on the ten impact factors from the perspective of "employees", "processes" and "customers", in relation to 54 criteria. In addition, three questions assess the company's human image.

The assessment is done online and takes about 20 min per employee. The result of the evaluation is the map shown above.

This illustration (Fig. 5.13) displays the evaluation results of a fictitious company. A traffic-light colour code is used.

Green: These are the three strongest fields of action.
Yellow: These are the four average fields of action.
Red: These are the three fields of action with the greatest need for action.

The colour code is created by positioning the survey results relative to each other. The three strongest (green), the four intermediate (yellow) and the three weakest (red) mean values are calculated and the fields of the map are coloured accordingly.

On the map shown in the example, one can thus see at a glance how the company is currently perceived by its actors. The company in this illustration has the greatest need for action in the area of cooperation and alignment through leadership. It rates itself quite well in the area of expertise. The strategy and the mission & vision also seem to be clear. The "human image" (the framework around the matrix), individual skills, the capability of the organization as a whole, and the culture and values are in the middle range.

How Can the Map Be Used to Bring About Change?

In the section "Developing Organizations", the consideration was advanced that change must always have two objectives in mind: on the one hand, the goal of the immediate change that is being worked on at the moment; on the other hand, the big medium- and long-term goal of the whole organization and its current situation, as shown on the Potentialum map.

According to these two target levels, the organization can now implement its measures in many places at the same time and in a coordinated manner. Co-creation can be put in place on the macro level, using the Potentialum map to identify fields of action and to assess the change by means of the Potentialum measurement. Co-creation can also be implemented at many different micro levels. This is guided, on the one hand, by the goals of the micro level and, on the other hand, by the goals of the macro level. The latter serves as an orientation to keep checking whether the micro-level measures are contributing to the development of the company as a whole.

The assessment of the company's ten impact factors can be done from different perspectives. Depending on whether the perspective of the employees, the customers or the processes is taken, different assessments can result. The "balanced scorecard" lays out these various perspectives, and the following section explains how the impact factors can be viewed through this lens.

5.1.5 Impact Factors and the Balanced Scorecard

The balanced scorecard (BSC) goes back to Kaplan and Norton (2018). With the help of the balanced scorecard, companies can measure and document how well they succeed in implementing their vision and strategy. The first-generation balanced scorecard measured four aspects:

1. Financial: determine relevant financial figures, such as cash flow, sales growth, operating profit, return on equity.
2. Customer: measures to answer the question "What is important to our customers and stakeholders?" Examples: percentage of sales of new products, adherence to deadlines, percentage of purchases by important customers, ranking by important customers.
3. Internal business processes: measures to answer the question "What do we need to excel at?" Examples: cycle time, unit costs, yield, new product introduction.
4. Learning and growth: actions to answer the question "How can we continue to improve, create value and innovate?" Examples: time to develop a new product generation, lifecycle to product maturity, time to market compared to competition.

The dimensions of the BSC are determined individually for a given application. However, they practically always include the financial perspective (return) and the customer perspective (output), and usually also the process perspective (process) and the potential or employee perspective (input) (Wikipedia).

In order to further differentiate the impact factors, each of the nine factors was differentiated at the item level, in line with three of the four BSC perspectives:

Table 5.5 Differentiating factors

Employees	Places the field of action (e.g. knowledge), under the BSC aspect "employees", in the context of value creation. Example: "Our employees have sufficient knowledge to fulfil their tasks".
Customer	Places the conditions and effects of the field of action (e.g. knowledge), under the BSC aspect "customer", in the context of value creation. To take the example of knowledge: "Customers perceive our employees as well trained".
Process	Places the field of action (e.g. knowledge), under the BSC aspect "processes", in the context of value creation. Example: "We have processes (exchange of information, Erfa groups, etc.) in which learning takes place systematically".

Table 5.6 Knowledge

		Knowledge: individual knowledge, the basis of skill.
Employees		Individual learning through formal and informal learning opportunities. The aim is for staff to have sufficient knowledge to fulfil their role/function.
Customer		Knowledge that the employee must have in order to be able to create the greatest possible benefit for the customer.
Process		Staff development process Informal learning process Formal learning process, etc.

- Employees
- Customer
- Processes

The Potentialum analysis makes a statement about the company's potential in its overall result. The "financial" aspect of the BSC is the result of the utilisation of potential. Hence, in order to avoid confusing cause and effect, no financial key figures are determined in the Potentialum analysis.

Each of the nine impact factors is thus differentiated according to the three factors: customer, employees, process (Table 5.5).

In the case of the impact factors, the details are as follows (Tables 5.6, 5.7, 5.8, 5.9, 5.10, 5.11, 5.12, 5.13, and 5.14):

This concludes the list of the nine impact factors that compose the model and which form the basis of the Potentialum analysis.

As announced at the beginning of this chapter, McGregor's theory XY will be discussed again. It is integrated into the Potentialum model as the tenth impact

Table 5.7 Co-operation

		Co-operation: having, knowing and understanding the rules of cooperation.
Employees		Shared understanding of how to work together in the organization. The rules of cooperation form the basis for this.
Customer		From the customer's point of view, the cooperation within the company must function smoothly and give the customer the certainty that they will receive the expected products and services.
Process		Meeting procedure CIP, kaizen Mutual updates

Table 5.8 Capability

		Capability: the performance capacity of the entire organization
Employees		Define the required knowledge and the basics of cooperation that are needed from an overall organizational perspective in order to successfully implement the strategy.
Customer		An innovative and competent company, from the customer's point of view, that is a reliable partner in the long term.
Process		Innovation process Personnel development process Organizational development process

Table 5.9 Skill

		Skill: individual ability to apply knowledge in a value-adding way.
Employees		Conversion of situational and declarative knowledge into practical knowledge.
Customer		Solutions that are implemented with great precision and accuracy.
Process		Order clarification Solution development Implementation/delivery

Table 5.10 Co-creation

		Co-creation: value-added teamwork.
Employees		Subjective relationship between people who come together in thought for the development of their shared creative potential.
Customer		Solving complex problems by connecting experts. The client receives innovative and viable solutions to novel problems.
Process		Group processes Self-control Holacracy, agility, etc.

Table 5.11 Strategy

		Strategy: describes how value creation should happen.
Employees		Clarity about the direction of individual and collective action. Guiding star in light of which actions are aligned.
Customer		Market-driven product range that captures customers' current and future needs.
Process		Strategy definition process Goal definition process Objectives and key results—OKR process

Table 5.12 Leadership

		Self-discovery and self-leadership: employees steer their actions in a common direction. Leadership through culture and values: reflective surface for guiding actions and members of the organization.
Employees		Aligning the actions of individuals and teams to achieve the goals defined in the strategy.
Customer		Aligning service delivery with the needs of clients and the organization.
Process		Leadership skills Leadership process Leadership development

Table 5.13 Values

		Values: principles governing interactions with all stakeholders. Culture: shared norms, values and beliefs.
Employees		The values communicate to the members of the organization characteristics, qualities and beliefs that are considered desirable and good.
Customer		Create orientation and focus on what is meaningful to the interests of the customer.
Process		All processes in which the organization's values are defined and introduced, and their meaningfulness and compliance checked.

Table 5.14 Vision and mission

		Vision: the organization's lighthouse that gives orientation and direction. Mission: sets out in writing the actions to be taken in the future.
Employees		Describes the vision for the organization's members: what the organization wants to be for its members, what the relationship between the two sides should be and what the common future should look like.
Customer		Describes the vision for current and future customers: what the company's services and products should be, do and provide in terms of benefits.
Process		All processes in which the organization's vision is defined, introduced, and its meaningfulness and relevance are checked.

factor, providing the framework for the other nine impact factors. How management views people affects how employees implement the other nine factors.

5.1.6 The Tenth Factor: The Human Image

Companies demand a high level of commitment from their employees. This is reflected in the fact that, these days, it is no longer employee satisfaction that is measured, but "commitment". However, only people who think independently and act on their own responsibility are willing to commit themselves. At this point, the question of whether organizations need people who think independently and act on their own responsibility or people who follow orders as employees seems to have been decided. As early as 1960, Douglas McGregor addressed this question in his book The Human Side of Enterprise.

Fig. 5.14 Human images X and Y (McGregor, 2006)

McGregor distinguishes human images X and Y (Fig. 5.14):

McGregor's insight is not just a mere description of the two ways of looking at people. The core message of the model is that people conform to the expectations placed on them. One might say: "When companies shout into their organizational forest, the same sound echoes back". If companies see their employees as recipients of orders, then they will behave like recipients of orders. If, however, they give them trust and personal responsibility, they will live up to this responsibility.

Theory X and Y is used in the Potentialum model as the tenth impact factor. It provides the framework for the other nine impact factors. How management views people directly affects the performance of the other nine factors.

In saying this, I want to make clear that it will be difficult to introduce co-creation into a company if the company management has the human image corresponding to theory X. The following example illustrates how theory X can still be experienced today.

EXAMPLE

A company was planning a leadership programme for the top managers. Leadership development programmes already existed for the two lower management levels, teaching basic leadership skills. So this programme was not designed to teach classic line management, but rather how the top managers could manage complexity on a global level. To do this in a practical way, a topic critical to the success of the company was chosen: the identification and promotion of talent. The 1-week programme was structured in such a way that at the beginning, there was an introduction and an examination of the subject "talent management". By the middle of the week, it was theoretically clear to all participants what was important. The task of the second half of the week was for the participants to organise themselves in such a way as to reach an agreement on concrete measures for talent development. The participants were given a setting with roles that corresponded to the company. At the same time, they were able to learn on a meta-level how to deal with the complexity of their company. After a somewhat turbulent initial phase, as expected, the participants had soon developed good self-organization. Towards the end of the week, they had concrete ideas on how to promote talent management. The mood was euphoric among the vast majority of participants. However, a few of them were somewhat unsettled and wondered whether the process was intended to work like this or whether the trainers had simply neglected to plan properly. The group had learned something on two levels:

- On the substantive level: How can we identify and promote talent?
- On the meta-level: How would we have to manage our interfaces in the company in order to solve complex problems?

Two weeks later, the lead trainer was invited for a meeting with the client to evaluate the pilot event. He was greeted with the words: "Well, that didn't amount to much". This surprised him greatly, as the feedback had been consistently good to very good, and the atmosphere had also been excellent.

(continued)

The client's assessment was based on the impressions of a few participants who felt that the process was not very structured. The trainer explained to him that this had been done on purpose, in order to trigger "meta-innovations" among the participants. The client listened to his explanation of self-organization in the programme with interest, but concluded: "I understand the idea, but it doesn't work for us, because our people are simply not capable of it".

Does this story sound somehow familiar to you? If so, then you have experience with the human image corresponding to theory X. Corporate leaders who judge people according to this image do not have bad intentions. On the contrary, they are concerned about and care for their employees. They want everyone to be successful, to feel good and to remain loyal to the company for a long time. It's just that they prefer to control rather than to trust. A process of co-creation, in which all employees can contribute, does not correspond to this mentality.

Impact factor 10 "human image" therefore provides the framework for the Potentialum model. For each of the factors, it determines the degree to which employee involvement is possible. If it is evident that the management is strongly attached to human image X, then a cautious approach should be taken. It is definitely advisable to clarify with the management what organizational and decision-making freedom they envision for co-creation. It may be that the leadership is willing to experiment and allow co-creation in one part of the organization. It can be particularly effective to involve the top management itself in the co-creation process, so that the leadership can assess how and where co-creation can be used.

This concludes the section on Potentialum. Potentialum is an organizational model that provides a shared perspective on the company. In using it, actors quickly come to speak a common language about their company. As an analytical tool, it can help an organization to hold up a mirror to itself. The results can be used to reach an agreement on the way forward. In the process of co-creation, the map is an important orientation tool for choosing and implementing fields of action.

In the first five chapters, the basics of the co-creation process were derived and presented. The sixth chapter now describes the co-creation process itself.

The Co-creation Process

6

Abstract

The aim of co-creation is to connect people to a shared consciousness so that they can let the future emerge. Mindset, values and principles are the basic attitudes and assumptions upon which co-creation is based. By means of the co-creation process, co-creation should be able to be employed as a method.

The co-creation process has four phases with all in all eight steps. Each phase and all steps are listed and described to give you an idea of what exactly happens at each phase in the process. If you run co-creation workshops yourself, it can also help you to prepare for the individual phases. An interview with Anke Bridge and their experiences at bank Credit-Suisse gives an example of applying co-creation.

Keywords

Workshop · Phases · Process

At the beginning of the book, the co-creation process was briefly described. In Chaps. 2 and 3, the levels of mindset, values and principles were described. In this chapter, the phases and the associated process steps are presented in more detail.

The co-creation process has four phases with all in all eight steps. In this chapter the four phases are listed and described. The aim of this chapter is to give you an idea of what exactly happens at each phase in the process. If you run co-creation workshops yourself, it can also help you to prepare for the individual phases (Fig. 6.1).

The chapter closes with an Interview of Anke Bridge and their experiences at bank Credit-Suisse while applying co-creation.

G. Michalik, *Co-Creation Mindset*, Management for Professionals,
https://doi.org/10.1007/978-3-031-21191-1_6

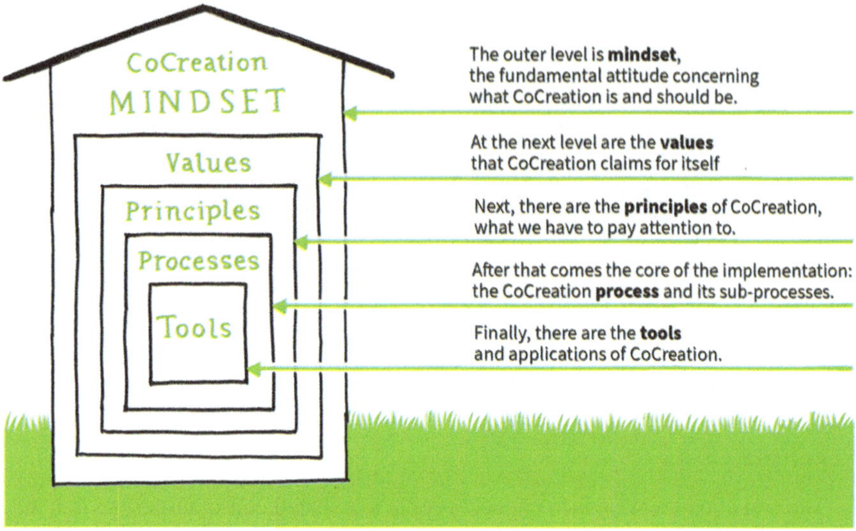

Fig. 6.1 The level of the co-creation process

6.1 Phases and Process Steps in Co-creation

The aim of co-creation is to connect people to a shared consciousness so that they can let the future emerge. Mindset, values and principles are the basic attitudes and assumptions upon which co-creation is based. By means of the co-creation process, co-creation should be able to be employed as a method.

The co-creation process is the implementation of co-creation in workshops. What are the basic assumptions necessary for co-creation to happen in a workshop? Essentially, there are three elements that have to happen for the future to emerge from a shared consciousness:

1. *Connection:* Participants are connected to each other on different levels.
   - They are connected with themselves and mentally present. They are completely present.
   - They are connected individually with the other participants. They know their essential personality traits.
   - They are all connected to each other as a team to form a whole. They are aware of potential dynamics and have a shared idea of how to deal with them.
   - They are connected to the goal on the individual level. They see the benefit of achieving the goal for themselves or for their own work.
   - They are collectively connected to the goal. They see the benefit of the goal for themselves as a group. They are aware of the benefits that all the other participants see for themselves.

2. *Simultaneity:* The participants move in synchrony through the process.
   - In its functioning, the group should be connected through a collective consciousness. This requires everyone to go through the stages of the process at the same time.
   - On the emotional level, the participants experience the process at the same moment. Highs and lows are felt at the same time.
   - To ensure simultaneity, the process can only function co-creatively as long as all the members are together. The team should live the process cohesively.
3. *Analysis and innovation process*
   - The participants go through the process of understanding and finding solutions at the same time. The process helps the team to mutually reinforce their thinking, feeling and decision-making.
   - The process is logical, complete and conclusive in itself.
   - The process finds acceptance from all personality types. It is logical, innovative, builds rapport, creates clear responsibilities and gets to the point quickly.

A participant in a co-creation workshop once explained the principle as follows: "The process is emptied of emotion, which gives us a clear view of what can be changed". I wouldn't put it quite like that, but the statement nevertheless picks up on an important aspect. By connecting so thoroughly and pursuing a common goal through an intuitive process, the group is able to leave certain egotistical behaviours behind. By this, I mean behaviours that are concerned with social positioning within the group. This does actually make it easier to have a clear view and to engage fully with the issue.

The co-creation process is structured in a systematic way. It is divided into four phases (Fig. 6.2), containing a total of eight steps (Fig. 6.3). The first step is then repeated at the end, so that the participants actually go through eight steps. In addition, there is a preparation and a follow-up to the process.

When approached from the centre outwards, the co-creation process contains:

1. The name of the process
2. The four phases of the process
3. The eight process steps
4. A brief explanation of the process steps

The structure of the co-creation process can be presented in four phases:

- *Phase 1: Connecting*
  - Step 1—"Connect" at the start of the process: connect people and ideas in relation to the goal.
  - Step 8—"Connect" at the end of the process: connect people for the implementation.

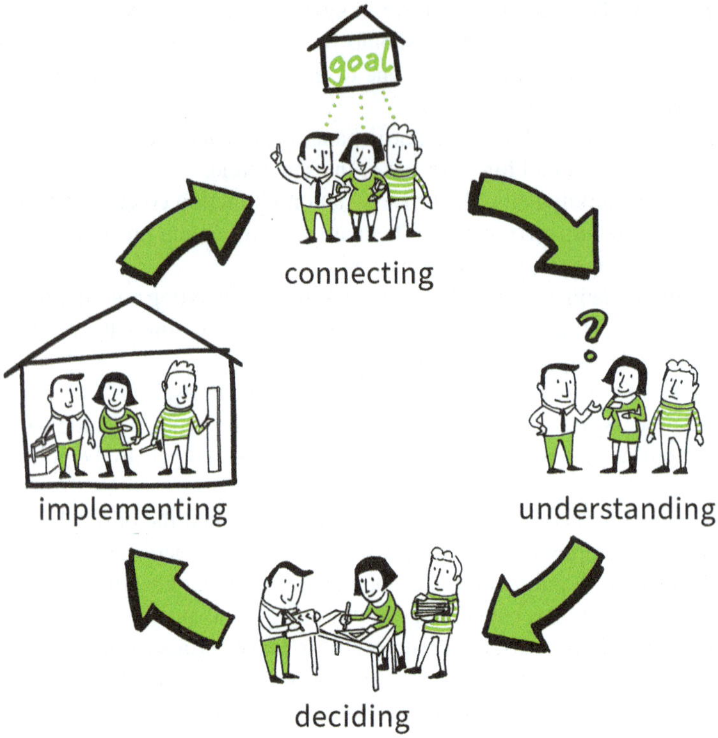

Fig. 6.2 The four phases of co-creation

- *Phase 2: Understanding*
  - Step 2—"Discover": discover the facts.
  - Step 3—"Explore": understand the background.
  - Step 4—"Share": share the conclusions.
- *Phase 3: Deciding*
  - Step 5—"Agree": decide.

- *Phase 4: Implementing*
  - Step 6—"Create": create solutions.
  - Step 7—"Do": implement solutions.
  - Step 8—"Connect": reflecting collaboration

6.2 Description of the Four Phases of the Co-creation Process

The four phases of co-creation can be described as follows.

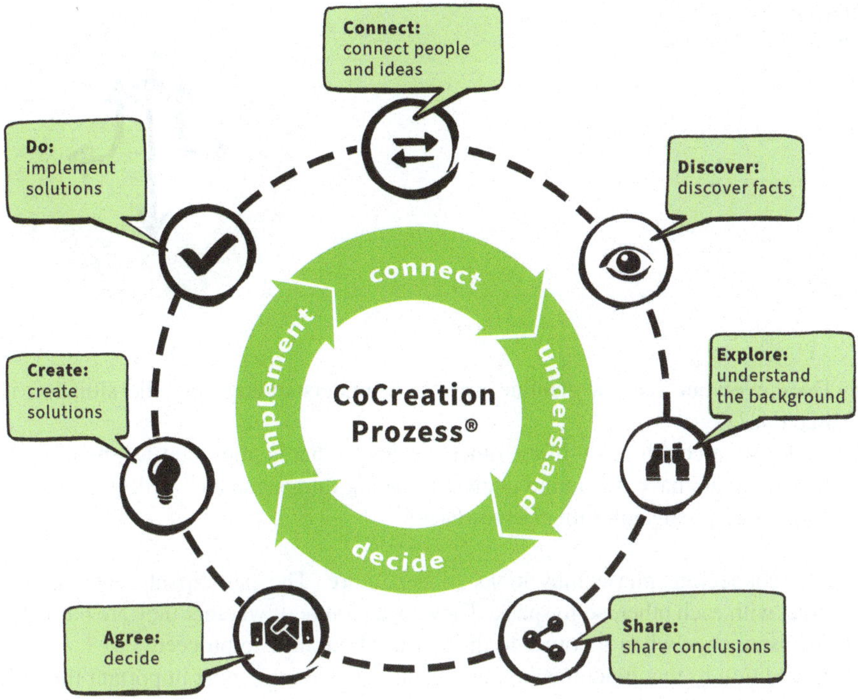

Fig. 6.3 Co-creation process

Fig. 6.4 Connecting as the basis for further work

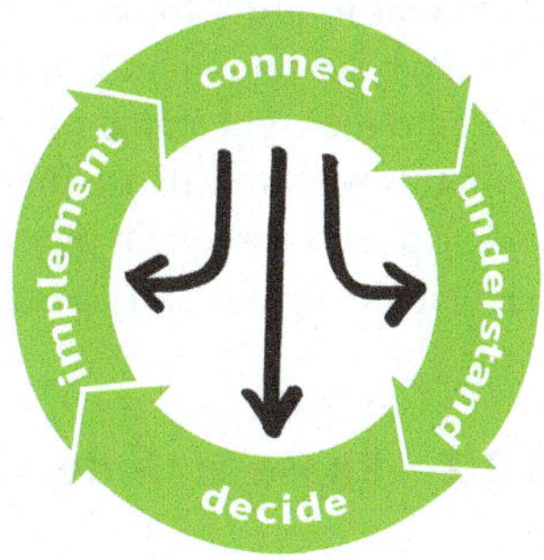

6.2.1 Phase 1: Connecting

Connect ensures that all people can fully engage in the subsequent phases. In doing so, they realise that they are all pushing in the same direction (Fig. 6.4). Each participant may have different reasons why the goal is important to them, and everyone should know these reasons. Trust does not just happen. What questions should the participants be able to answer?

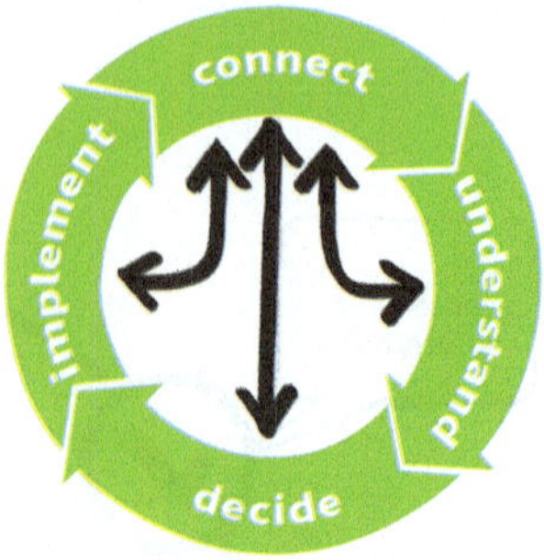

Fig. 6.5 The anchoring function of connecting

- Does everyone have a genuine interest in understanding why the situation is like this?
- Under what conditions will the others decide? What is important for them?
- Do the others have a genuine interest in seeing things change? Will they remain committed to engaging themselves later?

The connecting phase thus looks to the future. The participants enter into a contract with each other, so to speak. They get a picture of whether they are basically on the same page when it comes to their ideas about how to proceed.

In addition to this fundamental alignment, however, the most important thing in connecting is to commit to a common goal. This should create a common image of a "golden future" among the participants. They can go so far as to picture a journey into the future. In this way, everyone is anchored by the same image. This is important in order to have the goal as a guiding star in the following three phases. The analyses and ideas can take their lead from this guiding star. It helps people to "get into the right frame of mind" together.

In this way, this phase functions like an anchor, which participants return to again and again in subsequent phases (Fig. 6.5). A kind of control loop is created, in which the results are checked at each phase to see if they correspond to the goal.

6.2.2 Phase 2: Understanding

The task of the understanding phase is to recognise how the situation compares to the goal (Fig. 6.6). The relationship between connecting and understanding involves a comparison between "should" and "is". Connecting gives the goal, i.e. what "should" be the case, while understanding looks at the current situation, i.e. what actually "is" the case. To avoid jumping to conclusions, understanding is divided into three process steps: "Discover", "Explore" and "Share".

The "*Discover*" phase only looks at the pure facts: What information sources are available and what do they tell us? Only information is gathered at this point.

Next, this information is explored in more depth through a root-cause analysis in "*Explore*". The participants explore what the root causes of the circumstances are.

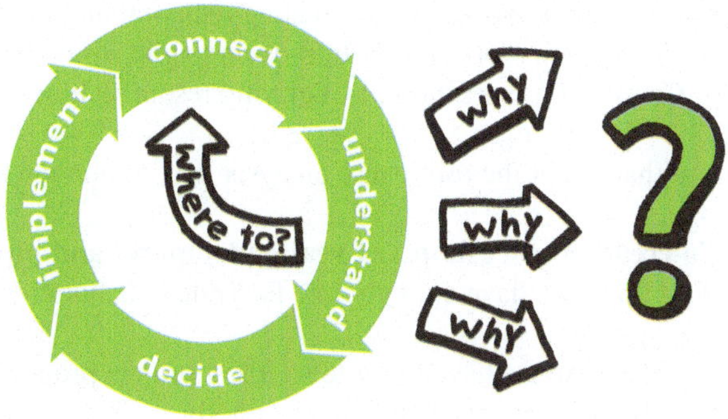

Fig. 6.6 Understanding cause and effect

Finally, in the third process step, "*Share*", the root causes are evaluated: What conclusions does each individual draw from the root-cause analysis? What are the most significant conclusions? Which of these should be given special consideration in subsequent decision-making?

As shown in the diagram, understanding consists not only of gathering information, but also of the recurrent sorting of this information. On the one hand, there is the repeated asking of the "why" question, which is typical of root-cause analysis. This gives a deeper understanding of the actual causes. On the other hand, there is the question of "where to?", which aims to ensure that the analysis is congruent with the goal. What information is relevant to the shared goal?

In the understanding phase, the cause-effect relationship is examined. Only causes that are significant for the shared goal and that can be influenced are pursued further in the co-creation process. This leads to the question: What causes are significant for the common goal? Let's take the following example: an organization has started the co-creation process as a form of strategic cultural development. The goal is to work together in a more agile way. In a cascading manner, issues were identified that were then further specified in the second and third rounds of co-creation. The objectives of the second round were more specific than those of the first round and the topics that emerged out of the third round were even more specific. For example, let's assume the following objective for the first-round co-creation workshop:

The first-round objective of the co-creation workshop was: "Create a culture of agile collaboration". From this, the following topics were derived for the second-round co-creation workshops:

1. Creating temporal and physical spaces
2. Creating agile structures
3. Resource allocation

This then led to the following second-round co-creation workshops:

- Co-creation workshop 1: Creating temporal and physical spaces
- Co-creation workshop 2: Introducing agile structures
- Co-creation workshop 3: Clarifying resource allocation

What might the root-cause analysis look like in the three workshops?

Co-creation workshop 1: Creating temporal and physical spaces
Why don't we have enough time for agile collaboration?

- ... because we have to write so many project proposals and get results.
- ... because we manage our time poorly.
- ... because we're overloaded with administrative tasks.
- ... because we don't coordinate enough among ourselves.
- ... because we can't set boundaries.

What criteria does the group now use to decide which of the five possible causes it wants to pursue? There are two main criteria that can be used to reach a decision:

1. Reflection on the goal (as described above)
2. Assessing one's potential influence

This is the decision matrix "Value × Influence", which was already described in the third chapter in the co-creation principles.

Potential Influence:

EXAMPLE
In one co-creation workshop, the group came out of the analysis having identified the following causes:

- We have too little guaranteed funding.
- Our management communicates poorly.
- The projects are so time-intensive that we can't implement them.

You will notice that the group would not have got very far with this. I asked them to look again for causes and to ask themselves: Which causes are simply given and which can be influenced?

Stephen Covey formulates the question as follows: "What is your Circle of Influence and what is your Circle of Concern?" People should expand their Circle of Influence and shrink their Circle of Concern. They can do this by focusing on what they can actually influence (Covey, 2018). In root-cause analysis, this means looking at the root causes over which we have more influence rather than at those

Fig. 6.7 The want/can decision matrix

over which we have less influence. It should be remembered that co-creation is ultimately about creation, so there must be opportunities to create.

The two criteria that help the group to choose the root causes they want to work on are their goal ("what we want") and their potential influence ("what we can do"). In the end, the choice is a simple want/can matrix (Fig. 6.7):

If we apply the decision matrix to the root-cause analysis from our example, it might look like this:

- ... because we have to write so many project proposals and get results.
  "Writing project proposals and delivering results is actually the core reason for our existence; we can't change that and actually don't want to".
- ... because we manage our time poorly.
  "We could really do better to some extent. And since we all find it kind of a burden, we would also be willing to learn something here".
- ... because we are overloaded with administrative tasks.
  "We would really like to get rid of the administration. However, that would mean hiring more people in the central areas and that again is difficult for us to influence".
- ... because we don't coordinate enough among ourselves.

"If we're honest, we're so absorbed in our own stuff that we don't think about coordination enough. It would be really nice if we worked better together. Of course this is something we can influence: if not us, then who?"

- ... because we can't set boundaries.
  "When it comes to setting boundaries, one the one hand, yes, we want them, but on the other hand we want to stay on the ball. And then there are also many things that we can't just stop doing, so our influence is limited".

From this classification in the matrix, "because we don't manage our time well" and "because we don't coordinate enough among ourselves" emerged as the two root causes where there was the most will and capacity for change. The discussion then enters the next round and would possibly come to the following conclusion:

"'Managing time' is important, but, on the other hand, it won't bring us the big breakthrough. Besides, anyone who wants to get better at it can do it themselves. We have courses on this in our training programme. But we all have to participate in order to coordinate among ourselves. So let's continue to look into this cause".

The root cause thus enters the second "why" round in the following form:

"Why are we not coordinating enough?"

- ... because we primarily have our own results in mind.
- ... because we're losing sight of each other more and more on a human level.
- ... because we'd rather write emails than go to each other's houses.

And so on.

The understanding phase is therefore animated by the fact that the participants question the existing situation more and more deeply, while at the same time connecting themselves again and again with their goal and their possibilities. In this way, an analytical process can emerge at the end of which the essential and, at the same time, influenceable causes are identified.

6.2.3 Phase 3: Deciding

The understanding phase is the preparation for the decision-making phase. The team works out the causes that are important and can be worked on. Deciding represents the midpoint in the overall process of co-creation. The goal-setting and analysis phase ends and the implementation phase is about to begin. Now the team has to decide which of the causes they actually want to pursue.

The conclusions that are available for selection are all those that have already gone through the decision matrix "Value × Influence". Now, out of the collective consciousness, a shared clarity should emerge as to which field or fields of action should be pursued further (Fig. 6.8).

The "Deciding" phase not only connects "Understanding" and "Implementing" in the phase model of co-creation, it also usually represents a psychological hurdle for

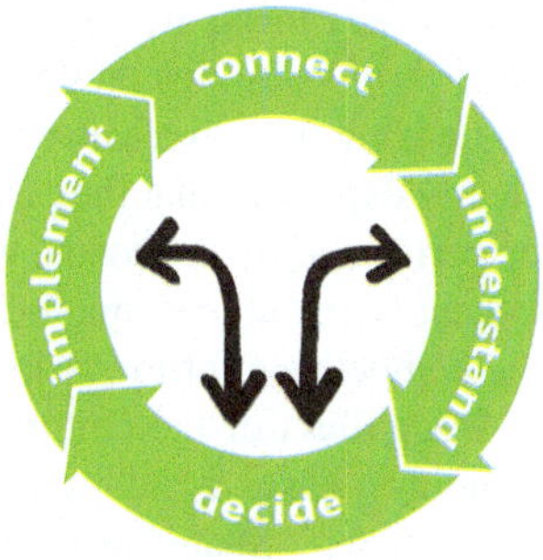

Fig. 6.8 Deciding—combines understanding and implementation

the participants. The participants feel that the time of rather non-committal reflection is drawing to an end and that they now have to start acting.

This is a new experience for them within the process, one for which they have respect. The analytical thinking necessary earlier in the process could still be easily separated from the individual's own potential responsibility. In the worst case, the repression of responsibility can go so far as to lead to the development of a shared blind spot. The following example illustrates this:

EXAMPLE

A co-creation workshop was held with the leaders of an organization. Previously, the managers had not been involved in decisions that affected the development of the whole organization. They were not used to taking the initiative and initialising projects themselves beyond their immediate area of responsibility. When decision-making now required committing themselves as a group, they were astonished. Only a few had grasped that it was now really about being the ones to take action and responsibility. For most, co-creation had been an "academic exercise" until that point. As it turned out in an open discussion of the process, they had the expectation that "someone from the central units would take it from there, like they usually do". The managers then complained to the clients and the coach that they should have been told this more clearly at the beginning. This was exactly the impression the coaches had: it had actually been said clearly several times, but because of the history of the organization, it had not been heard or understood.

The lesson learned from this example was that in hierarchical organizations newly embarking on the path of co-creation, sufficient time must be allocated at the beginning to clarify people's responsibilities in the process.

If goal setting is the most fundamental phase of co-creation, "decision-making" is the most sensitive phase in terms of group dynamics. It takes patience and tact to give the team the space to take responsibility and begin making decisions themselves. In companies where the culture of shared responsibility is less pronounced, there needs to be an open discussion with the participants at the beginning about what responsibilities they will be willing to take on.

Leading this discussion can only be successful if the management is present and clearly expresses that they expect there to be shared responsibility. This role cannot be performed by the coach, who lacks the legitimacy to do so. The participants need to hear from "above" that it is desirable for them to get involved, that they also have the competence for the task and should take responsibility for it.

Regardless of the culture, good preparation through the connecting and understanding phases is helpful for all teams. The more clearly the conclusions of the process step "Share" are aligned with "Value × Goal" and visibly formulated, the easier it is for the participants to decide on the field(s) of action.

6.2.4 Phase 4: Implementing

In the final phase "Implementing", the solutions are worked out and responsibilities are defined (Fig. 6.9). In the previous phase, the team agreed on the fields of action. Now concrete ideas for their implementation are extracted. For the members of the co-creation team, this is a high point in the process they have been working towards. For performance-oriented people, it can even be a moment of liberation, when they are finally allowed to get to the solutions. They may have had to restrain their impulse to propose solutions all day long, because that can sometimes take until late in the afternoon in a 1-day co-creation workshop.

During one co-creation workshop, a performance-oriented leader came into the room in the morning waving a paper. Beaming, he said, "Well, guys, this is the solution. My assistant researched this. It's all in there. We can take a look at it, divide up the tasks and in 2 h we'll be done". To our relief—and that of the co-creation team—he didn't actually mean it himself. And yet it indicates to what extent some participants have to hold themselves back, in order to engage in the process. Hence, it is only understandable if they breathe a sigh of relief when it is finally time to find a solution.

Finding a solution is no longer a major challenge. The process usually goes quickly. The team has dealt with the issue so thoroughly that it is clear to everyone

Fig. 6.9 Implementation—determining the next steps

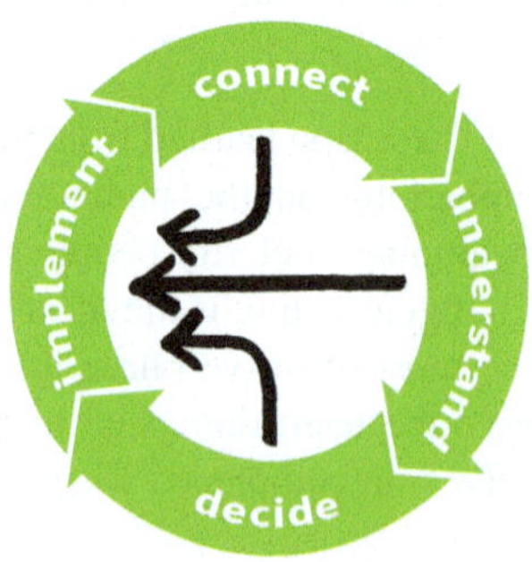

which direction they ought to take. Often all that follows is a summary of the elements that have been discussed.

Now we reap the rewards of possible differences in perception having long since been eliminated and having fixed a common goal from the beginning. One might say that the investment made in the first three phases is now paying off.

The euphoria about the successful solution reinforces a very important point in the implementation. When tasks are distributed in the "Do" phase, the members of the team willingly take responsibility. They will weigh priorities and give priority to the jointly achieved result, if at all possible. Through the result created in the collective consciousness, a shared sense of responsibility for the team and its effectiveness has emerged.

6.3 Guest Contribution: Anke Bridge Haux—Credit Suisse

Interview with Anke Bridge Haux—Head of Digitalisation & Products, Credit Suisse

Driving progress forward—this is the mission that Anke Bridge Haux and her team have embarked on. She is Head of Digitalisation & Products and a member of the Executive Board of Credit Suisse (Switzerland) Ltd. She also heads the Digitalisation Commission of the Swiss Bankers Association.

Within Credit Suisse, more than 160 colleagues work with her in a unit that is unique in Switzerland and is organised in terms of "client journeys", thus focusing on client needs. Anke Bridge Haux and her team see themselves as the contact point between the bank and the client. Needs-based products and solutions are developed in a co-creation style.

Anke, you have been working in the financial sector since 2005. Which developments have particularly surprised you and why? The ever-shorter half-life of knowledge, skills, processes and products. As the famous quote by the journalist Graeme Wood articulates so well: "Change has never been so fast and it will never be so slow again". The increase in speed in recent years is unparalleled. What in this is "flavour of the day", hype or megatrend? What is uncertainty or a great opportunity? And particularly relevant for me and my team: What is a genuine customer need?

How do you react to this change and the increasing speed? First and foremost with the realisation that we need to change how we work and our own attitude in order to keep up with the pace. We can't stop or shape a dynamically changing environment—but we can change our reaction. A change on the outside also requires a change on the inside, in our own "mindset". In order to be and remain successful, a new leadership approach is therefore necessary.

(continued)

Is this conviction the cornerstone of your co-creation journey? Together with my management team, I was looking for an approach that would include all of our employees. A faster pace means a shorter and shorter reaction time. In our business, decision-making and idea generation must therefore be possible in all directions: sideways, diagonally and especially "bottom-up". Our task was to create a space for collaboration and innovation, where each individual can make their best contribution and feel comfortable doing so. That was the birth of co-creation at Digitalisation & Products.

What were the initial reactions to your initiative? At the beginning, we did a site analysis in the extended management team: Where are we starting from and where do we want to go? What is our mission, what are our values and what initiatives should we focus on? To change direction, we need a common language and a map. After that, we presented co-creation to my whole team. Reactions ranged from enthusiasm and curiosity to scepticism. The positive voices clearly outweighed the negative ones. For me, this was confirmation that I was on the right track.

This was at the end of 2018. What happened next? After our co-creation kick-off in a large group, the entire team was able to freely divide up into eight initiatives, and from then on to determine the design, focus and pace at their own initiative. At regular intervals, invitations were sent out for "co-creation sounding boards", where previous results were shared and joint decisions were made involving everyone. Especially after our 2-day co-creation workshop—focused on our values and culture—ideas for strengthening collaboration just bubbled up. This strengthened collaborative spirit is now what sets us apart.

What is the perception of "Co-Creation @Digitalisation & Products" within the bank? Co-creation has already been implemented by a number of well-known companies worldwide. Within Credit Suisse, we are among the first. In doing so, we have exposed ourselves to a certain extent and also taken a risk. We are certainly being watched more closely. Our team works with more than 1000 colleagues in cross-functional teams and successfully implemented almost 100 initiatives last year. This is an enormous number that can only be managed with agility and sustainable teamwork. The first results of the cultural transformation are already visible. Our approach is becoming better known throughout the bank: co-creation is now a household word, and the first teams are starting to mirror our approach. And most importantly for us, it allows us to offer our clients even better solutions.

If I may say so: co-creation seems to have really inspired you. I think back to November last year... Thanks to the enormous trust, encouragement and positive feedback we received over the year, the decision to transform organizationally by adopting a co-creative approach was easy. In doing so, we would like to come even closer to our goal of "happy customers who feel understood". If you listen to the organizational development revolutionaries, each of

(continued)

us can only feel completely at ease in our jobs if we are in a trust-building environment with a sense of purpose and fulfilment, doing work that has an impact. We want to give everyone in the team this opportunity and have therefore also given everyone another chance to express their personal job preference. This is so that everyone in the team can become the best version of themselves and make the best contribution.

Is there any advice you would give to future co-creation travellers? Every change of structure goes hand in hand with the inner transformation of each individual involved. This makes open, clear and reflective communication all the more important in order to meet the different individual needs. I am sure that we picked up everyone in the team at a different point and, in turn, everyone went through different phases in the course of co-creation.

How did you find that out? Personally, it is important to me both to ask many questions and to listen carefully. The question "How do you experience our transformation?" may sound simple, but it is especially close to my heart. Empathy is the glue that holds a team together, enabling openness, trust and security. When the team started to openly express thoughts, concerns and feelings, our own distinctive co-creation culture began to emerge.

We are at the beginning of a new year. Will you stay faithful to co-creation in 2020? Our journey has just begun, and we have almost as many new ideas as calendar days to continue to focus on co-creation. We are just at the beginning. One focus will be the work with CREATE. But co-creation also paves the way for another conviction: diversity is a critical part of our business and one of the most important drivers of innovation—if not the most important. Diversity, in my eyes, goes beyond gender diversity to cognitive diversity: How does a person think? How does she solve problems? A team that is as diverse as possible in this sense will produce the best results. The prerequisite for this is a jointly defined goal and a trust-building culture. We make this possible through co-creation.

Thank you, Anke, for your valuable insights. To conclude our conversation, may I ask you to complete the following sentence "For me, co-creation is ...": . . . an agile culture that puts true teamwork at the centre, that understands innovation as a reaction to customer needs and that makes it everyone's task.

The Eight Steps of the Co-creation Process 7

Abstract

The aim of co-creation is to connect people to a shared consciousness so that they can let the future emerge. Mindset, values and principles are the basic attitudes and assumptions upon which co-creation is based. By means of the co-creation process, co-creation should be able to be employed as a method.

The co-creation process is the description of a structured procedure for how co-creation workshops can be carried out successfully. The sequence of and the specifics of the eight process steps are explained in detail.

Keywords

Procedure · Co-creation workshop · Process

The four phases of co-creation have shown the basic interrelationships and interactions seen in the process of co-creation. The co-creation process is the description of a structured procedure for how co-creation workshops can be carried out successfully.

The sequence of process steps was presented in the introduction and in the last chapter. In this chapter, the specifics of the process steps are explained in detail.

7.1 Creating the Eight Steps of the Co-creation Process

To visualise the steps of the process, we will use photos from a workshop conducted with our partner PLAYROOM. For them, space, time and culture are essential factors in the innovation process. Every company needs to develop its own innovation culture and therefore needs agile methods and systems to support it. This idea was the starting point for creating a physical representation of the co-creation process in space. A "terminal" made of light and movable material,

G. Michalik, *Co-Creation Mindset*, Management for Professionals,
https://doi.org/10.1007/978-3-031-21191-1_7

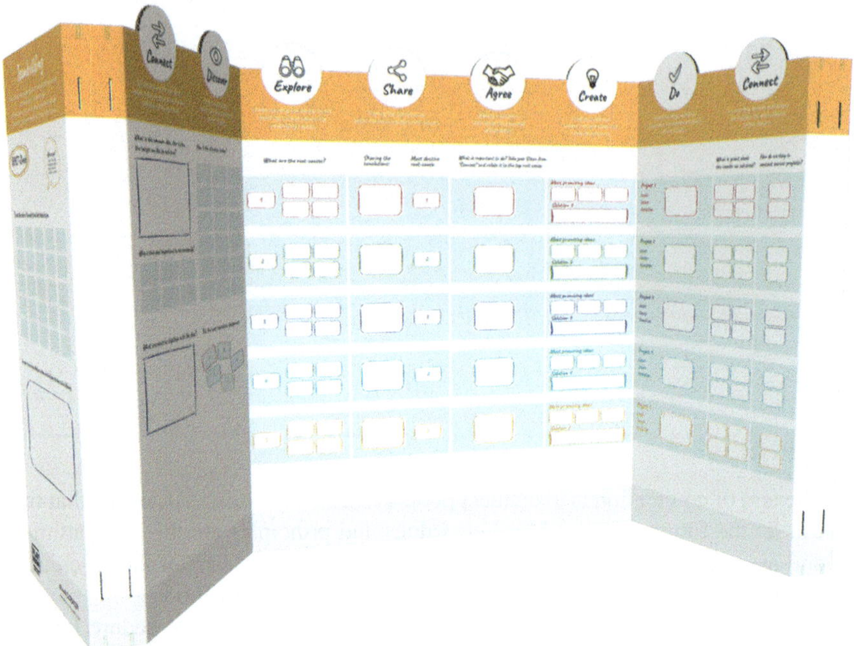

Fig. 7.1 CREATE

which we call CREATE. On it, thoughts become visible and cross-references are made simple.

CREATE looks like Fig. 7.1.

The pictures in this chapter show examples of work with CREATE. In Sects. 8.2 and 8.3, the importance of the co-creation space and CREATE will be discussed in more detail.

The first process step is "Connect": connecting people and ideas.

7.1.1 "Connect"

"Connect" is the most comprehensive part of the process. It has many different aspects that should be highlighted. This is because "Connect" is the foundation upon which the whole co-creation process is built. "Connect" is the implementation of the "Co-Creation Mindset" in a workshop.

The first two parts of "Connect" involve creating a shared sense of purpose among the participants and creating a bond between them that will tie them together during the co-creation process.

Everything starts with connection in the "Connect" phase.

Guest Commentary: Manuel Jork

If you want to act together, you must first act to create common ground.

People have a brain, which serves to allow intrinsic potential to unfold. The potential is the possible. People have an inexhaustible variety of possibilities. They are finely tuned living organisms, ones that are elastic and can withstand a lot. They are sensitive and empathetic, they can reflect on themselves and others, they can transfer knowledge and experience to different fields of action, and they can foresee the effects of their actions. They can thus do great things. But there is a catch.

No brain exists on its own. This sounds strange, especially for individualists, but it is true. Brains always interact with other brains. Consequently, possibilities only unfold through the most meaningful possible interaction between people. The more diverse the people, the more diverse the possibilities. People cannot interact. They have no choice at all about this. They have to cooperate. But they do not always want to. If they do cooperate, they prefer to cooperate with people who are similar to them. But that does not create diversity. Ideally, they would cooperate with different types of people. But they want that even less. At this point, fields of tension arise, filled with contradictions and sensitivities.

People connect in cooperation to act in a goal-oriented way on the basis of their knowledge and experience. This ongoing process leads to the expansion and completion of the foundation of knowledge and experience. Discoveries are made, sorted and classified. This is the inexhaustible source of human creative power, which must be secured and protected at the same time. Expansion and renewal emerge from this secure creative space. A continuous process that moves forward and unfolds in upward spirals. People combine the basic dynamics of "thinking—feeling—acting" in service of the common cause. In doing so, they proceed both with a plan, insofar as they seek the right measure of time (chronos), and spontaneously, insofar as they recognise and seize favourable opportunities (kairos). One person alone cannot do all this. Only conscious co-creation makes this possible, by linking five fundamental personality structures (Jork, 2019) that correspond with the aforementioned dynamics of experience and action. In order of frequency of occurrence, these are: relationship, order, performance, power and innovation.

People with a strong relationship component establish connections with and between others, integrate individual personalities into joint thinking and action, and seek solutions that can be endorsed equally by all. Together with performance-oriented personalities, goal-focused implementation and creative processes emerge, the results and findings of which are in turn logically sorted and classified by order-oriented personalities. In this way, knowledge and

(continued)

experience are collected, prepared and made available for further action processes. Power-oriented or territorial people secure and protect what has been created, expand and extend their sphere of influence. They look to make a "big move" and paint the "big picture". Expansion results in change and renewal, and thus ensures the further unfolding of intrinsic potential. In this way, everyone is involved in the joint development process. Co-creation creates the structured space within which these diverse human forces can balance and connect.

7.1.1.1 Personality Dynamics

The connection between the participants is made at the level of their personality dynamics. For this purpose, we work with the MOBIL personality model (Jork, 2019) or with the Clifton Strengthsfinder (www.gallup.com/cliftonstrengths). MOBIL is a psychometric procedure for distinguishing the reactions and behaviour of different people. David C. McClelland (Harvard University, 1957) articulated the relevance of the motivation complex as an important factor in social change and the evolution of societies. Manuel Jork took up the idea, examined it and expanded it to the scope it has today (Jork, 2019).

The German acronym MOBIL refers to the following personality dynamics:

- Power (*M*acht)
- Order (*O*rdnung)
- Relationship (*B*eziehung)
- Innovation (*I*nnovation)
- Performance (*L*eistung)

Even if every person basically has all five preferences within him- or herself, the most pronounced parts determine the typical, externally recognisable behaviour and the expected reactions.

Each person's personality profile consists of a combination of these five basic drive or action dynamics. The specific combination of these dynamics describes the individual personality of each person. Our strongest motivations or dynamics for action can be observed externally, in our characteristic behaviour. Actions, reactions and decisions are shaped by our personality profile.

The personality traits can be felt and observed as parts of the individuality of each participant in the co-creation process. It is therefore helpful if they are made transparent at the beginning. This requires the consent of the participants. They are invited to reveal as much of themselves as they feel comfortable with.

With this tool, it is possible to classify the participants' statements. This helps to avoid possible misunderstandings. The participants are taught a language that enables them to address things they notice in their colleagues. Since everyone knows the same language of personality dynamics, communication on the meta-level is now easier.

When participants see how their team members can openly deal with their dynamics, identify with them and talk about them, it creates closeness. It helps the participants to connect with each other on a human level. They now have the ability to classify the thoughts and assessments of the other participants, and thus to better accept them.

In the "Connect" phase, we respect the fact that people will initially have to spend time getting to know each other until they have a good enough feeling about who they will be working with. In order to do so, they pay attention to many signals that the other members of the team give off. People look for security, which they find when they discover common ground.

This can be done in a relatively short time. It is possible to establish such a relationship with a team of seven people within about 30 min. This is possible even if they previously only knew each other superficially. Since their need for information about the other team members has been satisfied, they can now concentrate fully on the matter at hand.

There are two ways to work with the personality procedure. Participants can create their personality profile either before the workshop or at the beginning of the workshop.

If the personality profile is created in preparation for the workshop, then the participants are given access to the Clifton Strengthsfinder. The result is evaluated together with a coach in person or by phone.

However, the analysis can also be done as a short self-assessment by all participants together at the beginning of the workshop.

Both approaches achieve the following results that are important for the "Connect" process:

1. The participants become aware that not all people tick in the same way. They realise that other people see the world from a different perspective.
2. They have a better reflective understanding of their own personality preference.
3. They come to know the preferences of their colleagues in the workshop.

On this basis, they can now connect and gain clarity as a team about what to look for with their respective preferences in working together.

7.1.1.2 The "Connect" Attitude

The attitude of "Connect" can be expressed as "being the whole together with others". It describes how the individual can connect with others during co-creation. To do this, participants should understand that the depth of connection with others mainly has to do with one's own attitude. Becoming aware of this and developing one's own attitude is part of the workshop. Connection is, in its own right, a "discipline" necessary for success. The "Connect" model of co-creation describes in seven phases how individuals connect, maintain this relationship and disconnect again (Fig. 7.2).

Intention: The participant's "intention" in co-creation is the phase before co-creation even begins. What attitude does he have when he enters the

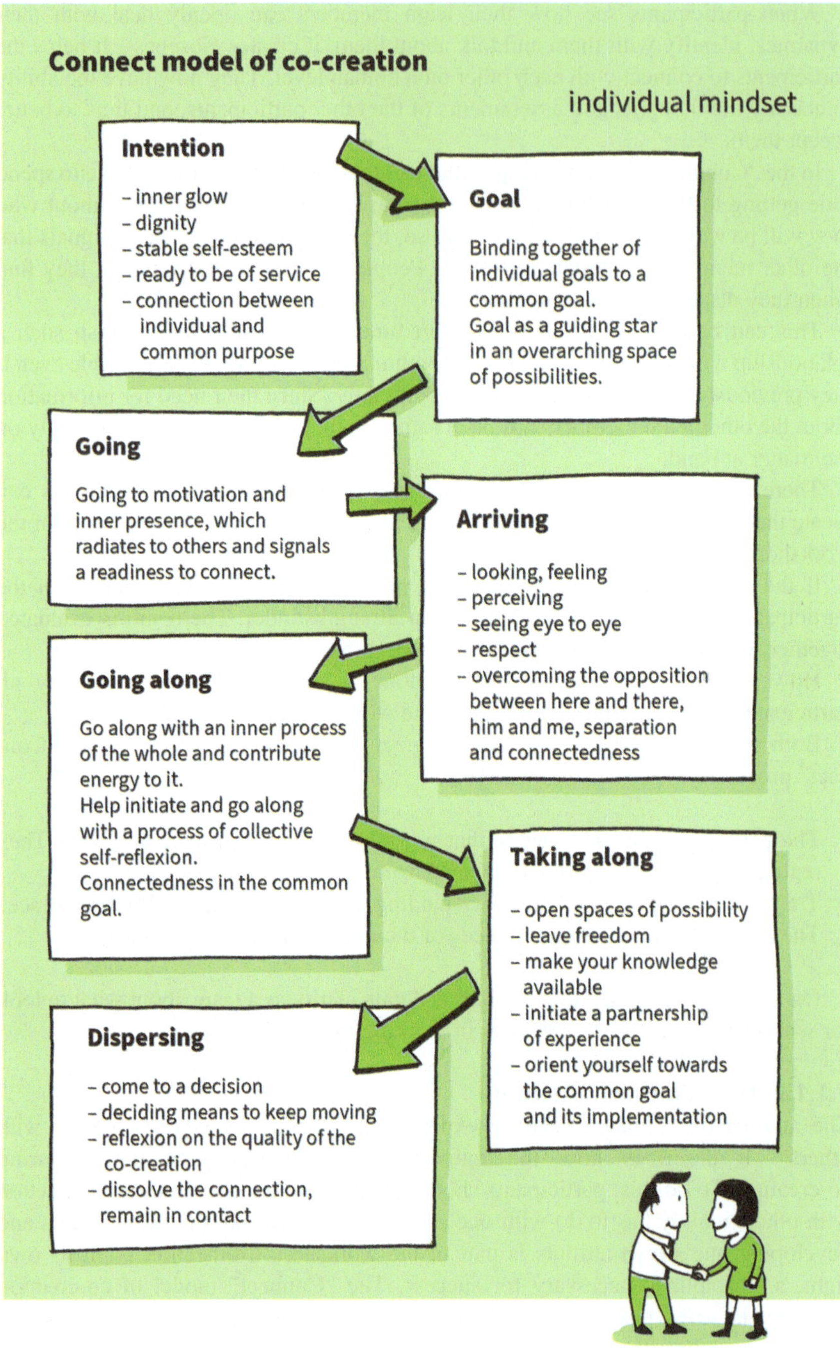

Fig. 7.2 The "Connect" model of co-creation

co-creation process? What are his expectations and how does he see himself in relation to the group? Is he concerned with pushing through his own goals or is he prepared to be part of a whole and to contribute to the success of the whole? This requires a willingness to compromise and a positive mindset—an inner glow that is also felt by others—in which one's own needs are considered just as legitimate as the needs of the other individuals and those of the group. This is easier for individuals with stable self-worth. People who have self-doubt find it harder to let go and to receive and evaluate external arguments without fear.

Goal: At the level of goals, co-creation means precisely not forgetting one's own goals. On the contrary, they are the essential individual aspects of the common drive. A common value and a guiding star should emerge from their connection, creating a space of possibility that goes beyond individual interest. A willingness and an understanding of why this is important should be awakened in the participants. The goal serves as a guiding star, in light of which everyone can orient themselves. In the beginning, there is a detailed discussion of what the guiding star should be. Once it has been decided, it should be maintained throughout the process. If the shared understanding arises that the goal should be revised, then it should be possible to go back and redefine the guiding star. It is nice when the goal does not have to be negotiated. In negotiations, sometimes certain negotiating partners lose out, which is a bad starting point for co-creation. It is better if the common goal emerges from the connection. Meaningful work can only continue if the group succeeds in determining the common goal.

Getting there: The attitude behind this stage is: "I take the first step" and I do not see this first step as an "inner overcoming", but rather look forward to mastering the upcoming challenge together with the team. Getting there requires an inner presence and presentness. I should be in the here and now, and my presence should be palpable. In this way, the participant signals to the other participants: "I'm here. I'm ready to embark on our adventure together, and I am looking forward to joining you. Come on, let's get started together".

Arriving: In the first three phases of the "Connect" step, the participants are still very much preoccupied with themselves. This is the case even when they already have the team and the whole enterprise firmly in their sights. In the arrival phase, they now enter into contact with the team. From now on, direct contact takes place and everyone should allow it. Distinct perceptual and emotional sensory systems now meet and get a feel for each other. Who are the others who I can now work with? Are they similar to me? Can I trust them? Manuel Jork (2019) calls this the "inner scan". Through the inner scan, we try to get as much information as possible from our counterparts in a short time. Based on this information, we make a decision, initially a very simple one: Are they trustworthy or not? Over time, the decision becomes a bit more differentiated, such as: "Basically trustworthy, especially when it comes to the subject area, but at the same time a bit lame and not my first choice when it comes to having a beer after the workshop".

> Deep down, human beings are looking for connections with other people that are secure, meaningful, lasting, reliable and beneficial. Details matter and that is why his radar is also

very finely tuned. Now there are an infinite number of signals that affect the human being. Man's natural innate radar sorts these numerous signals according to an order of importance. This order varies depending on the type of person and the situation. But it essentially consists of the following criteria:

Is the other person a danger to me or is he sending out signals of peace?

Is the other person present at all? Is he "with me" or is he just preoccupied with himself?

1. Does he see me or does he only see himself?
2. Is he interested in me as a person or does he only see a concrete "benefit" in me?
3. Does he treat me with appreciation and respect or does he behave critically and deprecatingly?
4. Can I assess him easily or does he behave ambiguously and unclearly?
5. Is he like me?
6. Is he competent? Does he have something that is useful for me?
7. Is he also prepared to give me that? Does he feel that my interests are at least as important as his own or does he perhaps even put my interests first?
8. Can I rely on him consistently or do I have to reckon with him not keeping his promises or not being there for me at all tomorrow?

Only when all these criteria are fulfilled—I repeat, only when ALL these criteria are fulfilled—will the person feel safe and comfortable and start to build trust. If one of these criteria is not fulfilled, he will become irritable and his inner scan will continue. This costs energy and is disruptive. These disruptive feelings can hinder the building of trust and stable relationships if they are not cleared out quickly.

The Ultra-Fine Radar—Manuel Jork (2019)

Going along and taking along: Both take place. There are phases in which the person goes along with the group and there are phases in which he feels that he now has to take the others along with him.

Going along: Going along with the group is an active and not a passive act of connection. By actively going along with the group, people give strength to the group or to the person who is currently guiding the group. They provide support by making their energies available: "In co-creation, I invest a part of myself". This is a completely and perceptibly different behaviour than "just being there". You could say being a "source of strength instead of a deadweight". Economically speaking, they have given a part of themselves and thus invested in the group and the common success. Now they can no longer be indifferent to what will happen with it. The participants become almost physically a part of the whole. They can then be moved by the following thought:

"In going along with the group, I can actively observe where we are going. Are we still on the path we have chosen? If I have the feeling that we are moving away from it, it is my job to speak up and trigger a joint self-reflection process. In doing so, however, I always remain connected to the group. I may have a different perception or view at that moment, but that doesn't lead me to see myself outside the group".

Taking along: When participants are in the role of taking others along with them, they feel the urge to take a step forward with the group. They share their insights, their ideas and their vision, in order to open a space of possibility for everyone. But they leave the other team members free to go along with this perception or thought. It is then not a matter of winning others over to your own views, but of creating a new perspective from the wealth of perspectives. And everyone has the task of always paying attention to whether the principle of "Value × Influence" is still in place. If it is threatened, the task is to lead the team back to the shared, realisable path.

Resolving: At the end of the joint co-creation, the joint connection must be brought back to a level suitable for everyday life. This can only be done satisfactorily for everyone if the co-creation has been completed, that is if the team has made a decision on how to proceed going forward. If this decision has been reached together, everyone involved can leave the co-creation process with confidence. In order to do so, the team must do two things:

1. Reflection round on cooperation:
   (a) What did we do well in this co-creation session?
   (b) What should we do the same next time?
   (c) What was not yet ideal and what could we do better next time?
2. Disconnect by agreeing on how to stay in touch with each other from now on or in the interval until the next co-creation.

7.1.1.3 "Connect" in the Process

The co-creation process begins with the "Connect" phase. Standing above everything is the creation of connection between three subjects:

- The individual "I"
- The group "We"
- The goal

The combination of these subjects results in six questions to be answered in the "Connect" phase (Fig. 7.3). Three questions used to determine the goal, the individual and the group and three questions about the connection between the parts. In co-creation, we work on the questions in the following order:

1. Who am I?
2. Who are we?
3. What connects me with the group?
4. What is the goal?
5. What connects me to the goal?
6. What connects us in relation to the goal?

Who Am I?

The first question is: Who is the "I" who wants to embark on this journey with my colleagues to this exciting destination? How do I function, what is important to me and how am I when I am involved in cooperation?

Most of us will already have gone through one or more psychometric procedures and will be able to roughly assess what type of person we are. Nevertheless, it is

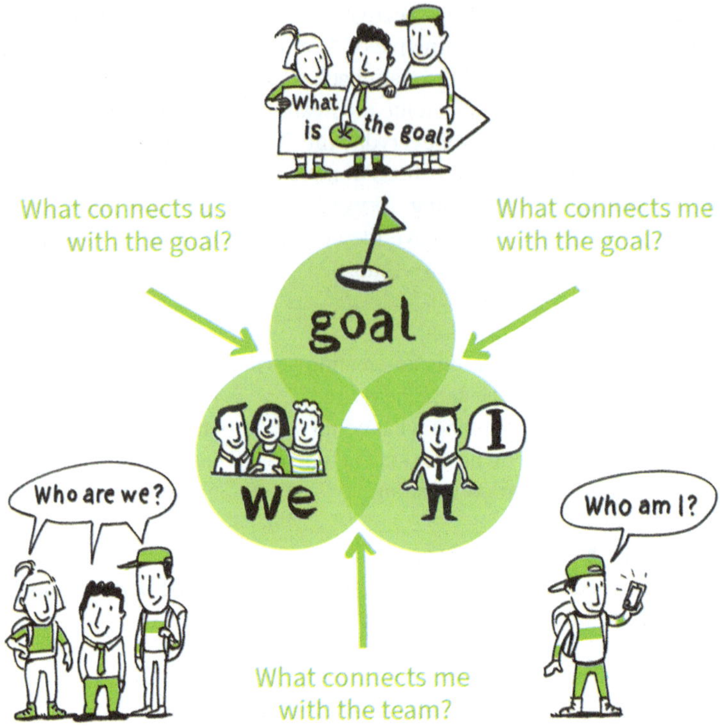

Fig. 7.3 The journey begins with the "I"

helpful to refresh this awareness of oneself at this point. For this, we will use the MOBIL model (Jork, 2019).

Depending on the available possibilities, we recommend conducting the MOBIL analysis as preparation for the co-creation and to have already gone through an accompanying evaluation interview.

In the beginning, the participants introduce themselves based on their personality factors:

- What is important to me in the cooperation?
- What can I contribute to success?
- What is less important to me?
- How do I react when I get stressed?

Who Are We?

After introducing the individuals based on their personality profiles, they look at the interactions and possible synergies that result from the sum of the individual profiles. These are great moments of shared energy. All the participants are fully engaged. The group is now at the filling station and draws strength for cohesion in the coming steps. Questions that the coach can ask the group at this point include:

- What makes each participant individual?
- Where have you been able to observe this?
- How do you personally react under stress?
- How are you likely to react as a team under stress?
- What synergies can you use in your team?

What Connects Me with the Group?

These questions then lead to a kind of "small team development". The participants are led from the focus on "I" to the focus on "we". It is now obvious to everyone that the individual perspectives an overarching perspective emerges. The basic question is: What do you want to pay attention to for successful cooperation as a group?

The team or the facilitator can later refer to this result if things start to go wrong during the co-creation or if the group is at a loss.

This is not the end of the "Connect" process. The "I" and the "we" take place on the level of human relationships. But that is not enough. The third element is still missing: connection in light of a common goal.

With the goal, the level of the subject matter is added as a connecting element. This is essential so that the participants realise that they are here to fulfil a mission. It is not just about having a good time together. It is rather about using the good time together to achieve exceptionally promising and binding results.

In the following sections, as part of the first step of the process, goal setting is explained in detail. This is not a new process step that has nothing to do with the "Connect" phase. We are still very much in the "Connect" phase, answering the three questions that are still open:

- What is the goal?
- What connects me to the goal?
- What connects us in relation to the goal?

"Connect" is only successful when people have connected both with each other and together with a view to the goal.

7.1.1.4 Setting the Goal

What Is the Goal?

It should be clear to all participants why they are going through this process. The goal should be set very carefully. As part of the "Connect" step and as a guiding star, it constitutes the essential element of co-creation. As a rule, the participants come to the workshop with different ideas about what is to be achieved. The coaches' task is then to support the participants in working out the goal. From their experience with traditional meetings, they are used to the goal already being set or being set very quickly. In co-creation, it can take a considerable amount of time to agree on the goal together. If there is already a fixed goal, it takes time to clarify its meaning.

If it is the first in a series of co-creation workshops, then the basic goal for the entire process must be determined at the beginning. The subsequent co-creation workshops will be guided by this goal. An explicit time window is needed for this. The strategic goal is then defined with the client, who is often the management or the board. In the past, it has proven useful to dedicate a half-day, or at least the evening, before the initial co-creation workshop to setting the goal. The agreed-upon goal then has time to settle in overnight for all the participants. The next morning, at the beginning of the co-creation, the participants can be called on to share how they feel about the goal after having slept on it. At this point, corrections can be made. This creates confidence in the process among the participants, since an important goal has not been set hastily.

This is the procedure to be followed when the initial situation is open. But how does the "Connect" phase take place when a goal already exists? When the goal is already given, the main thing is to create clarity and a shared understanding of this goal among those involved. This means clarifying with those present whether they have understood the goal and how they assess it.

Targets are set when it is not the first round of co-creation, but follow-up workshops. A cascading roll-out of co-creation workshops can help the organization to disseminate the topics at issue widely throughout the company. Then even more levels of management and staff can get involved in the overall co-creation process (Fig. 7.4).

In cascading rounds of co-creation workshops, the results of previous workshops become goals at the next level. Depending on the role of the participants in the organization and the overall process, the target is given in varying degrees of detail. For this reason, it is not always clear whether the target is the actual goal or whether it is just a general topic area in which the co-creation team is working. It is also possible that it is already a given solution that is to be concretised. At this point, we will explain how the topic, goals, sub-goals and projects are connected in a multi-stage co-creation process.

7.1.1.5 Topic, Goals, Sub-goals and Projects

The following diagram (Fig. 7.5) shows the structure of a co-creation process that goes through several stages. This helps to explain the differences between the topic, the goals, the sub-goals and the projects:

In the beginning, there is a topic that is to be worked on. The goal is then defined in light of this topic in the course of the first co-creation session. When starting an overall process, the goal can be very fundamental—it can even concern the basic purpose of the company itself. People like to talk about the "purpose" of a company: the "why" question and its answer, according to Sinek's "Golden Circle" (Sinek, 2009). Possible fields of action are then derived from this purpose. These can lead directly into ideas for action and finally into actions that organise themselves into projects. They may possibly become goals for the second round of co-creation.

These are then the sub-goals of the overall goal. In the second round—in a number of co-creation workshops that is to be determined—on the basis of the sub-goals, either goals for the next round of co-creation are derived again or the projects are defined as shown in the illustration. The co-creation takes place with

Fig. 7.4 Setting the goal together

different participants at different times. A feedback and coordination meeting makes the findings and results transparent between the co-creation workshops and coordinates the final projects. In the presentation, two rounds of co-creation have been assumed. Of course, three or more rounds of co-creation are also possible. However, this also increases the need for coordination. If the cascading continues through three or more rounds, it makes sense to divide up the original goals according to content or organizational areas. This reduces the need for coordination, and the overall process is more agile.

In Fig. 7.6, a fictitious example is applied to the preceding schematic representation.

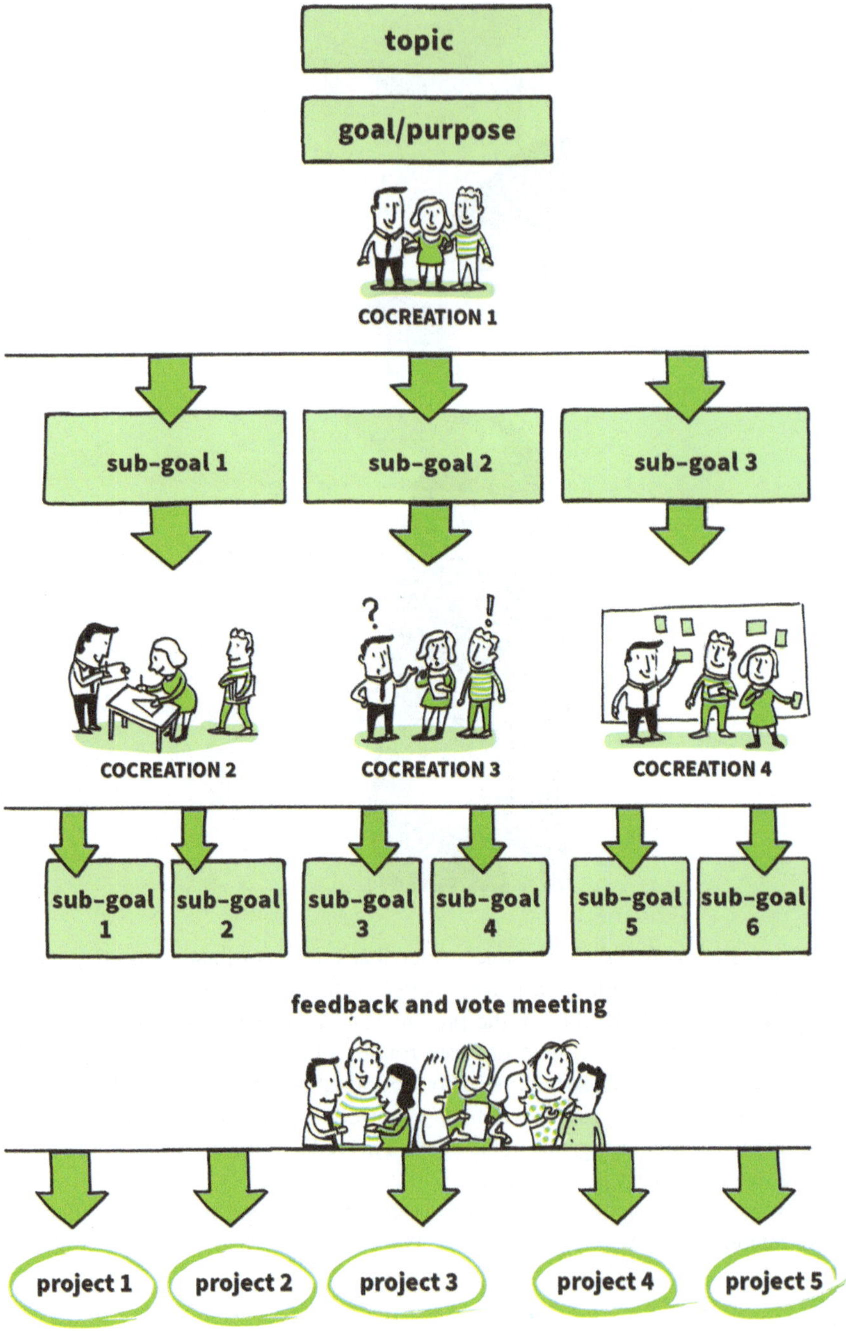

Fig. 7.5 Co-creation process in the organization

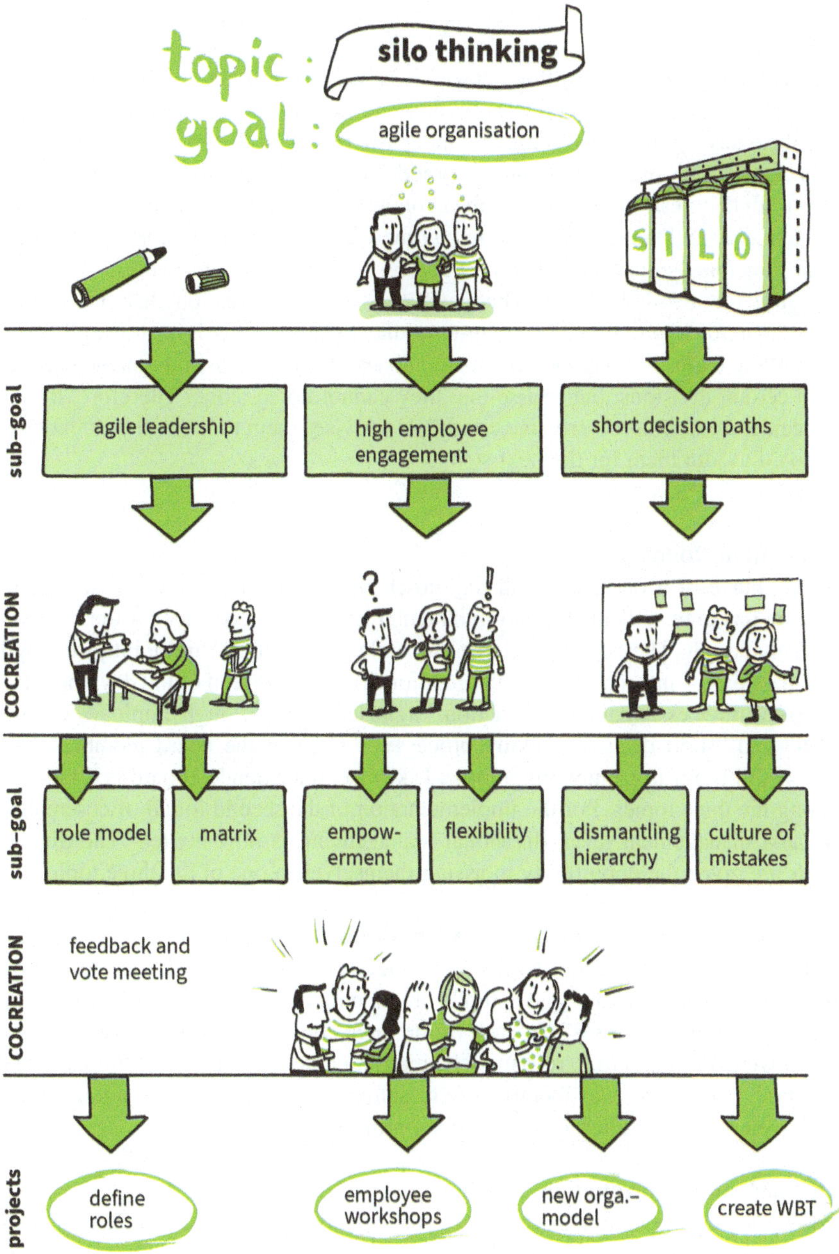

Fig. 7.6 Example of the co-creation process in the organization

Example

A company suffers from the fact that it is actions are rather clumsy, that the business units are not well coordinated and that there are reservations about colleagues in the other units. In the past, this was disturbing, but it was accepted. The order situation was good, and the results were alright in the end. In the meantime, however, the economic climate has changed. Growth is stagnating and the company has to pay more attention to its figures. The board of directors—consisting of three people—retreats to a hotel with a seminar centre for a 2-day offsite. There, they discuss the situation that has been obvious for a long time. They come to the conclusion that it is above all silo thinking that is holding the organization back. They want to end this mentality in certain divisions, but realise that they cannot do so alone. Therefore, they decide to call in a "co-creative coach". He advises them to invite the extended board to join them for the next step.

Co-creation Round 1

In the course of a one-and-a-half-day co-creation workshop, they realise that the solution has to be looked at on a fundamental level. It is necessary for the company to receive a jolt. They agree to create an "agile organization" and jointly set "agile organization" as the goal for their co-creation. Towards the end of the day, they have identified three essential fields of action: "agile leadership", "high employee engagement" and "short decision-making processes". Each of the board members takes responsibility for implementing a topic. Likewise, the extended board is divided up among the three topics. For the implementation of the second round of co-creation, the next management level, divisional management, is now invited. The division heads are given the opportunity to assign themselves to one of the three topics.

Co-creation Round 2: Co-creation Workshops 2, 3 and 4

In three 1-day co-creation workshops, the three groups work on the above-mentioned topics: "agile leadership", "high employee engagement" and "short decision-making processes". In each of the three co-creation sessions, two fields of action were identified (e.g. role models, matrix, empowerment, etc.). For each field of action, one project was identified (e.g. defining roles, creating an organizational model, etc.). This resulted in a total of six projects.

Feedback and Coordination Meeting

Before the implementation starts, all the participants meet to present their results and potential projects to each other. It is determined that empowerment and making working conditions more flexible are very close to each other in terms of content and should be packaged together into a single project. The same applies to the matrix organizational model and the dismantling of hierarchies. These projects are so closely interlinked that splitting them up does not make sense. The responsible project leaders are appointed from the circle. They involve other experts and managers from the organization in the elaboration and implementation. In addition, a joint authority is created for project acceptance.

In the example described above, co-creation was carried out over two levels in a total of four co-creation workshops and one coordination meeting. In the end, four projects emerged. It is now necessary to decide whether these projects should be implemented directly in project management. Alternatively, co-creation workshops could be held with the responsible project members.

7.1.1.6 Connection via the Goal

What Connects Me with the Goal? What Connects Us with the Goal?

In practice, it has been shown that goals are sometimes very general. Sometimes they are unclear or have not even been set. In this case, it is advisable to pick up the participants in their "cold state". The aim is to achieve individual and joint identification with a goal. The co-creation coach asks the following questions:

- What does each of you understand by the goal?
- What could a vision or a particularly motivating goal look like?
- What do you see as the common denominator that unites your individual goals?

When the participants think about the goal, they are still unreflective about what types of goals there are. The coach is familiar with three types of goals in this phase:

- Compulsory goals
- Problem goals
- Heart goals

Compulsory goals are those that had to be done anyway. Topics to be worked on can usually be assigned to certain functions in the organization. The responsible individuals, or at least a representative from the relevant divisions, should take part in the co-creation. If it is a human resources issue, perhaps the HR manager or an HR specialist will join in. If it is an image issue, a representative from communications will certainly be present. These representatives usually come to the co-creation meetings prepared and present their goal for the co-creation. For example, if the topic is "people in our company" and the HR manager is part of the group, he may bring up topics such as: introducing working from home, enforcing casual Friday and enabling mobile working. Surely, you have noticed that these are approaches to solutions and not goals. Mandatory goals are therefore the tasks that have to be implemented in the respective areas of responsibility anyway.

Problem goals are those that are simply the "annoying or really difficult things in our environment" for all those involved. In the beginning, these are often thrown out there quite randomly by the participants, in order to vent or to find allies to deal with a vexing issue. A more constructive approach to arriving at the guiding star via problem goals is for participants to consider what is not working and to look for examples. The example should then underline how important it would be to do something about the problem.

Problem objectives rarely move the group forward, as they are usually personal issues that are not always important to everyone. Moreover, they are often described in detail as examples and cost the team valuable time and energy. They are difficult for the coach to handle. He will quickly recognise them as problem goals, and yet cannot simply exclude them without unduly interfering in the choice of topics. Moreover, the participants are just now opening up and too forceful an intervention could interrupt the positive dynamic. Now the coach needs empathy to support the opening, to stay focused and to engage the participants for further discussion.

Heart goals are the goals through which progress is almost always achieved. These are goals that look to the future, that provide perspective and that people can get excited about. They are therefore rarely deficiency-oriented, but rather mainly growth-oriented. If they do not already have a positive connotation, they can at least be reformulated so that they acquire one. Heart goals manage to rally the participants behind them in no time and to create a glow in their eyes. Once the group has found a heart goal, the whole process is carried along by a higher purpose. Connection, commitment and trust then grow seemingly by themselves.

The following situation describes an (a)typical goal-setting process:

Example

A medium-sized metal processing company with 120 employees is already in its fourth generation. It is solidly positioned in the market with a niche product range. It could probably continue to operate for the next few years. However, the younger generation that has now taken over the management wants to achieve more: "We haven't studied and gained experience in other companies, just for things to continue as they are". While the brother and sister in the company management see considerable potential, they fail to let the necessary ideas for new products emerge. They also perceive a certain lethargy in the company. They want to change the situation and invite the first two management levels to prepare co-creation workshops. Before they begin, everyone should be informed about the project and the major goal for the journey should be determined.

The managers are positive about the idea. However, when it comes to setting goals, they go round and round in circles. Again and again, the time-consuming decision-making processes are explained in detail with examples and the wish is expressed that decisions be made more quickly (problem goals). The HR manager announces that they are thinking about digitalising the company suggestion scheme and that this will probably lead to more ideas for new products (compulsory goals). The discussion has now lasted almost 3 h, and the managers are growing increasingly impatient, especially as it is already approaching 7 pm. Finally, they agree that there is still enough time in

(continued)

the workshop to think about the goal, when the service manager stands up. In an agitated voice, he makes the following appeal: "I am 63 years old and know the shop since the times of the senior boss. I have never seen another company from the inside. My grandson—Stephan is his name—has now started working in an IT shop. He is very happy there. He explained to me how they organise themselves, that there are no bosses anymore and that it all works very well. I couldn't believe it and it's still hard for me now". Turning to the two managers, he continues, "Birgit and Peter, I appreciated your father very much. He was my boss for 24 years. There was no one else like him. And yet, he was a different type of guy. For him there was always only one truth. But I can see that times are different now. It's no longer enough for the boss to tell you what to do. The same applies to me in Service. My people usually have better ideas, and I have to be careful not to get in their way. Birgit and Peter, you are young. And we have many other young people with us. And even the old-timers are not that old in the head (laughter). Why don't we do it the way we do it in Stephan's IT shop: we let our people organise themselves and take a step back as managers. I think we can—in fact I think we have to". The service manager then sat down again and after a moment of silence, the first comments came from the other managers. Some concerns, questions and suggestions surfaced, but everyone was enthusiastic (heart goal).

The example illustrates how important it is to give space to goal setting. We have often had the experience that the goal was as clear as day for everyone; it could just be written down and everyone was fully behind it. Sometimes the situation is different. Then it takes a lot of time to listen and also to give space to emotions. It takes trust in the group that they want to achieve a common goal.

How can the coach support the goal-setting process? The goal stands at the beginning of the process of group formation, and maybe the group is not yet able to achieve this. Perhaps the participants are not yet connected deeply enough to each other for the really important issues to come to light. In that case, it is advisable for the facilitation to start at the issue level, and thus on relationally safe ground. When discussing the issue level, the participants learn from each other about different perspectives and new arguments. They can get a picture of how the others argue and how they see the problem. They get an impression of "how the others are on it in the first place". In this way, the participants reduce their inhibitions and, over time, the really essential ideas for a goal come to the surface. For successful facilitation, it is now important to listen carefully:

- Which issues are substantial and presumably headed in the right direction?
- Which issues are still poorly thematised?
- Which statements are mere commonplaces?

By asking questions and visualising, the coach can support the goal-setting process. A proven method is to formulate a promising statement as a possible goal. This makes it easier for the participants to imagine what they actually want and do not want. They will reject the proposal or come up with a revised proposal. If this, in turn, meets with the group's approval, the jointly formulated goal is not far away.

If at the end of the discussion, there is a goal that functions as a "working title", because the formulation is not yet completely satisfactory, then an important first step has been taken.

As will be explained later on, in Chap. 11, the coach functions as an energy manager. Basically, this means finding the balance between being there and keeping a critical distance. In goal setting, this task is demanding. On the one hand, he is concerned that the group finds a tangible goal; on the other hand, this goal must, of course, be the group's goal and not the coach's goal. For this to happen, the responsibility for goal setting must lie with the group in a way that is clear to everyone.

7.1.1.7 Connecting Contents

The cascade model of co-creation over several levels raises the question of how the contents are connected in the ongoing process. This is the coach's job. During the second round of co-creation, it is possible that only the coach knows what happened in the previous co-creation workshops. So his task must be to create transparency between the co-creation workshops while they are still running. This cannot wait until the feedback and coordination meeting. The participants need an overview of the goals, analyses, decision-making and implementation phase from the other workshops. Otherwise, it is possible for two groups to set themselves the same goal and arrive at the same results. In one sense, this is a good sign, but it can also be frustrating for the participants.

So far it has been assumed that there is only one goal per co-creation workshop. But what if there are different goals? In the phase model of co-creation, it was shown that co-creation is an ongoing process in which different perspectives and ideas are incorporated. Part of the process is then to agree as a team on which ones are really important. To come to this decision, the "Value × Influence" matrix helps.

This can be applied as early as the goal setting. The coach can confront the group with the question: Which goal is more relevant to the topic and how do you already assess the possibilities of realising it? This makes it clear from the beginning that the group has to focus.

Now it may be that, even after this, the group concludes that there are two or three goals, all of which are equally significant and likely to be similarly realisable. How should we then proceed?

If there are several destinations, there are two possibilities:

- If it is a small group, with up to seven participants, they can agree to work on the goals sequentially, in other words, to meet for another co-creation session in order to then work on the other goal.

- With a group of eight or more, the processes can be done in parallel until the "Do" process step. The participants allocate themselves to the goals in light of their energy and interest and then work as a separate group until they have agreed on the next steps to take at the end. There, the two sub-groups should then come together again and align themselves. There may be overlaps and the projects can be partially combined.

7.1.2 "Discover"

The second process step is "Discover": discovering the facts (Fig. 7.7).

In "Discover", the participants collect the facts. They get an initial picture of what the situation is like.

"Discover" is the first of three process steps in the understanding phase. Understanding was deliberately divided into three sub-steps:

- "Discover": discovering the facts
- "Explore": understanding the background
- "Share": sharing the conclusions

This should make it possible for the participants to concentrate completely on a given step. Otherwise, there is a danger that different mental processes will be mixed up or confused with each other.

"Discover" is about the pure collection of facts, impressions, situations, etc. This should be as non-judgemental as possible. In "Explore", the participants try to better understand certain relevant impressions. Here, it is a question of analytical

Fig. 7.7 "Discover"—discovering the facts

thinking—a completely different mental process than the collecting done in "Discover". Finally, in "Share", the participants reveal themselves. They combine the analysis with their personal evaluation. Here, they make their own personality visible. This requires inner clarity and courage.

What is the goal of data collection? "Discover" collects data that is as value-free as possible, which should tell the team something about what is hindering the achievement of the goal today. But it should also show where there are positive developments. The view of the actual situation should be as open as possible.

In Chap. 5, the Potentialum analysis was presented. The results of the Potentialum analysis are a comprehensive source for forming an overall picture of the organization. When working with Potentialum, now is the time to present or review the results.

If the participants did not work with the Potentialum analysis, they now take a direct look at the relevant areas of the company. Since the participants are already influenced by the definition of the goal, it is now particularly important to approach the data collection as openly as possible. How can this openness be achieved?

In order to get the broadest possible view, it is recommended that the group first think about where they can look in the first place. Friedrich Nietzsche is quoted as saying: "I suppose that we only see what we know". Therefore, only what is known can go into the data collection. What is information that can say something about the actual situation? The participants can think about which sources contribute something to the actual situation. These can be, for example, reports, figures from controlling, expert interviews, results of employee surveys, customer studies, etc.

Next, the sources are evaluated. What statements do they contain that have something to do with the goal? These statements are written on post-it notes and collected on a whiteboard or CREATE.

It is clear that the collection and evaluation of data can be time-consuming. How do we make it so that, on the one hand, there is an adequate database and, on the other, enough time for the other steps of co-creation?

Even if the objective has not yet been agreed, the topic is usually already known before the co-creation meeting. Hence, a preparatory task could be to ask the participants to read up on a topic and bring information about it. They could be asked to think about what sources say something about it and present them in the workshop.

The most dynamic and least time-consuming variant is to ask the participants in the "Discover" phase to collect their own individual impressions on post-its. The advantage of this approach is that it happens within the framework of the process itself and fits in well. It is spontaneous and not time-consuming. At the same time, it must be taken into account that important information may not be included in the analysis.

You also have to keep pointing out to the participants that there are not only things that do not work. It is equally important to recognise what is already being done today or what is available that can support the team. After all, it is not about reinventing the wheel. Therefore, the positive aspects should definitely be included.

The collection of data almost always brings together more information than can be processed at once. How can the relevant information be selected?

First, the participants should briefly present the notes they have stuck on CREATE to the rest of the team. This way everyone understands what is meant by the content on the post-its. This is also an opportunity to ask comprehension questions.

Once the meaning of the information has been clarified, it can now be brought together in clusters.

The coach can provide guidance to the group about how to cluster the cards. However, the coach should not cluster the cards himself, not even if the group asks him to. It has proven useful to have the team station itself at CREATE and group the cards together thematically. This creates a mental representation of the topic areas. The group knows the deeper meaning of the notes and can sort them out quite quickly.

After clustering, it is helpful if the team takes a step back and looks at the big picture again. If the Potentialum model was used, everyone now looks at the map and understands the interactions between the impact factors.

It is now clear to everyone at a glance how the existing situation is characterised. However, the results of the "situation analysis" are not yet very tangible, because they are in the form of clusters. So each aspect is still distributed on many different cards or post-its. Therefore, the last task of the "Discover" is to summarise the results of the "situation analysis" in a maximum of five core statements.

Here, a principle of co-creation becomes visible: the opening of space and the subsequent condensation of the results (see Sect. 3.1.3). Shared consciousness now comes to its third conclusion in the overall process of co-creation:

- First conclusion: Who we (the co-creation team) are.
- Second conclusion: What we jointly want (i.e. the goal).
- Third conclusion: What we see as the key factors supporting or hindering the achievement of goals.

The result of the "Discover" step says nothing about what is to be done. While the results are very important, they are also very superficial. They only say what is obvious. They do not say anything about the reasons why. Since we want to bring about a sustainable change, we now have to look at the underlying causes in the third process step.

7.1.3 "Explore"

The third process step is "Explore": understanding the background (Fig. 7.8).

In "Explore", the participants get to the bottom of the facts. They form hypotheses about the underlying causes. In co-creation, they work with different forms of root-cause analysis.

Fig. 7.8 "Explore"—understanding the background

The most thorough approach is the Potentialum analysis, as described in detail above. If this does not take place in advance, a root-cause analysis can be carried out in the workshop itself using a wide variety of methods.

7.1.3.1 The Five Whys Method

One of the best-known approaches to root-cause analysis is to repeat the question "why". It is a method used in kaizen or lean management (Quality Services & Knowledge) (n.d.). In the "five why questions" method, you keep asking until you find the real cause of the problem. Each time we reach an answer to the why question, this answer is called into question with a new why formulation. Let us take the following example:

Example

In a co-creation workshop during the "Discover" step, it became obvious that there was little commitment among the staff. It seemed that most of them just came to work to do their job.

The root-cause questioning technique would proceed as follows: The employees show little commitment.

1. Why do the employees show little commitment to their work?
   a. Because they have little scope for decision-making.
2. Why do the employees have little scope for decision-making?
   a. Because the decisions are made by the leadership.
3. Why are decisions made by the leadership?
   a. Because we have numerous processes that dictate that.
4. Why do we have numerous processes that dictate that?
   a. It is always been that way; nobody knows why...

In this example, it did not take five steps to get to the root of the problem. After four questions, it is relatively clear that there is an evolved process culture that has also extended to decisions. It seems to have taken on a life of its own, and there is no real reason for this handling of decision-making processes. Of course, one could now ask the fifth and sixth questions:

1. Why has it always been like this?

or

2. Why does no one know why this has always been the case?

But that does not really help. After the fourth answer, the situation is clear: we have reached the point where if we do something, it can change the decision-making culture and thus also employee engagement.

In this way, one penetrates deeper and deeper towards the actual cause of the problem. In the co-creation workshops, the participants come up with several conceivable causes. Which of them should they use to ask the second why question? Lean management offers an alternative method here that maps this complexity: the Ishikawa diagram, which offers branching and thus takes a more differentiated approach. However, we need a less time-consuming method, so that the co-creation process does not get off-track and the dynamic is maintained. The group thus needs certain criteria to decide what the decisive root cause is.

In the end, the group has to decide what the essential root causes are. How is this possible? In order to do so, it needs the common recollection of the goal, it needs a mental—or better even a physical—representation of its guiding star so that it does not get lost on its way. Therefore, the goal should always be clearly visible in the workshop. If there is enough time, it is good if the participants visualise the goal using the means available.

The same principle applies to decision-making: What decision should we make? Which field of action should we pursue? Representing the goal helps with the choice, and ultimately also with finding ideas and allocating tasks: Which of the ideas brings us closest to our goal? With this picture in mind, the "Value × Impact" question can then be answered more clearly. The "Connect" phase forms the basis for a control loop that helps to achieve in the end what everyone wanted to achieve at the beginning.

7.1.3.2 The Fishbowl Method

The five whys method cannot be used in the same way with large co-creation groups. Let us say there are 25 people in the co-creation process. We can divide them into groups according to sub-goals. However, the understanding phase encompassing "Discover", "Explore" and "Share" should be done together, so that a common picture of the current situation and the fields of action can emerge. In the implementation of the fields of action and further planning, work can then be done in sub-groups again.

How can you create common understanding with such a large group?

The first step, "Discover", can be done in small groups and the results can be consolidated at the table. Then the most important points are collected in the plenary session. However, this approach cannot be used with large groups in the "Explore" stage, since it involves looking together at the deeper causes. Dividing into small groups would prevent the collective consciousness from emerging at a crucial moment.

To solve this problem, we work with the fishbowl method. With this method, it is possible to simultaneously conduct a root-cause analysis with larger groups. We have carried out root-cause analyses using the fishbowl method with 60–80 people in the context of large co-creation workshops.

A fishbowl is a form of dialogue that can be used when discussing issues in large groups. The advantage of this method is that the whole group can participate in the conversation.

Four to five chairs are arranged in an inner circle. This is the "fishbowl". The remaining chairs are arranged in circles outside the fishbowl. Four to six participants are chosen to fill the fishbowl while the rest of the group sits on chairs outside the fishbowl. Two chairs inside the fishbowl remain empty. The coach introduces the topic, and the participants start discussing the topic. The audience in the surrounding circles listens.

The topics concerning the current situation collected in the "Discover" phase are discussed. They were gathered together from various small groups and organised into the most important clusters. The "fish" use the five whys method in their discussion. This means that they carry out the root-cause analysis on behalf of the whole group.

However, the listeners in the surrounding circles can also participate. A listener can occupy one of the two empty chairs at any time and join the fishbowl. After his

Fig. 7.9 The fishbowl method

contribution, he leaves the centre again, freeing up the chair for others. The discussion continues with the audience entering and leaving the fishbowl (Fig. 7.9).

A volunteer was chosen to record the main statements made throughout the discussion on a flip chart for all to see. Ideally, the root causes are summarised on the flip chart at the end. When the time is up, the fishbowl is closed and the person taking notes summarises the results of these notes, i.e. the root causes.

After the root-cause analysis, the participants now have a deep, shared understanding of the problem. But how is this to be classified?

Imagine the process you go through in understanding an important problem. First, you become aware of the insights you have gained from understanding the problem. Then the question arises: What do I do now? That is, you are one step away from making a decision. With individuals, these steps happen very quickly, and we probably cannot tell them apart at all.

In order for the collective consciousness to have the chance to form, these steps must be made conscious through group processes. This requires a simultaneous process of comparing the thoughts and feelings of the individual participants. This happens in the next step: "Share".

7.1.4 "Share"

The fourth process step is "Share": sharing the conclusions (Fig. 7.10).

At the "Share" stage, the participants consider which of the root causes are the most important. Then they decide on a maximum of five root causes. In the next step, fields of action are defined for these.

"Share" is the third process step of the understanding phase, bringing it to a conclusion. When it ends, the midpoint of the co-creation process has been reached. This is followed by the decision-making phase and then the implementation phase. "Share" thus concludes the analysis and prepares the transition to "Do".

Why is this part of the process called "Share"? As the explanation says, it is all about sharing conclusions. How can a group do that?

Fig. 7.10 "Share"—sharing the conclusions

7.1.4.1 The Hinge Function of "Share"

As illustrated in the principles of co-creation, each process step is an "opening" and a "closing". At each step, the field is first opened up and then compressed again. One might say that the process "breathes". Metaphorically speaking, in the "Share" step an "exhalation" takes place in the middle of the whole process. Sharing means, in a deeper sense, that now that the end of the analysis has been reached, the individual perspectives of the participants must become visible. Sharing makes it necessary for everyone in the group to position themselves with their assessment. What is the personal conclusion reached by each individual at the end of the analysis? This also determines in which direction the measures should subsequently go.

"Share" has a kind of hinge function between analysis and action. It takes us through, and puts a final point under, the understanding phase. What exactly has to happen in "Share", so that the process step can successfully fulfil the function of acting as a hinge between these two major parts, understanding and doing?

The "Share" stage is where the analysis comes together. In the end, the (at most) five most important underlying causes should be identified.

For a better overview, here are once again the three analytical steps in context:

"*Discover*" asks which facts and situations help or hinder the implementation. The result of "Discover" is a collection of phenomena that are grouped into a maximum of five topic areas (clusters). In the end, the team has to give names to these different areas.

"*Explore*" asks what the underlying causes of the issues are. It carries out a root-cause analysis for this purpose. The result of "Explore" is a collection of root causes that are grouped into causal fields (clusters).

"*Share*" asks the team to formulate an understanding of what the conclusion is for achieving their goal from each of the causal fields from the "Explore" step. On this basis, the most significant cause/root cause for each causal field is then determined. In the end, there are a maximum of five causes that need to be addressed if the goal is to be achieved.

7.1.4.2 Completion of the Understanding Phase

"Share" concludes the understanding phase.

The following example illustrates the kind of discussion that takes place in "Share".

Example

"Discover": For example, a lack of ideas was noted in relation to the first of the (maximum) five topic areas.

"Explore": The analysis of the underlying root causes revealed that:

- There is no common thread.
- Things have always been like this.
- Reactive behaviour prevails instead of the proactive proposal of ideas.
- Ideas are not wanted.

"Share": The conclusion drawn from the various causes in the causal field is that things are still too reactively issue-driven and opportunistic. The most significant cause was identified as the fact that the responsibility for ideas anchored in the community is unclear.

7.1.4.3 Maximum Five Options

The example shows the common thread in the understanding phase. This process takes place a maximum of five times. This means that co-creation is limited to working out no more than five topic areas with their causal fields, conclusions derived from them and the essential cause in a single co-creation workshop.

The reason for this lies in relevance and feasibility.

Relevance: As mentioned before, co-creation is also a process that leads the team to decide what is essential. The more issues are identified, the less important each issue is. The co-creation team should limit itself to working on the most important issues.

Feasibility: It must also be kept in mind that the results are ultimately to be implemented by the group. With the limitation to five topics, the team will have to restrict itself to five fields of action in the following stages and to five projects at the end of the process. With a small co-creation group of five participants, each would eventually have one project to work on. That is a lot. In the workshops, the coaches encourage the co-creation team to commit to fewer issues and to implement them consistently.

At the end of the "Share" step, the participants have set the course. Through their analysis, they have laid the foundations for the decision to be made in the next process step, "Agree".

7.1.5 "Agree"

The fifth process step is "Agree": deciding (Fig. 7.11).

Fig. 7.11 "Agree"—making a joint decision

In "Agree", the participants look back over the understanding phase and at the goal. Then they look at the results of "Share". They see what has emerged as the (maximum) five most important root causes. For these, the fields of action are now to be defined in the "Agree" step.

7.1.5.1 Fields of Action

What do we mean by fields of action and how do they differ from future actions?

Fields of action open up the space for action. They create possibilities, without the team already committing to specific actions. Through this intermediate step, the co-creation team approximately translates the results of the analysis into possible actions. The openness still allows for many options, and thus fosters the creativity of the shared consciousness.

Let us take an example from everyday life to illustrate the difference between a field of action and an action.

Example

A person started a new job in sales support a year ago. The longer she does the job, the more valuable her contribution becomes to the salespeople she works with. At the same time, the expectations placed on her also increase. In the beginning, everything sort of happened without her giving much thought to how to organise her work. But lately, she feels that everything is becoming too much. She comes to the conclusion that it is because of her lack of organization that she cannot stay on top of things.

Transferring this to the process steps of co-creation, the person would now have identified the root cause: "Because I have not got the basics in order, my processes are not efficient".

In the next step, the person would first determine the fields of action, before collecting ideas about how to increase their efficiency. Possible fields of action include:

- Improving process flows in sales support
- Introducing time management
- Distributing tasks among colleagues

Ideas for action corresponding to the first of these fields could include:

- Identifying critical points
- Inviting affected colleagues to vote
- Agreeing on a process together

We can see two things from this example:

1. Fields of action are less concrete than actions.
2. A decision is needed on which field of action to start with.

Fields of action are not yet ideas about how to tackle a problem. They only say something about what should be done. One could also explain them using Sinek's "Golden Circle". Fields of action correspond to the "how". They determine what is to be done in principle. Only later, in the "what" phase does it become clear in precisely which way this is to be accomplished.

The example above makes this clear. "Improving process flows in sales support" only gives the general path. The next step is for the person to ask him- or herself what the process looks like and what could be improved about it. The same goes for the second point: "introducing time management" does not yet make clear what can be done concretely at this moment. It only becomes clear that this is a field of action that needs to be made more specific through ideas in the next step.

7.1.5.2 Joint Decision

In the example above, a person has come up with three possible fields of action. Will she tackle all the fields of action at the same time, or would we advise her to choose one? We would probably advise her to choose one. To do this, she could ask herself which of the three fields of action is most valuable for her goal and which one she has the most influence over, using the "Value × Influence" matrix already mentioned several times.

To illustrate the basic thinking and decision-making process, this simple example of a single person was chosen. In the co-creation process, however, it is a group of people with a collective consciousness. The group consciousness needs explicit steps in the thinking and decision-making process, because the team needs to coordinate its individual aspects and keep them synchronised. Therefore, the steps transferred to an individual would seem somewhat "artificial", as people do this automatically for themselves without giving it much thought.

In co-creation, too, the team now creates various possible fields of action or spaces for action and in the end must decide on a maximum of five fields of action. This is why this process step is called "Agree".

The team says "yes" to a limited number of specific fields of action. Saying "yes" to one or more fields of action is a conscious act of commitment. It goes beyond committing oneself to a few areas but is also a "yes" to collective action. Now the participants engage in self-commitment. In the co-creation workshop, this is clearly noticeable in this situation. The participants pause. They become aware at this moment that they are in the process of creating a part of their future. This can then result in extra work and a change in their priorities.

7.1.5.3 The Role of Leadership in Decision-Making

What role could leadership play in this? Making a joint decision is completely different from making a decision on one's own. Is it not the leadership's task to decide which field of action to choose?

Prof. Peter Kruse asks what legitimises leadership (Kruse, 2013). Our image of leadership is that it should provide orientation and security: "Surely, it must know where the journey is headed". Kruse argues that in the past, leadership had the necessary knowledge to make decisions. However, Kruse continues, leaders are stuck in the complexity trap: our issues are becoming more complex and the outcomes are non-linear. It follows that complexity + non-linearity leads to unpredictability. Therefore, the role of leadership is changing. Its task should be to provide orientational knowledge that serves as the basis for jointly taken decisions. Leadership would then develop from all-knowing decision-making to shaping knowledge relationships. For this, social competence is needed. This means above all the ability to perceive one's own reality and those of others. On this basis, it can support co-creation. In this sense, co-creation can be seen as bringing about joint decisions.

It is becoming increasingly significant that people decide together and unconditionally stand by a common "Yes to...". To be able to do this, they have to go all the way to the level of collective consciousness and adopt the inner disposition of the whole. Only then will people change their patterns in their connection with other people.

> A human being is a part of the whole called by us universe, a part limited in time and space. He experiences himself, his thoughts and feeling as something separated from the rest, a kind of optical delusion of his consciousness. This delusion is a kind of prison for us, restricting us to our personal desires and to affection for a few persons nearest to us. Our task must be to free ourselves from this prison by widening our circle of compassion to embrace all living creatures and the whole of nature in its beauty.
>
> (Einstein, quoted from Sullivan, 1972)

A kind of "reprogramming" of human consciousness, as Einstein suggests, can only occur in a space of trust. A space of trust is the community between people in which everyone is accepted as they are.

Co-creation creates such a space of trust. It starts with community and commonality. It then looks to the common goal, which must also be represented in each individual. Together, the individuals who compose this community go through a multi-stage process of understanding. If one accepts Kruse's understanding, then the team creates the necessary orientational knowledge here, with which they bring about the joint decision in "Agree".

Equipped with the necessary knowledge and strengthened by the joint decision, the co-creation team is now ready to take the next step, creating ideas as solutions to the fields of action.

7.1.6 "Create"

The sixth process step is "Create": creating solutions (Fig. 7.12).

In "Create", too, the process "breathes" again. First, the participants open up the room. They collect ideas on how the fields of action could be implemented. Afterwards, in the "exhalation", the ideas are condensed. The participants decide

Fig. 7.12 "Create"—creating solutions

Fig. 7.13 How ideas are created

on the three most-promising ideas. From these three ideas, they then choose the solution. Of course, it is also possible that they create a solution out of a combination of ideas.

You can see in the photo above that there is a "1" on the left and a "2" hidden underneath. These numbers refer to the underlying fields of action. Behind field of action 1 there is now a whole collection of ideas (Fig. 7.13). The participants think about which three are so promising that they would like to choose them as the basis for the solution.

The easiest way is for participants to write down ideas for themselves and post them on CREATE. They can also do the same thing as a joint brainstorming session.

Brainstorming or clustering ideas is not necessarily known as the most creative way of collecting ideas. In "Create", however, the situation is different. What is missing in classic brainstorming is everything that has happened before in co-creation: the deeper engagement with the goal of an in-depth analysis of the problem. Likewise, there is no comparable synchronous understanding on the part of the participants. None of this can be compensated for in classic brainstorming. That is why other methods have prevailed for innovation processes.

So far, we have described co-creation as a way in which the team forms a collective consciousness. What happens in the subconscious during this collaborative process? In the shared subconscious, the solution matures. As you can see in the photo, it is still being expressed in different formulations. However, it is clear on the level of content.

The "Create" process is very different from meetings where colleagues come together to come up with a solution. There, finding a solution is exhausting and very open-ended. Very different ideas emerge, which are difficult to evaluate in terms of which is more promising. In co-creation, the participants simply write down which ideas are obvious, even if they have not yet been formulated. They only have to put the obvious into words.

The "Create" process is, therefore, more like an opening up than a strenuous exercise: "Finally, we are allowed to write down what has been on our minds for a long time anyway". Now, too, comes the hour of the participants who have a high-performance component in their personality. Their evaluation of the process often looks like this: "We already knew what had to be done before the workshop even started. But it was good that we went through it together, because the solutions are more differentiated than the original ideas were".

Next, it is important to evaluate the ideas in relation to their field of action and feasibility. This means that the "Value × Influence" matrix is used again to determine which ideas are particularly promising as solutions for the field of action and which are more likely to be implemented than other ideas. In "Create", the participants take a look back at the overall process, review their thoughts and then choose the path they want to take together.

"Create" paves the way for the next-to-last of the eight process steps: clarifying responsibilities. "Create" provides the basis for this. Now that it is clear what is to be done, the "Do" step can be carried out to plan the implementation.

7.1.7 "Do"

The seventh process step is "Do": implementing solutions (Fig. 7.14).

"Do" defines the basic project responsibilities for each solution:

1. Choose the project name
2. Project management
3. Members of the project team

Fig. 7.14 "Do"—implementing solutions

4. Timeframe: what should be done by when
5. Basis for the next co-creation round

What should be considered in relation to each of the four components?

Project name: The name of the project is derived from the field of action or the solution idea. It should be short and catchy. It should be clear to the other projects which project it is. This facilitates coordination.

Project management: Project management can be taken on by any participant in the co-creation session. It is even conceivable that, in the course of the project, a person who was not originally present during the co-creation process takes over the project leadership.

If the responsible entity is represented in the co-creation team, it might be appropriate for them to become project leader. Let us say a project plans to introduce "reverse mentoring". In reverse mentoring, younger employees become the mentors of older employees. The younger generation is networked with experienced staff, in order to introduce current trends into the company's thinking. One would assume that such a measure would fall under the personnel division. Hence, if a human resources employee is part of the co-creation process, this person could take over the project management. This would ensure that the co-creation project is aligned with initiatives happening in HR.

Project team members: The first question is the size of the project teams. This depends mainly on how large the co-creation group is and how many projects have been selected.

Considerations about the number of members of the co-creation team will be presented below.

The number of projects should not exceed five when working with CREATE. CREATE provides that, at the end of the co-creation, work will continue on a maximum of five projects. We have already mentioned this number in the explanations concerning opening and closing in the process steps. This means that the team should limit itself to a maximum of five topics from a larger number of possibilities.

In co-creation workshops, it has been shown that the participants almost always use the full number. Occasionally, there are also four projects, since one or the other can be merged at the end.

This means that with 6–10 people and four to five projects, there are on average two people per project. Hence, the project team is quite manageable at this stage. In some co-creation teams, the members work on several projects, so the number per team increases.

Basically, there are only a few people per project at the end of the co-creation. This provides the opportunity to involve other people, who were not part of the co-creation at an early stage in the process. If the project teams were made up of six or seven people from the beginning, there would be little incentive to bring in people from the outside.

Timeframe: In the timeframe, the project members agree by when the first results should be achieved. What results are conceivable at this early stage of the project?

If time is running out at the end of the co-creation process, the project team should at least agree on when they will meet next. This date should be agreed on and entered into calendars. If there is more time left, then it can be decided who else should be invited. This also includes clarifying who will invite and brief the additional people.

If there is still an hour or more available, it is advisable to use this time to start the first project meeting right away. First, however, the conclusion with the second "Connect" step must be carried out with the whole group. Directly afterwards, the project teams can have their first project meeting. Which topics could be clarified with each other in a first project team meeting?

- What do we understand by the project? Even if everyone in the project team was involved in the co-creation and thus helped shape the creation of the goal, it is now important to clarify the common understanding once again.
- What do we want to achieve with the project and by when? What is the basic goal of this project and by when could this goal fundamentally be achieved?
- What could the milestones on the way to the goal be? This question goes a level deeper and takes a corresponding amount of time. The milestones provide the framework for a coordinated approach and should be chosen carefully.
- Who should be involved? Which individuals or institutions would be valuable feedback providers? Which opinion leaders and decision-makers should be involved? How and when should they be integrated?

Basis of the next co-creation round: As already described in detail above, the results of one co-creation process can also form the basis for another round of co-creation. In that case, more people from the organization would be integrated into future projects through co-creation. The project leaders become the "clients" for the next round of co-creation. They take "their topic", for which they have project responsibility, and transpose it to the next level of co-creation, where they present it. This includes not only the result, but also the presentation of the overall goal and the results of the phases of the preceding co-creation workshop.

"Do" concludes the co-creation process on the level of content. However, the team process is not yet concluded. In the final "Connect" step, the team looks back over the collaboration before the co-creation workshop can be brought to an end.

7.1.8 "Connect"

The final process step is "Connect": connecting people and ideas (Fig. 7.15).

The co-creation workshop opened with "Connect" and it also closes with "Connect". Co-creation stands and falls based on the quality of the connection. In section "The Principles of Co-Creation", it was explained that co-creation has a clear beginning and also an end. The participants have fully engaged in this process and should say goodbye to each other with gratitude.

The end should be such that the participants appreciate their respective contributions. They should learn from each other that they have passed through the co-creation together and be grateful to the others for making it possible.

Fig. 7.15 "Connect"—connecting at the end of co-creation

The message is clear: "We did good work. It was not always easy, but we did it and I think it has moved us forward. It was great to meet you in this way, and I look forward to the next time".

This is typically how the personal message at the end of a co-creation workshop sounds. On the level of content, the conclusion should answer two questions:

1. What is really good about the results we have achieved?
2. How do we stay in touch with each other afterwards?

The answer to the first question reinforces the experience on the level of content: "It was not only good to work with you, but the results have moved things forward". The question already made that clear. It is not about a neutral reappraisal. What is important now is to reinforce the experience. If the coach wants to conduct an additional qualitative feedback round, he can do so afterwards.

The answer to the second question links co-creation to the way forward. It clarifies how the participants, now that they are in different projects, will stay in contact with each other. This is also important for technical reasons: they can agree on how to coordinate the results of the projects with each other and on who is the contact person for questions.

In order for the project participants to actively approach each other, they must have decision-making authority in the implementation of the project. If they only carry out what others decide, it will be much more difficult to achieve an active exchange between the projects.

Co-creation was described as a complete process that can be rolled out at other levels. If the implementation is to be successful, it would be better if it did not remain a one-off event. The co-creation teams should meet repeatedly for co-creation workshops to work together on the big goal. The design of a follow-up co-creation workshop is presented in the next section.

7.1.9 Follow-up Co-creation Workshop

Follow-up workshops can take place at the project level or with the whole co-creation team. What are they for and how do they differ from the first co-creation session?

The goal of co-creation is to let the future emerge from a shared consciousness. As we have seen, this does not just happen but requires the right attitude and approach. We can ask ourselves whether it makes sense to conduct every meeting in this way. If the goal and the way to the goal are clear to all the participants and everyone is in agreement, then it may be more efficient to use classic formats. However, it is also advisable to live the co-creation mindset here, to connect with each other in an appreciative way, in order to accomplish the next task. This has become the culture of the team, and it would feel strange to behave differently now.

But when is it advisable to work with the co-creation process in the follow-up workshop as well? The answer is simple: whenever it is unclear what the future should look like. Because precisely this is the task of co-creation: to let the future emerge. The way to do this is through purposeful, human connection.

Let us imagine the following scenario. The aim of a co-creation workshop was to change the external image of a company. At the end of the co-creation process, five projects resulted, which were then implemented. At this point, the question arose among the participants and the client as to where to go from here. This is exactly the right time to come together for the next co-creation.

How should the second co-creation workshop unfold? Only the opening "Connect" step changes. All the other process steps remain the same. In the follow-up workshop, "Connect" should be carried out as follows:

Connection of the Participants

In the "Connect" step of the first workshop, the process began with the participants connecting with themselves and with the others on the level of their motives. In the follow-up workshop, people's preferences are known and the process does not have to be repeated in the same sense. However, this is different if the composition of the group has changed. It is not unlikely that new members have joined. If so, it makes perfect sense to integrate the new group members at the level of motivational preferences.

Review of the Interim Period

The most obvious difference between an initial workshop and a follow-up workshop is the review of the interim period. This deals with how the cooperation has gone since the last co-creation or project meeting. From the results of the reflection, conclusions can then be drawn about how to work together in the future. What should remain the same because it has proven successful? What could be done even better?

In co-creation workshops, we use a method from the agile toolbox, the "retrospective" or "retro" for short. There are different ways to conduct a retro. In co-creation, we work with the "starfish", which mixes simplicity and completeness (Fig. 7.16).

The starfish is performed as follows:

1. Clarify the common goals of the retrospective.
2. If this is the second retrospective, review the agreed-upon actions:
   a. What measures were agreed?
   b. Which ones have been implemented?
   c. What changes have been brought about by this?
3. Retrospective of the collaboration:
   a. Draw a star on a flipchart
   b. Individual work: write a post-it about each of the five areas
   c. Everyone presents their post-its and sticks them on the wall
   d. Sort and prioritise all issues

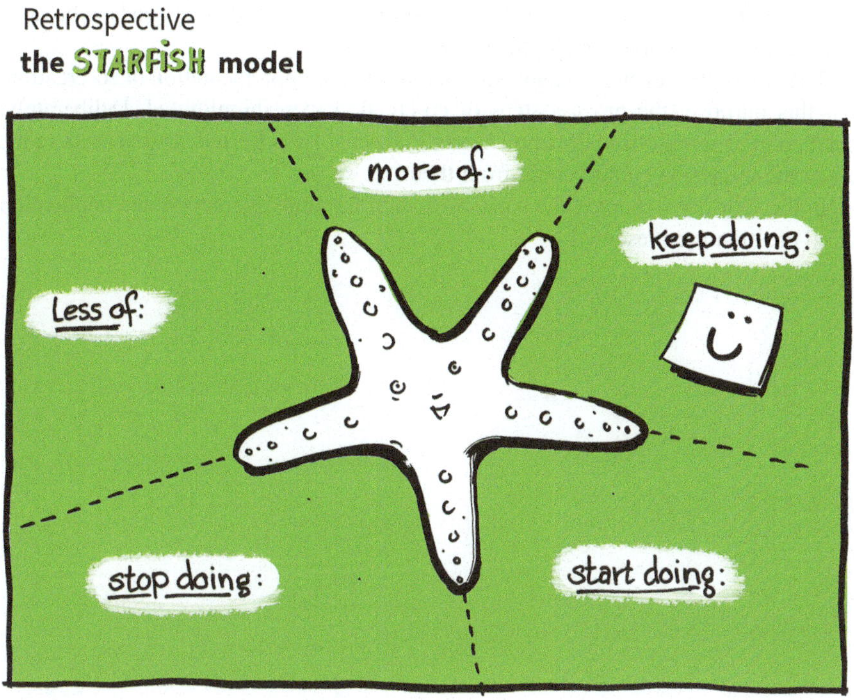

Fig. 7.16 Retrospective using the starfish

e. Discussion and decision about two to three concrete measures concerning what should be changed

Target Review

Since the last co-creation, measures have been agreed on and implemented in the projects. Their implementation should have an effect. How does this change the goal? Is the goal still the same or has it changed? It is possible that the perspective has also changed and that the participants now see the goal with different eyes. This can also result in the desire to adjust the goal.

Regardless of whether the goal remains the same or has changed, the participants should once again clarify for themselves why it is important to them. This refreshes and strengthens the common connection. The group thus acquires the energy for the steps ahead.

After "Connect", the process continues as in the first session. After "Connect", the participants get a picture of how the situation is at the moment in "Discover". What has changed since last time? What are the differences between the current situation and the target situation?

Depending on how much the goal has changed or remained the same, this round may take less time than when it was first carried out. If the goal has remained the same, then the main focus is on the impact of the projects and what needs to be done now to further promote development.

The aim of the seventh chapter was to describe the implementation of co-creation. For this purpose, the process steps of co-creation were highlighted. Deliberately, detailed experiences from the implementation were also reflected, so that users of the co-creation method could benefit from them.

In the following chapter, the basic aspects of the implementation and application of co-creation are presented.

Transformation of the Organization

8

Abstract

When people connect with each other in relation to a goal, with the determination to do things differently, they have the power to transform organizations. Co-creation builds on the connection between people and their aspirations, in order to make their intentions a reality. Co-creation can also help people to transform organizations. In order to do so, they must have the will to bring about transformation, to implement it and to sustain the new culture. The formats of transformation refer to the application-oriented aspects of co-creation, which mainly revolve around the space, the time available and the possible forms of co-creation. Important aspects are employees and the corporate culture, the role of leadership in changing the corporate culture and how HR can support this.

Keywords

HR management · Leadership · Roles · Transformation

When people connect with each other in relation to a goal, with the determination to do things differently, they have the power to transform organizations. Co-creation builds on the connection between people and their aspirations, in order to make their intentions a reality. Co-creation can also help people to transform organizations. In order to do so, they must have the will to bring about transformation, to implement it and to sustain the new culture.

In this eighth chapter, we first want to take a look at the formats of transformation. This refers to the application-oriented aspects of co-creation, which mainly revolve around the space, the time available and the possible forms of co-creation.

In the later chapters we then look at how this can help the transformation of the organization to succeed. We start with the employees and the corporate culture, look at the role of leadership in changing the corporate culture and ask how HR can support this. In order to do so, we examine the role of leadership development,

G. Michalik, *Co-Creation Mindset*, Management for Professionals,
https://doi.org/10.1007/978-3-031-21191-1_8

organizational development and finally the role of the co-creation coach and process facilitator.

8.1 Space

Let us start by describing the space in which co-creation takes place (Fig. 8.1). Consciously integrating the space into co-creation is a prerequisite and an essential ingredient for success in our approach. In space, we work with an element that is of crucial importance for creating the collective consciousness: "CREATE". CREATE is a visualisation and process tool for spatial work.

People live and work in spaces. We are not two-dimensional beings, and yet our forms of discussion have shifted to the two-dimensional world. PowerPoint has become the tool for visualising things. In the virtual world, our communication has become two-dimensional, such that we do not use our capacity for three-dimensional thinking, our spatial imagination.

> Spatial imagination [. . .] can generally be described as the ability of humans and other living beings to see and think spatially in the imagination. This ability includes the acquisition, organization and active handling of imaginary images stored in memory. [. . .] The focus is on recognising the position and relationship of bodies in three-dimensional space. There are different perspectives on spatial imagination, as described in a large 1985 meta-analysis by Linn and Petersen: the psychometric, differential, cognitive and strategic perspectives. (Wikipedia).

In this description, it becomes apparent that thinking and feeling in space means much more than being able to imagine three-dimensional objects. Rather, it is about

Fig. 8.1 The co-creation space

the holistic ability to create relationships. Connecting things with each other in order to create something new from them is a creative process. In this creative process, alternative ways of solving problems become visible.

The space in which co-creation takes place creates an additional medium as a projection space. Not only can people interact with each other via a two-dimensional image, but they move together in the third dimension. They use the environment to represent things there, to create references and to let their thoughts and sensations connect with each other in space. They can look together at what is being created. The parts become a whole in space. In this way, the whole becomes its own thing. It detaches itself from its individual origin and acquires its own identity. Everyone can work on this at the same time. They look at what has been created, talk about it, modify it and occasionally marvel at what an amazing thing has happened.

The co-creation space provides room for people to move, both physically and in their perspectives. It makes it possible to create references. It inspires and makes room for thinking. It is bright and warm. It is flexible and should be adapted to the people, not the other way around.

In co-creation, we also create space on another level: the space in which something new can come into the world. This is the space between people and between people and organizations. Organizations are also three-dimensional entities. Forcing them into matrices usually does not do justice to their complexity.

8.2 Guest Commentary: René Massatti (PLAYROOM)

About: PLAYROOM is an innovation design company based in Vienna and Berlin. Here, designers and economists work together to develop future-oriented co-creation formats. Since its founding in 2016, the company has developed over 100 co-creation spaces of various dimensions for clients throughout Europe and Asia (www.playroom.rocks).

The story of PLAYROOM begins in the playroom. How do children come up with new ideas? They go to a safe place (a playroom), where, unlike in other areas of the house, they have the freedom to think and create. Often, they develop their ideas alone or with others over an extended period of time. So far, so good. How do adults develop new ideas in a corporate context? They book a meeting room, organise a workshop, digitise the results and hope for change.

Workshops are a legitimate tool for developing new things, but they are only one aspect of co-creation. If they want to live this approach, companies need fixed physical locations where teams can dedicate themselves to innovating through co-creation at different intervals. These physical spaces

(continued)

dedicated to co-creation work are not a replacement for the necessary digital spaces and communication platforms but should be seen as a supplement, contributing to the satisfaction of deeply rooted human needs for communication.

The use of analogue tools to master the challenges of digital transformation seems paradoxical at first. However, the desire for real collaborative work has been flourishing for years now. In a study by PwC*, 60% of millennials and 72% of all respondents expressed a preference for face-to-face collaboration over other forms of communication in the work environment. From numerous conversations with clients, we can confirm this desire for the physical presence of all participants in a setting specifically configured for the task.

Under the popular buzzword "agility", we find not only processes that should become more flexible and adaptive, but space too. For future-oriented companies, this means building a modular principle at the elemental level of processes and space that can be used to respond to a wide variety of requirements, in terms of tasks, processes, time constraints and team sizes.

Cultural transformation processes in organizations have many aspects. However, space is a factor that is increasingly playing a decisive role in the way in which change processes happen and are perceived in companies. Here, it is not so much the elaborate architectural design of the space that plays an essential role, but rather the disclosure and transparency of the processes.

This entails the fusion of space and process design, resulting in the design of distinctive physical process modules in the space, which are visible and comprehensible to everyone and which, in contrast to the classic use of paper canvas in workshops, also remain sustainably anchored in that space.

The use of process modules, such as CREATE, that are physically present in the space changes the way in which people work together. The problem of distance, which is typical for large organizations, can be addressed by the transparent use of spatial processes, in order to undermine hierarchies that hinder the change process and thus to more efficiently achieve the goals that have been set. In a rapidly changing, increasingly digital and disruptive world, physical spaces with clearly structured processes thus also serve as protective spaces, in which factors such as interpersonal communication and empathy once again play an essential role in the sustainable development of any company.

8.3 CREATE

In the photos used in this book, there is always a place where co-creation is visualised. We call it "CREATE". CREATE is a terminal that combines three elements: space, time and thinking together (Figs. 8.2 and 8.3).

Fig. 8.2 Working with CREATE

Fig. 8.3 CREATE—a representation of shared memory

Space: CREATE helps us to make use of space. As described in the previous section, space is a central element of co-creation. It can be used as a projection space for three-dimensional thinking. Within this space, CREATE is the surface onto which the thoughts of the group members are projected.

The idea of a collective consciousness is a common thread running through co-creation. It takes people to a higher level and creates the potential to solve complex problems. However, consciousness is neither visible nor tangible. This is why it cannot be packed into existing workshop formats. But how can you work with a collective consciousness if it is not visible?

In more complex discussions, we refer, somewhat helplessly, to previously expressed opinions or thoughts: "What you said earlier about working together as a team. . .". This is complicated because we always have to take a trip down memory lane. The point has to be recapitulated clearly, so that we can understand who said what and how.

This process could be made easier if the participants repeatedly described their thoughts. They could assign keywords to individual thoughts. When they wanted to come back to a thought, they could recall it by means of the keyword. The participants would then have their own image of the thought. However, working like this is time-consuming and carries an ongoing risk of misunderstanding.

Alternatively, you can make the thoughts visible. You can work with a flipchart and sketch the group's thoughts on it. Flipcharts are standard equipment in most meeting rooms today. However, working with flipcharts quickly reaches its limits: they provide little space, only a handful of thoughts are visible at a time and when changes are made, things quickly become messy and confusing.

Working with CREATE is different. It is a three-dimensional component of the space, and thus part of the working environment. It provides space for many thoughts that can be changed at any time: writing and drawing can be done on CREATE itself. Through this shared representation, thoughts and ideas grow together with the project.

As can be seen in the photos, co-creation is presented as a self-explanatory process. CREATE makes it possible for people to quickly orient themselves, without requiring a long introduction.

Using CREATE, participants can classify their thoughts into a system that follows the co-creation process. This opens up a second dimension alongside space: time. The results of the collaboration can be arranged on a timeline. Thus, in addition to a shared imagination, a shared memory is also created. This memory is immune to forgetfulness and confusion, since the essential elements of the process are always visible to everyone at a glance.

This photo illustrates the collective memory of CREATE. The participant seems to say: "Look what we said there. . ."

The following experience left a lasting impression on us coaches. At the end of a 1-day co-creation workshop, after everything had been completed, the participants were still standing together. The CREATE had been photographed with the day's results and the post-its had been removed. It had thus been returned to its neutral, unlabelled state. An idea came to the participants and the discussion was engaged again. To make his point, one participant said to the group, "Do you remember what we wrote down there. . ." He pointed to the lower part of the "Explore" stage, where the results of the root-cause analysis had been 30 min earlier. But now they were no longer there. At least physically they were no longer on the CREATE, but in the participant's memories, they were still visible on the wall. And so the participant could point to the spot and everyone knew what he meant.

By following the timeline, CREATE not only allows participants to go back in their minds but also to look into the future. The subsequent course of events is visible, in the sense that everyone can imagine what will come in the next step or the step after that. This also allows projections into the future. This can help us to run through our own thoughts and to consider where an idea will lead.

The function of CREATE is to shape the interrelation between the actors, to serve as a medium that offers them new possibilities of togetherness. Now they can think aloud when interacting. It is a reciprocal relationship between actors. In the interaction with CREATE, space and time come together. The participants can move around freely in this zone with the help of CREATE.

As individuals, we do this all the time. We go back in our memories. We think about what the future might look like. We mentally go to places that inspire us. We look in our diaries at what we had written down earlier.

With CREATE, it becomes possible for people to do this not only as individuals, but also as a community. With CREATE, their inner process is externalised. By being able to represent the collective thought process, the collective consciousness can work effectively. CREATE can serve the function of an external cognitive representation in co-creation, the group's transparent memory.

The co-creation process is, in itself, a logical process of problem-solving. People go through this process when they want to systematically overcome challenges. When they work with CREATE, they quickly recognise their inner process in it.

When they recognise their inner process in space, they realise that they can externalise their inner thinking. They then know that they do not have to do any translation work to communicate their thoughts to the others. This means that they do not have to first finish their thought for themselves and only then put it into another external format, because the outer format corresponds to the inner format. Working together via CREATE gives them the opportunity to think out loud.

8.4 Forms of Co-creation

In explaining co-creation, we have so far limited ourselves to 1-day co-creation workshops. However, there are other possible formats. They differ in terms of time, space and the form of interaction:

- 1-day co-creation: co-creation in 1 day
- CC 60: co-creation in 60 min.
- Virtual co-creation: co-creation at a distance
- Coaching co-creation: co-creation for coaching support
- Leadership co-creation: co-creation between manager and employee

These variations are described in this section using the following criteria:

- Application: opportunities for this format
- Format: basic process of co-creation in this format

- Time: time commitment and allocation
- Space: framework, location, tools

8.4.1 1-Day Co-creation

Application: The 1-day co-creation workshop is the basic form. The experiences described in this book are derived from it. It is always suitable when the fundamental course for the future is to be set. The future should emerge from the collective consciousness of those involved. Typically, this is the prelude to a series of co-creation workshops. Here, the overall goal of the co-creation is agreed upon and the sub-goals are worked out.

The 1-day workshop is also suitable when team building is important. For example, let us say a company board has only worked together operationally in the past, and now there is a need for the silos to be overcome, making closer cooperation possible. If the board members knew each other better, this would be a good prerequisite. Through a 1-day co-creation workshop, they can connect the factual and the relational levels. They experience each other as colleagues, free of political reservations in their motivation and attitudes.

Format: The format of the 1-day co-creation workshop has already been described in detail. The number of participants is usually in the size range of a team, i.e. 5–10 people.

For large groups, the 1-day format can also be adopted. By a large group event, we mean an event where the group size is too large to work with CREATE. Groups of 60 or more are perfectly suitable for co-creation workshops.

In large groups, considerable time is needed for coordination between the working groups. This must be taken into account in time management. For this, the overall process must be more structured, meaning that the goals are therefore less open. A large group thrives on the dynamics between the people. It can focus on the implementation of issues.

Time: A possible format for a 1-day co-creation session is to start at 9 am and end at 5 pm. In between, there is a 30-min break in the morning and two 20-min breaks in the afternoon. The lunch break lasts an hour. We discourage a "sandwich lunch" in front of CREATE. It is good to change the location for lunch.

Inclusion of the previous evening: in certain circumstances, it has proven useful to have the 1-day co-creation start the day before, in the late afternoon or evening.

Having the co-creation start already on the afternoon of the previous day can be useful if a little more time is to be invested in team development. The participants can take more time for the personality analysis and present their profiles to each other in one-on-one conversations.

Making use of the evening before is a good idea if the goal to be achieved with the co-creation is still open. Before and after dinner, the group can think in a relaxed atmosphere about the basic direction it should take. This preliminary discussion helps make it possible to formulate the common goal the next day. During breakfast on one such occasion, a new member of the executive board came up to me and said:

"You know, it was really great that we were able to talk about our goal last night. Now I've slept on it and can go into the co-creation workshop today with a good feeling".

In a 1-day workshop, there is time to connect the participants and build the collective consciousness. The 1-day format has proven successful for this. However, other time windows are also conceivable. It can also take one to two half-days. Or it can be adapted to any other time window. As long as attention is paid to the attitude, values and principles of co-creation, the most important framework conditions are in place.

Space: The 1-day co-creation event is ideally designed with a CREATE. This may differ for large group co-creation events. The room should offer enough space to set up the CREATE so that people can move around freely in front of it. In creative spaces set up for this purpose, there is the possibility of flexibly adapting the space to the group's needs.

8.4.2 CC 60

Application: CC 60 is co-creation in an hour. This makes it possible to use co-creation in standard meetings as well. CC 60 assumes that the participants are already well connected, since it is not possible to both create a deeper connection and go through the co-creation process in the short time available.

Format: The 1-h format focuses on the structured process. In 60 min, all eight co-creation process steps can be gone through. CC 60 gains its strength from a different source than the 1-day workshop. In 1-day co-creation, the payoff lies in the collective consciousness, from which the future emerges in the course of the process. The strength of CC 60 lies in concentrating on what is absolutely essential.

CC 60 follows the timeboxing approach: a pre-defined number of minutes are available for each of the process steps. Given this compressed timeframe, the co-creation process must breathe more quickly. This means that there is only a brief amount of time to open the space and then to close it via a group decision. If the group has a whole day, then the breathing tempo is that of a quiet endurance run, whereas if the group only has an hour, then its breathing is like a 100-m sprint.

Timeboxing is the strength of the CC 60. A strong argument that is obvious to everyone prevails. It provides the basis for the next step. CC 60 is thus still different from standard meetings, because it is highly structured and goes through all the phases of defining the goal, understanding, deciding and finding a solution.

Time: The hour allocated to the process is divided between the eight phases as in Table 8.1.

Each step is divided into sub-questions. A certain number of minutes is also available for answering the sub-questions.

Space: The same conditions apply when it comes to the space as in the 1-day co-creation. Due to the high level of dynamism, it is advisable to conduct the CC 60 at standing tables. If a CREATE is available, this is an advantage, as the participants can quickly post their notes themselves at the right place in the process.

Table 8.1 Schedule CC 60

0:00	CONNECT	8 min
0:08	DISCOVER	5 min
0:13	EXPLORE	9 min
0:22	SHARE and AGREE	10 min
0:32	CREATE	9 min
0:41	DO	10 min
0:51	CONNECT	5 min
0:56	Buffer	4 min

If the overall process is visible, this makes it easy for the participants to navigate it in a short period of time. In addition, post-its can be removed or reposted as necessary.

8.4.3 Remote Co-creation

Application: Co-creation thrives on the connection between the participants. At the same time, collaboration via digital media is becoming increasingly important. Competence and responsibility are often spread around the world, and it is necessary to organise accordingly. Therefore, meetings increasingly take place in the form of video conferences. How can co-creation with real connection between people happen under these circumstances? Is it conceivable that co-creation can also happen virtually without the participants being in the same room?

The co-creation process maps out a complete and systematic problem-solving process. People recognise their inner process and agree to proceed in this way. The clarity of the process steps and knowledge of what the next steps will be creates trust among the participants. If different people agree that the process is a good fit, then the connection between them can also take place through the goal and the process.

As already stated in the chapter on the importance of connection, process is the third level of connection in co-creation:

- Connection from person to person
- Connection via the common goal
- Connection via the co-creation process

All three forms of connection are also possible in digital space.

Format: What form can remote co-creation assume? As in the physical workshop, there are moments in the co-creation process when the team works for itself, and other moments when it shares the results and coordinates. Online platforms take over part of the function of CREATE. The input of the participants can be collected there.

In order for the collaboration to function in a coordinated manner, facilitation is indispensable. A facilitator must accompany the process. He senses when conflicts arise, when time limits are not being respected or when the content does not meet expectations.

Time: The advantages of remote co-creation are the relative independence from spatial proximity and the decoupling of time. The steps between the coordination sequences can be completed by the participants when it works best for them. This is especially easy if the participants are in different time zones.

Space: The virtual space can be exploited through different tools and platforms. The chosen tool should enable both real-time collaboration and individual work at different times on one platform. For example, we work with Mural, Teams or other whiteboards as visual platforms, and use Zoom or Skype for the accompanying communication.

Even in virtual collaboration, oral communication remains important. This is why we speak of remote co-creation and not pure virtual collaboration. Whenever intermediate results need to be interpreted, this enhances collective awareness. Otherwise, the probability increases that the participants will misunderstand each other and fail to realise their shared potential.

8.4.4 Coaching Co-creation

Application: Co-creation involves creating something together. "Together" means that more than one person has to be involved. What if the challenge involves a single person? What if a situation can only be dealt with by one person? That is, if a coaching framework is present, can co-creation be applied?

Co-creation always involves a common goal. However, the coach is neutral towards the coachee's goal. How does this work with co-creation? Could the coach take on the role of a "co-" without actually being one? In this case, the coach would function like a sparring partner.

First of all, it should be said that there is no such thing as "coaching". Coaching is used to refer to a range of different counselling methods.

Coaching conversations have a certain structure. That is, they follow a process. One of the best-known structures is the GROW model (Withmore, 1992).

Format: The GROW model follows a four-step process:

- G: GOAL—Define and agree on goals!
- R: REALITY—What is the situation at the moment?
- O: OPTIONS—What are the alternative courses of action?
- W: WHAT—What does the coach want to do? WHEN does he want it done by?

This structural understanding coincides with the co-creation process. Here, too, it is a question of developing one's own solutions. Co-creation also provides a clear structure. The four steps in GROW correspond to the eight steps in co-creation.

What about the role and attitude of the coach? His task is to accompany the coachee in developing their own solutions.

Does the co-creation coach adopt a different stance than a classic coach with a systematic background? Gerhard Neumann, an experienced coach, describes his own attitude as follows:

> My task as a process facilitator is to reflect on the client's constructions of reality and to work out how and what he observes, what explanations he gives for his observations and what he bases his decisions on. I hold back on explanations and ask questions instead. I accept the client as an expert with respect to his reality constructions, which he wants to check and possibly change through coaching. But I can question, suggest different things, offer ideas or ask about consequences and effects of possible actions, etc. But if someone is sure that they are on the right path, it is not my place to know better. (Neumann in Barczynski, 2014).

The co-creation coach does what Gerhard Neumann describes. He "offers solutions" without pushing them. In principle, the co-creation coach is very similar to the team members in a co-creation workshop. They too offer points of view, their own points of view. Which ones are selected and followed up on in the end is determined in a second step.

Co-creation can therefore also be used for individuals in the form of coaching. In order to do so, the coach takes on the role of the team member in the co-creation session. He thinks his way into the topic and takes a stand. However, the decision as to which option is chosen for the next process step remains with the coachee.

Time: The time required for co-creation coaching is the same as in ordinary coaching. Here, the possibilities vary widely, from a brief intervention to a whole-day coaching session. There should, however, be at least 1 h to proceed through the CC 60 process.

Space: The same conditions apply when it comes to the space as in any other form of coaching. However, the coach may have the option of using a CREATE. If this option exists, other opportunities arise than would be the case with only a flipchart. Similar to the use of CREATE in co-creation workshops, coach and coachee then have the possibility to constantly move back and forth in their visualisation of time.

8.4.5 Leadership Co-creation

Application: With co-creation coaching, a "1:1" format for co-creation was described. Is the "1:1" format also applicable to conversations between manager and employee?

Whether and how leadership co-creation works depends on what image the manager and staff have of leading and being led. Let us assume that there is a challenge or a "problem" that needs to be discussed. There are three possible attitudes in a "1:1" relationship:

1. The manager looks at the employee's problem.
2. The employee looks at the manager's problem.
3. The manager and the employee look at the problem together.

In most cases, managers would endorse attitude three: "We look at the challenges together and work on solutions in partnership".

For the sake of completeness, all three attitudes should be checked to see whether co-creation is possible there.

1. *The manager looks at the employee's problem.* This corresponds to the classic image of leadership, and often also to what leaders actually do. There is an imbalance here that can be felt by everyone, a difference in level. The manager looks down on the employee and his problems. He feels responsible for solving them. If necessary, he solves them himself. If this happens more often, then the employee quickly becomes the problem, and not the problem itself.
   Co-creation cannot arise on the basis of such an attitude. In co-creation, the participants engage eye to eye. They do not just say it, but they actually feel that they are on the same level.
2. *The employee looks at the manager's problem.* In the classic picture of leadership (point 1), this corresponds to a large extent to reality. If the manager has a "problem" with the employee's performance and challenges, it is often the manager who has the real problem. The person being managed quickly realises this and has the opportunity to make life difficult for their boss. From their point of view, bosses can be quite demanding. This results in an imbalance, as in the first point. Then the problem is no longer the problem; the boss is the real problem.
   Co-creation cannot develop on the basis of such an attitude either. Because here, too, the manager and the employee do not see eye to eye.
3. *The manager and the employee look at the problem together.* This is the attitude of co-creation and the only way in which co-creation can be applied in leadership.

But are not leadership and co-creation inherently contradictory? After all, leadership means that one person leads the other, and thus they are not on the same level.

If we were to assume that "leadership" means managing people in the sense of "I know better than you what to do", then this would indeed be an unresolvable contradiction.

However, leadership can be much more than that. Leadership in co-creation can mean that the leader takes the initiative and facilitates the process. In co-creation, they can then look at the problem together with the employee. In this way, the leader preserves his role as a leader and simultaneously reflects on the common problem at the same level as the employee. In this way, role clarity is maintained, but the two parties still engage eye to eye.

Format: Depending on whether the leadership co-creation concerns one staff member or a whole team, the formats look different.

In the case of leadership co-creation involving a single staff member, the format is similar to that of co-creation coaching. It is a "1:1" situation. However, there is a difference between the coach and the manager. The manager has a personal interest in solving the problem, while the coach has a professional interest in solving the problem. This means that the manager is directly affected by the outcome. The coach is concerned, because he wants to be a good coach. It is therefore important to him that the coachee is satisfied with the result, but the result itself is not important to him. During their collaboration, this should hardly be noticeable, however, because the coach also has to immerse himself completely in the role of the "co-". The manager should bring his own leadership perspective into the co-creation. He is thus fully part of the co-creation, with full awareness that he is taking on a different role in the organization.

A leadership co-creation session with one's own team corresponds to the format of a "normal" co-creation workshop, i.e. the 1-day co-creation or the CC 60. The manager can take on the role of a facilitator. However, he does not have to. He can also assign the role to a team member or a coach. However, he should always authentically represent his perspective as a leader.

Time and space: The time and space requirements correspond to the comparable formats mentioned above. In other words, in 1:1 sessions, the timing should correspond to a coaching session, while in divisional workshops, the timing should correspond to a 1-day co-creation workshop. If possible, CREATE should also be used in leadership co-creation.

Later on in this chapter, the "role of leadership" and "leadership development" will be addressed again. So far, we have looked at the importance of space as a projection surface for our shared consciousness. For this purpose, CREATE, a tool that helps us to make use of space, was introduced. CREATE can be used as a visible collective memory. It enables a journey through time that also allows projections into the future.

Finally, five different co-creation formats were discussed. These can be used in different contexts: as all-day workshops with numerous participants, as a 1-h meeting format, as a method to make virtual collaboration as inclusive as possible, as a coaching format and finally also as a leadership tool.

The book so far has taught the basics of co-creation. These are the aspects of attitude, the effect on the individual, team dynamics, how to create an evolving map in order to orient oneself towards it as a whole system, how to carry out co-creation and which other framework conditions have to be taken into account. In the following, we report on the practical experiences of how co-creation can make the transformation of a company possible.

8.5 Roles in Transformation

The individuals in an organization take on specific roles in the transformation. In what follows, we will describe what they have to pay attention to in their roles. Subsequently, the co-creation transformation process shows how the introduction of co-creation can succeed in eight steps.

If we consider the transformation of an organization through co-creation as a project, then roles can be derived from it and responsibilities assigned. A project has at least three roles: the client, the project management and the project staff.

Client: In the co-creation transformation, the client is the highest decision-making entity involved. To find out who this is, it is necessary to ask oneself what the most far-reaching changes that can be imagined are. What financial and time resources would these changes require? The client should be the body or person who would have to agree to release the funds and accept the changes. Very often this is the CEO. Since in this case, the board members would also be part of the co-creation and the

CEO has the authority to give them instructions, this can have a detrimental effect on the co-creation process. Therefore, it may be advisable to either involve the supervisory board in the decision or to be collectively responsible as a board for the approvals and decisions linked to the co-creation.

Project management: Project management is primarily responsible for the implementation of the project according to the plan. Here we do not mean the transformation projects that are the result of the respective co-creation workshops, but the "introduction of co-creation" as an overall project. Project management plays a leading role in the overall planning, implementation, monitoring, control and completion of the transformation. This includes managing, reviewing and prioritising the co-creation projects with the aim of staying on time and on budget. Almost more important than this, however, is to ensure the coordination of project outcomes. This requires organising the necessary decision-making bodies and ensuring the flow of communication. Who could take on this task in the organization? If there is a separate organizational development department in the company, this would be the first choice. This is usually part of the human resources department. If it does not (yet) exist, then the necessary competences and resources would have to be created within the HR department.

Project staff: The project staff are all those who are involved in the projects resulting at the end of the co-creation process. Initially, these are the managers, but as co-creation is rolled out in the organization, experts and other staff members also become involved.

The senior management as the client, the HR department as the project leader, and the managers, employees and internal/external experts as project collaborators are jointly responsible for making the co-creation transformation possible.

8.6 Employees and Corporate Culture

Business transformation is intensive work that requires one's full attention. One of the most important principles is to involve the employees in the change, rather than handing them a ready-made concept.

Transformations have certain conditions for success. Successful companies, for example, need visibly committed C-level leaders who communicate clearly about the changes ahead. C-level support is a condition, but it is not sufficient on its own. To be successful, employees at all levels of the hierarchy need to play a certain role and everyone needs to know how to contribute.

A study by McKinsey (2017) shows that in successful transformation processes, employees were significantly more engaged than in unsuccessful transformations. However, especially at the level of staff and team leaders, the difference in engagement was more pronounced than in the senior management or in certain supporting functions:

When it comes to the CEO and senior management, visible engagement was 94% for successful transformations and 83% for unsuccessful transformations. This means that visible engagement is high in senior management regardless of whether the transformation is successful or not.

The situation is similar with respect to functions that support the process. Perceived engagement in the transformation office was 89% for successful transformations and 79% for unsuccessful initiatives.

Also not showing a particularly large difference between success and failure, but with a significantly lower level overall, was the perceived commitment among HR managers: 67% and 54%, respectively.

However, the situation was quite different for first-line managers. Their commitment differed significantly, ranging from 82% for successful initiatives to only 57% for unsuccessful ones. The same effect can be seen in employees: 73–46%.

Now, unfortunately, these figures say nothing about the direction of the impact. Was the transformation successful because engagement was higher? Or was staff engagement higher because the transformation was successful? Both explanations are conceivable. Presumably, it is a self-reinforcing dynamic that can lead to either success or failure.

Employees are by far the largest group in the company. The management margin, i.e. the number of employees per manager, is, for example, 26 on average in German mechanical engineering production. In other countries, this is significantly lower (Switzerland 13, USA 8) (Fokken, 2017). In the more communication-intensive areas of administration, sales or development, the management margins also tend to sink below 10 in Germany: "I am of the opinion that the management span should be in single digits. The number 7 plus minus 2 seems to me to fit quite well..." (Geropp, 2019).

Even if we assume a factor of "only" seven, the importance of employees and first-line managers is still clear. According to estimates, the number of employees and first-line managers in companies is at least 80%, if not higher. Especially in this group, there is a clear difference in commitment between successful and unsuccessful transformation projects. If one were to determine a "commitment in relation to transformation success" factor for the company, one would find that the success of the transformation depends on the capacity to inspire employees and first-line managers to realise the change.

Senior management must start the transformation with conviction, communicate about it and take the first steps. However, the transformation will only be successful as a result of employee commitment.

Winning employees over for transformation is not always easy. They have already experienced a lot. They have seen various initiatives come and go and ask themselves why they, of all people, should change anything, when the fish stinks from the head down: "Actually, it would be great if our boss didn't only care about his own career". "Our old board was still able to deal with people. Today's management just talks things up. They don't care about us at all". "We have people in the company who don't look to the left or right". or "Those who need to attend a communication training course are the ones who send us to the training courses".

These words, which you have probably heard in a similar form, speak of frustration and doing things by the book. Here, there is still little sign of enthusiasm for change. We hear such statements above all when the employees have the impression that they are the ones who are supposed to change, that they are the problem.

Even if most employees would agree that change is needed and that they also have to do their part, they want to help shape things, instead of being shaped. They want to be taken seriously and integrated into the process, and they want leadership that credibly exemplifies what they want.

8.7 Guest Contribution: Schmid-Huberty, Beatrice-Matter, Utzinger (Swiss TPH)

Organizational development at the Swiss TPH with co-creation: Matthias Schmid-Hubert, Sabina Beatrice-Matter and Jürg Utzinger

The Swiss TPH (Tropical and Public Health Institute) was founded in Basel in 1943. It is an associated institute of the University of Basel. With over 800 employees from 80 nations, the Swiss TPH is one of the world's most renowned institutes in the field of global health. Special attention is paid to low- and middle-income countries. The history of the Swiss TPH goes hand in hand with research partnerships in Africa.

With a unique combination of research, teaching and services, the Swiss TPH contributes to improving the health and well-being of people locally, nationally and internationally.

Four factors prompted the Swiss TPH to take an in-depth look at the topics of leadership, culture, structure and, finally, co-creation.

Change in the physical working environment: By the end of 2021, the Swiss TPH had moved into a purpose-built, multifunctional building. It was decided early on in the building project that there would no longer be small, individual offices, but rather an open and flexible working environment.

Market pressure and acceleration: As a research, teaching and service organization, the Swiss TPH is exposed to the dynamics and complexity of global markets and the network economy, as well as being confronted with the shortening of the half-life of knowledge on a daily basis. Rapid response, adaptability and innovation are key success factors for a knowledge-based organization like the Swiss TPH.

Generational change in the management: Within a few years, a generational change took place in the management. The new management also brought in a change in leadership culture. Diversity and inclusion became more central.

New strategy 2021–2024: The new Swiss TPH strategy 2021–2024 was developed in partnership in an iterative process across all hierarchical levels.

(continued)

This also led to reflections on values and culture and how to work together in the future to better meet new challenges.

As part of the general further development of the Swiss TPH, employees are invited to monthly lunch seminars. This included the contribution "Organization & Leadership: Approaches for Future Companies" by Georg Michalik. This laid an important foundation for developments in the areas of leadership, collaboration and organization.

Leadership development: During a leadership retreat, the need for in-depth leadership development was identified.

The need for an iterative method that takes diversity and complexity into account was obvious due to the interdisciplinary work of the Swiss TPH. Michalik's co-creation method thus complemented the current collaboration with its structured methodology.

In three-and-a-half-day co-creation workshops, each with 15–25 unit and group leaders, the participants sought answers to the question of how collaboration and culture could be made even more agile, innovative and engaging. The goal that ended up being formulated was: "We leaders create the nutrient fluid that forms the basis for an even more agile culture of cooperation".

Cooperation: Four thematic areas with a need for action were jointly identified and prioritised and corresponding action points formulated.

Vision, values and identity—How does the Swiss TPH maintain, promote and shape its culture, vision and values, and how can effective communication and internalisation be ensured?

Freedom for creativity—How do you create more freedom within the Swiss TPH, whether physical, temporal, emotional or intellectual, to further promote creativity and exchange at the Swiss TPH?

Rethink organizational structure—What options could there be for structuring the Swiss TPH to further promote decentralised decision-making and agile collaboration between departments?

Support leadership through a common practice of communication and collaboration skills—How can communication and collaboration be implemented on a broad basis for all Swiss TPH staff?

In four further 1-day follow-up workshops, in which the participants were allowed to enrol of their own initiative, possible approaches to solutions were again identified using the co-creation method. This resulted in a total of nine concrete project ideas.

Organizational development and change management: The delegation of the developed solutions to different functions and units was communicated with the corresponding prioritisation to everyone involved and the entire staff.

The focus is on collaboration, which is the common intersection of leadership, communication and processes. The sub-intersections also result in strategy (communication and leadership), structure (leadership and processes) and

(continued)

information (communication and processes). Thus, collaboration is influenced by three main factors (communication, leadership and processes) and three secondary factors (strategy, structure and information).

It is no coincidence that the focus is on collaboration, and thus also on co-creation. In order to achieve the goals set out in the new 2021–2024 strategy, the working environment plays a decisive role. This point has also been formulated in the strategy and creative, value-driven and iterative collaboration is the most important factor in this equation.

Conclusion: Active thinking and participation in finding solutions in the sense of co-creation corresponded to the usual way of working at the Swiss TPH. However, the fact that this was now explicitly desired by the management and exemplified in a structured way through the various workshops also contributed to the spirit of optimism at the organization. With a lot of enthusiasm, people across departments, units and groups worked together to create the future of the Swiss TPH. This dynamic is flowing intensively into the planning and design of the new building, especially in the working group "new working worlds".

A major advantage of the co-creation method is the guided and targeted discussion, the bringing together and thinking together on the part of employees who would otherwise never or only rarely have experienced a similar exchange in their everyday work. Thus, the consistent application of this method in a cross-structural workshop already had a unifying effect and promoted mutual understanding.

As a result of Michalik's co-creation, three main effects were observed at the Swiss TPH:

- Involving employees with the co-creation methodology led to the development of potential and an increase in self-efficacy.
- Active implementation, as well as the scope for creativity and self-efficacy on offer, were limited and/or hindered by constraints connected to resources, structures and time. Co-creation is therefore not a magic bullet, but a practical and pragmatic instrument.
- In an academic, knowledge-based organization like the Swiss TPH, where research and teaching are already highly networked and interdisciplinary, the co-creation methodology falls on fertile ground and provides a solid and pragmatic structure and guidance for analysing a problem in a goal-oriented and iterative way in a short time, defining a goal and jointly implementing the best solutions.

These effects raise the hope that in the future the strengthening of collective thinking will lead to a reduction in silo thinking. At the same time, mutual understanding could be further strengthened and complemented by methodological competence.

9 Co-creation: The Role of Leadership and HR

Abstract

The aim of co-creation is to connect people to a shared consciousness so that they can let the future emerge. Mindset, values and principles are the basic attitudes and assumptions upon which co-creation is based. Leaders need to create acceptance for co-creation. They are responsible for introducing the process of co-creation in the company and ensuring its sustainable application. Since in hierarchical organizations decisions are made from the top down, there is some evidence that it is primarily the role of leadership to initiate the change towards more co-creation. In the implementation, the leadership is supported by the HR department and its leadership development offers.

Keywords

Leadership · Hierarchy · Decision-making · Top down · HR department

What can the leadership do to create acceptance for co-creation?? Who is responsible for introducing the process of co-creation in the company and ensuring its sustainable application? Since in hierarchical organizations decisions are made from the top down, there is some evidence that it is primarily the role of leadership to initiate the change towards more co-creation. In the implementation, the leadership is supported by the HR department and its leadership development offers.

9.1 The Role of Leadership

In preparation for a day of co-creation on the topic of leadership, a participant sent us a link to an article with the following title: "Google Tried to Prove Managers Don't Matter: Instead, It Discovered 10 Traits of the Very Best Ones. Google's definition

G. Michalik, *Co-Creation Mindset*, Management for Professionals,
https://doi.org/10.1007/978-3-031-21191-1_9

of what makes the very best managers will help you be your very best" (Mautz, 2019). The "10 Traits" are as follows:

1. Be a good coach.
2. Empower teams and do not micromanage.
3. Create an inclusive team environment, showing concern for success and well-being.
4. Be productive and results oriented.
5. Be a good communicator—listen and share information.
6. Have a clear vision/strategy for the team.
7. Support career development and discuss performance.
8. Have the expertise to advise the team.
9. Collaborate.
10. Be a strong decision-maker.

These qualities can be seen, to a greater or lesser extent, as beneficial to a manager. Lists of qualities also exist for other areas of the organization: "What Corporate Culture Should You Strive For?", "Seven Criteria of an Effective Organization" or "What Motivates Employees?". These recipe books are appealing and stimulating. They have the advantage of receiving widespread agreement, as people will not object to what they say. Also, who could object when Google says that collaboration is important and that the boss should be a good coach?

In principle, managers know how they should behave, but the challenge remains in how to implement this in practice.

Individual managers should first ask themselves these three questions about their own implementation competence:

- How do I do what I should do?
  Of course, the manager immediately wants to know how she can implement the new behaviours.
  In the process, she notices that she is not as good at it as she might have thought and wants to know how she can learn.
- How do I learn what I should do?
  In order for her to learn meaningfully and effectively, she then asks herself what has prevented her from doing or learning this so far.
- What has kept me from doing this and learning until now?
  The answer gives her a clue as to what she has failed at in the past.

After the manager has gone through this process of self-reflection, she will realise that her personal transformation is an interesting, but unfortunately also costly task. It must therefore also be crowned with success, so that the effort is worthwhile. But this can only happen if she is not the only person in the company who wants to do things differently. So she will ask herself a fourth question:

- Should I make the effort? Because if I am the only one in the company who changes something, then the situation will not improve and my effort will be a waste of time.

What conclusion can we draw from these understandable reflections? In order to start the transformation and move it forward, it takes both the manager herself and all the other managers. So there is an individual success factor and a collective success factor: "Leadership in the transformation to co-creation".

9.1.1 Leadership as an Individual Success Factor

The individual success factor of leadership is about their personal commitment, values and skills. At this level, leaders can make their contribution to transformation if they both acquire their own implementation skills and recognise that transformation can only be successfully introduced if employees are empowered to take responsibility for their own actions.

In a study on the implementation competence of managers, Pelz (2017) was able to empirically confirm five factors that correlate with success. These are, in order of strength:

- Self-confidence and assertiveness: Is the person convinced of their own strengths and successes based on their experiences, and can they assert their goals constructively and prudently?
- Attentional control and focus: Can the person concentrate fully on essential, clearly formulated goals, even when influences occur that impair motivation and attention? Can they set clear priorities?
- Forward-looking planning and problem-solving: Is action fundamentally proactive (rather than reactive) and forward-looking and solution-oriented? Is the person well prepared for risks and problems?
- Goal-related self-discipline: Does the person have strong stamina until results are achieved? Do they recognise the deeper meaning in their activity? Can they deal constructively with others' disappointed expectations?
- Emotion and mood management: Is the person able to understand their own and others' emotions and motivations (empathy), and can they put themselves and others in a positive emotional state, as well as manage emotionally stressful situations efficiently?

One approach that has become known within the framework of hierarchical leadership for strengthening the self-responsibility of employees is transformational leadership. Certainly, there are approaches to self-organization today that go beyond this. However, leadership takes on a different role there. Holacracy, agile leadership and sociocratic systems are organizational forms that function in a completely different way and that are used by organizations that have already moved beyond hierarchies in the transformation.

Bernard M. Bass and Bruce Aviolo (1993) can be seen as the founders of transformational leadership in management. They distinguish less effective transactional leadership from more effective transformational leadership.

In transactional leadership, employee behaviour is controlled through an "exchange" of performance and consideration (transaction). An example of this is leadership involving target agreements and performance bonuses.

Transformational leadership has been given this name because it transforms behaviour: "The core question is: How can you make it so that employees are loyal, willing to take responsibility, develop team spirit, show self-discipline and respond to change with a willingness to learn and commitment? Traditional target agreements, praise, salary increases, bonuses and other 'rewards' will not bring about such behaviour in the long term. The most varied means of pressure also fall short" (Pelz, 2016).

Transformational leadership uses more effective methods of influence and motivation. Bass and Avolio (1993) have recognised that one of the most effective methods of behavioural change is the role-model function of the supervisor. He must inspire, spur on, empower, communicate fairly and build a foundation of trust.

On this basis, the leadership can observe and adapt its own behaviour, doing its best on an individual basis to contribute to a successful transformation. However, this alone is not enough.

9.1.2 Leadership as a Collective Success Factor

For the transformation to succeed, it should become a joint leadership "co-creation" initiative. Managers are embedded in an organization that has a significant influence on what they do and what they learn. At the level of the organization, i.e. at the level of all individuals and the given framework, the same questions can be asked as at the individual level:

- How do we do this?
- How do we learn this?
- What has kept us from doing and learning this until now?

Now it becomes clear where the implementation problem lies: we already know what is not going well, we just have no idea what we need to do and how we need to learn, so that together we are able to change.

This is where co-creation as organizational development comes in: co-creation connects individuals. Co-creation as organizational development goes a level higher and connects groups of individuals. As an organization of people, we will find out with our collective consciousness what we all want, how we need to do it and how we can learn to live it. Then we can all together set as our goal to be good coaches, to empower our teams and so on.

This requires a procedure that is comprehensible to all, a process that is described in detail in this chapter, and it requires functions that support the procedure. In traditionally organised companies, this role falls to the HR department and internal/ external co-creation coaches.

9.2 Role of the HR Department

At the beginning of the chapter, it was explained that the HR department has the role of project leader in the introduction of co-creation into the organization. How does this fit with the understanding that Human Resources (HR) has of itself?

One of the most common HR models is David Ulrich's HR business partner model. It describes the essential tasks and roles of the HR department (Ulrich, 2012).

The transformation of the organization has many dimensions. If transformation is also about engendering a co-creation culture, this always serves the ultimate goal of being successful in the market and serving customers even better. According to Ulrich, transformation is based on three pillars: talent, leadership and culture. These organization-related issues ensure that the strategy is implemented and the financial results are sustainable.

As we have seen, leadership is important for transformation and is one of the three focal points of HR work, along with talent development and the effective functioning of the organization. The role of business partner can be assumed in many HR areas. HR professionals usually fit into one of four categories: corporate HR, embedded HR, HR specialists and HR as a service centre.

HR as a strategic partner defines company-wide initiatives, represents the company to external stakeholders and provides support to the managers.

HR as change agents work as HR generalists in organizational units. They assist line managers in ensuring that their organizations add value to stakeholders by defining and implementing competitive strategies. They help shape business strategy, conduct organizational diagnostics to determine which capabilities are most critical, design and deliver HR practices to achieve strategic goals, coach leaders and manage the strategy development process.

HR professionals as administrative experts work in centres of excellence, where they provide technical support on HR issues such as human resource management, leadership development, compensation, communication, organizational development, employee benefits, etc. They deliver value when their recommendations provide answers to current challenges.

HR as an employee champion: HR professionals working in service centres add value by building or managing technology-based HR systems that organise contact between companies and employees. They manage activities such as processing benefit claims and payroll, as well as responding to general employee queries. These people can work inside or outside the company. They add value for all stakeholders by keeping costs low and providing accurate and timely services.

In which of these four roles can HR support the transformation into a co-creation culture?

1. **As a strategic partner:**
   Strategic partnership is expected from the leadership. It requires self-confident HR managers to hold a mirror up to it and remind it of its own intentions. Co-creation is widely accepted by the leadership partly because it can deliver quick and concrete results. As described above, the introduction of co-creation is the ultimate goal of collaboration in the organization. However, it is not a matter of days or weeks. We are talking about months and years until it is sustainably anchored. Who in the company can ensure that it does not run out of air and that it is systematically pursued? In a positive sense, this requires someone to act as a "mirror", who can perceive, assess and say what needs to be said with the necessary distance. The HR business partners are predestined for this.
2. **As a change agent:**
   HR professionals can be excellent change agents, because their perspective is people, a company's most important resource. Because they often have a good sense of social change and cultural politics, they are better able to predict the need for change—whether in corporate culture, employee motivation or work productivity—and suggest ways to implement it. They use their communication and interpersonal skills to understand the interface between leadership co-creation and employee buy-in. Change is much easier to implement when employees are involved in a respectful and trusting way.
3. **As an expert:**
   HR also includes experts in leadership and organizational development. Both are critical success factors for transformation. Creating effective leadership in organizations is by no means a new topic, but it is one of increasing importance. The goal of the human resource development experts in the co-creation transformation is to support the leaders in their development. This focus on developing effective and dynamic leadership offers HR the opportunity to move from being a purely administrative and technical department to becoming proactive business partners who make a real difference in organizations. We will say more on the topic of leadership development in the following section.

In order for HR to take on these roles, it should have the necessary prerequisites to do so:

- Being part of the transformation process from the beginning: If the business partner is involved from the beginning, he can represent the perspective of the processes and structures. In this way, certain blind spots can be avoided. In addition, his role as a strategic partner in the transformation can be clarified and defined with the other participants.
- Having some intellectual freedom and organizational independence: If the business partner's manager is involved in the transformation, then he finds himself in a dilemma. On the one hand, HR is supposed to be a critical observer and provider of feedback; on the other hand, he takes orders from his manager. The most effective way to resolve this issue is for the business partner not to report to any of the other project participants, for example, by coming from another division. At

the board level, it could be decided that in the project "Transformation through Co-Creation", the board members (including the HR director) will make decisions together with the CEO.

- Have sufficient staff and budget: In addition to the strategic partners' "mirror" function, they also have the task of ensuring that the processes in the preparation and follow-up of the co-creation workshops run smoothly. The different processes have to be coordinated and the next workshops have to be agreed upon. This does not have to mean that these tasks are all taken over by the HR department. However, someone must be responsible for clarifying responsibilities and ensuring that they are adhered to. To this end, HR needs the necessary resources to be explicitly made available for this purpose. In the end, it must not be said that "HR will do that too", without ensuring that there is additional capacity for it or that it is relieved of other tasks for it.

9.3 Co-creation and Leadership Development

At the beginning of the chapter, it was explained from a project management perspective that the leadership, as a client and as a project collaborator, takes on two of three central roles in the co-creation transformation. This task is demanding, requiring experienced and well-trained leaders.

This section shows how leadership development, as it is still offered in most companies today, would have to change in order for leadership to effectively lead the co-creation transformation. In doing so, we will proceed as follows: first, it must be clear what the fundamental role of leadership development should be. Then, we will outline which values of the co-creation mindset best represent leadership. The goal is to achieve eye-to-eye leadership, as it is lived in co-creation. Finally, we will infer how leadership could be an effective facilitator, and how it would need to be supported by leadership development to achieve this.

9.3.1 The Fundamental Role of Leadership Development

One of the fundamental characteristics of leadership is its role model function. It is a process whereby one person influences the behaviour and attitudes of others. It is not only what the leader says that is important, employees also pay attention to what the leader does. Albert Schweitzer is credited with the following quote: "Leading by example is not only the best way to influence others, it is the only way." If the leadership exemplifies co-creation, then it will be perceived as credible and authentic when it demands co-creation from colleagues and staff.

Through the authenticity of leadership behaviour, authority can be engendered naturally towards employees. This is the basis for the trust that employees develop towards their supervisors. Employees who trust their supervisor and see him as a "role model" are more likely to follow him and be willing to take responsibility for their activities.

The values of leadership play a fundamental role. If they are in line with the values of co-creation, then a culture of co-creation can develop. If the supervisor is guided by completely different values, then he will not be a credible advocate of co-creation.

The third chapter described the importance of the co-creation mindset and its values.

9.3.2 The Leadership Values of the Co-creation Mindset

Values are the fundamental attitude behind co-creation. They lead to people in the company connecting with each other in such a way that they can develop a common consciousness, from which the future can be allowed to emerge.

If the values of the co-creation mindset serve as a basic framework for orientation, a shared orientation in the process is possible. The following values are the cornerstone of the co-creation mindset: connection, trust and commitment.

For the transformation of the company to co-creation to succeed, the leadership must credibly exemplify these three values. In order to do so, the leadership must embrace these values. For leadership development, this consequently means that its content and the way in which it communicates its content is about connection, trust and commitment.

9.3.3 Leadership Development Today

Where does leadership development stand today? Do existing programmes build on connection, trust and commitment as core values? By this, I mean not only about the content of leadership programmes, but also the way in which they are conducted. After all, leadership development also has a role model function. Leadership and leadership development that builds on these three values lead employees and managers to engage eye to eye.

Companies love the idea, but not necessarily its application. Harnessing the potential of the company can mean letting go of comfortable positions of power. It also means re-evaluating beliefs and being open to other views. Breaking new ground means change, perhaps even chaos, and with it comes the fear of losing control. Instead of sharing responsibility, it seems quicker and easier for leaders to give an order through the chain of command. Similarly, it seems easier to aim for measurable results than to enter into a process of learning together.

Leadership seminars are always a place for reflection. Managers do not often take the time to look at their leadership work from the outside. Such programmes are particularly suitable for addressing a new leadership mindset with the participants. Having designed and led leadership programmes myself for many years, I have certain doubts as to whether the existing idea of leadership training does justice to the claim of creating "eye-to-eye leadership". There are two questions here:

- Does our understanding of leadership contradict the idea that employees and their bosses should engage eye to eye?
- Do the layout and structure of classic leadership training contradict this understanding?

If one comes to the conclusion that both questions must be answered predominantly with "yes", then it is possible to say that leadership development does not yet support the transformation to a culture of co-creation today.

9.3.3.1 Eye-to-Eye Leadership

On the first question: Do we have an understanding of leadership in organizations today in which managers and employees engage eye to eye? Of a relationship between managers and employees that is based above all on connection, trust and commitment?

Management conversations follow an inner logic. They have a certain direction and differ according to the type of discussion. The most common management conversations are the appraisal conversation, the feedback conversation, the development conversation, coaching, delegation and so on. In order to be able to conduct such discussions, managers need a not-inconsiderable amount of knowledge and practice. Both are offered to them in leadership programmes.

Now, when they carry out their leadership tasks in everyday leadership, they call on this knowledge, in order to achieve the goals that correspond to their role.

In this approach, however, the imbalance is inherent in the process itself.

When they apply the knowledge they have acquired in conversations with their employees, they create an imbalance between themselves and the employee. This is because the employees themselves do not possess knowledge of how such conversations are conducted, which gives the manager a knowledge advantage. The employees are also aware that their boss knows things about conducting conversations that they are not aware of. Thus, both sides know that there is an imbalance. This alone means that there is no longer a level playing field between them.

How do the employees deal with this situation? Maybe they think it is good that their boss leads them through the conversation so elegantly. Often, they also laugh about it: "Look out, the boss was in leadership training. It'll be interesting to see what's different in the next couple of weeks. I wonder how long it'll take until he's back to 'normal'". In the worst case, the employee withdraws, because he does not see himself being treated as an equal, and goes his own way.

Hence, there is an imbalance in the management conversation from the very beginning. This imbalance arises out of a kind of secret knowledge, knowledge about how to lead employees. It is only accessible to the leadership. The imbalance is known to all, but is not addressed. It is accepted as a given, and thus it is also accepted that the manager comes from a different caste. Taking this as the basis for an exchange between adults cannot lead to an eye-to-eye discussion. There is always someone who dominates and someone with second-class status. Leadership, however, should overcome precisely this.

Leadership fulfils a function. It should not be a promotion or compensation for long years of faithfully performing a duty. As long as there is hierarchical organization, there needs to be line management. Leadership is nothing more and nothing less than fulfilling this function in the best possible way.

Are there other ways in which this function could be carried out, eye to eye and without resorting to the "secret knowledge" taught in leadership seminars?

One obvious solution would be to turn secret knowledge into general knowledge, knowledge that is available to the leadership and the staff. This raises the question of why the inner logic of the conversations is not made transparent and accessible to both participants. This could be done, for example, by making the management conversation transparent in space, just like the co-creation process. This would make it possible for both the manager and the employee to look at the process together. This would mean that the manager would no longer have any prior knowledge, and the pervasive imbalance between the participants would be significantly reduced.

The leadership development programme would then become a programme in which leaders learn together with their staff to live the process at the same level.

This approach would also introduce solution orientation into management practice. As it stands today, one manager might say to another: "Later, I'll have a feedback meeting with a difficult employee". In the future, he would say instead: "Later, I'll have a discussion with an employee who is in a difficult situation". Then, it would be a matter of focusing on the actual problem and not the employee as the problem. In this way, both parties would look together at the cause and the solution, rather than at the person's supposedly difficult character traits.

The tools are all available for this. The co-creation process is not only suitable for team processes, but also for all forms of staff meetings. Transparency is created through CREATE. If managers and employees use it to work together on the situation, then they can connect and use their creative potential together to come to a solution. This creates a connection between them that builds trust and inevitably results in commitment.

As regards the question posed at the beginning of whether our understanding of leadership contradicts the idea that employees and their bosses should engage with each other eye to eye, the answer is unfortunately "yes".

9.3.3.2 Eye-to-Eye Leadership Development and Leadership

Moreover, the answer to the second question—about whether the layout and structure of classic leadership training conflicts with our understanding of engaging eye to eye—will also have to be "yes". I would like to give the following example from our training practice:

Example

Along with another trainer, I conducted a three-day leadership programme with first-line managers. It was the second part of the programme and the last

(continued)

of a total of 7 days. At the end of this period, the group had taken a significant step forward. They had changed how they perceived their role and their task. They had become professionals in assessing people and work situations. They had made significant progress in how they conduct conversations even in difficult situations. And finally, I think their self-perception had also changed. We had achieved all the programme's goals.

As we approached lunch break on the last day, we were doing so well for time that we could think about using an hour to introduce something new. My training partner had recently had his first co-creation experience with me and was enthusiastic about it. He suggested the following experiment: "Let's all sit down in a circle and ask the participants what their common goal could now be. We'll ask them how they could positively influence the organization with their newly created awareness. They've developed so wonderfully and see their leadership task so clearly. We'll let the spirit of co-creation breathe".

For us, this was the logical next step. If people have grown as individuals to the point where they can manage themselves and have their immediate tasks under control, then they should not only look up and down, but also to the left and right. They should be able to adopt a horizontal perspective, in order to optimise the overall system. The overall system creates the framework conditions for leadership in which they work with their teams. Leadership 2.0, so to speak: working on the system from the centre outwards, in order to improve the framework conditions for their work.

We wanted to find out what the group—now that they had realised what leadership is all about—could do together to optimise not only themselves and their own division, but to move the whole company forward. Leadership takes place more and more at the interfaces inside organizations. This also raises the question of whether traditional leadership development, even if it happens at a high level—and we aspire to this in our programmes—automatically leads to organizations developing as a whole. Or does it need something additional to develop the system?

After we had arranged the participants in a circle, we assured them that the seminar goals had been achieved. We explained that we now had some more time and that we wanted to give them the opportunity to discuss with each other what their common goal as leaders of this company could now be. How could they make an impact on the organization?

The outcome of this round was unsettling for the participants and instructive for us. What happened? About a quarter of the group tried to understand the question and make the best of it. Another quarter expressed their lack of understanding of the exercise, while the remaining half observed with interest what was happening. The group was overwhelmed by the question. Although the question was quite clear, they could not fit it into the familiar scheme of questions and tasks they had experienced over the past 7 days. Why could not

(continued)

they answer a simple question and what does that say about how leadership training, as practiced today, reinforces the experience of "not seeing eye to eye"?

What we observed throughout the entire process was that the participants were guided by us through the programme for almost 7 days. The guidance provided by us trainers corresponded to how these managers understood themselves: i.e. someone who "manages" them, who gives them tasks, tells them how to do it and afterwards tells them what worked and where they need to do more. In this setting, they felt at home right from the start and were able to "cooperate" very well. The impression we trainers got from the participants after 7 days—that they understood and were now ready for the next step—is comparable to the impression a supervisor has of his employees who carry out his orders more and more effectively: "This employee is developing wonderfully: she's already very independent and is performing great. She's ready for the next level".

In this assessment, however, we are subject to our traditional view of leadership as working vertically from the top down, sometimes through feedback loops from the bottom up. What staff members and managers learn in our organizations is to move vertically. In classical leadership programmes, through the way the programmes are designed, we repeat this pattern. That is why they work so well in themselves.

What the participants do not learn is to think outside the box and to take responsibility for the whole.

But does this reflect our reality? The application of the learning content in daily reality would probably be as effective as in the seminar environment, if reality were also vertical. But is it? Is our organizational reality really vertical? Or do we only think of it as being vertical, when reality has long since evolved into horizontal, diagonal or simply a kind of "fuzzy logic"?

The answer to both questions was "yes". It can therefore be said that leadership development, as it is practised today, does not encourage the transformation to a culture of co-creation. It creates a "two-tier society", and it fails to give managers responsibilities outside their own sphere.

9.3.4 The Contribution of Co-creation to Eye-to-Eye Leadership

The logic of a management conversation is the same as the logic of a general problem-solving conversation. The eight steps of the co-creation process also make sense for the management conversation. In the world of co-creation, the participants are part of the solution and not the problem. In the ideal world of leadership, this would also be true. The manager and the employee would look at the problem together and see themselves as part of the solution (Fig. 9.1).

Fig. 9.1 Eye-to-eye leadership

Leadership development should adapt to this reality, it should increasingly take care of the non-vertical interfaces, without neglecting the individual skills of leading conversations, recognising people and situations, self-knowledge, etc.

Co-creation is capable of mapping more than vertical or horizontal linear processes. It goes into breadth, works at interfaces and connects people quite independently of hierarchies. Results emerge from the joint connection. In order to do so, individuals learn to trust each other and to function as a whole. This is a learning process. It has to be initiated and people have to be prepared and guided towards it. If you do not do that, the result is what happened during the somewhat awkward hour in our training session—everyone sits around and asks themselves one thing: what should we do now?

What would leadership development have to do to support the co-creation mindset?

At this point, I would like to recommend rethinking leadership development, in order to think in a new way. We should start with the realities. These can only be simulated to a limited extent in seminars. Co-creative leadership development means starting with the leaders' reality, connecting with their environment and their interfaces, looking together for causes and solutions. And possibly one of the solutions has to do with the leadership qualities and skills of the leader himself, in which case one should also work on this. But very probably the solutions also lie in the dynamics of the infinite number of interfaces in organizations that cannot be regulated. If we proceed in this way, leadership development no longer stands isolated in space, but is given a context. The leaders can then better understand why and for what purpose they are learning leadership. They would then also have an answer to the question: "What should we do now?"

10 Co-creation and Organizational Development

Abstract

Hierarchically structured companies and organizations on their way towards flat hierarchies, agile working methods and dynamic interfaces mostly make use of Co-creation and Potentialum. They are in the process of transforming into less hierarchical structures and processes. This transformation is emerging from existing structures. It must therefore be the people in charge of the company who initiate this transformation.

The question is raised: Where do most of our organizations stand today and what impact has it on the way how we do organizational development? Kotter's Leading Change model is taken and transferred into the world of co-creation to lead change by using co-creation and following Kotter's eight steps at the same time.

Keywords

Change management · Kotter · Model · Organizational development · Agile · Transformation

Co-creation and Potentialum are mostly used by hierarchically structured companies and organizations on their way towards flat hierarchies, agile working methods and dynamic interfaces. They are in the process of transforming into less hierarchical structures and processes. This transformation is emerging from existing structures. It must therefore be the people in charge of the company who initiate this transformation.

In this chapter, the book reflects on the development of the whole organizations. In the beginning, different stages of development of organizations are described. The question is raised: Where do most of our organizations stand today and what impact has it on the way how we do organizational development.

G. Michalik, *Co-Creation Mindset*, Management for Professionals,
https://doi.org/10.1007/978-3-031-21191-1_10

In the following Kotter's Leading Change is taken and transferred into the world of co-creation. The book tries to explain how change can be led by using co-creation and following Kotter's eight steps at the same time.

10.1 Co-creation and Types of Organizations

In Reinventing Organizations (Laloux, 2015), Frederic Laloux describes four currently existing organizational models and outlines the contours of a future model:

1. **Tribal impulsive organizations ("Wolf packs")**
   Constant exercise of power by the leader to ensure the obedience of subordinates. Fear holds the organization together. Very reactive, short-term focus. Thrives in chaotic environments. Important breakthroughs are division of labour and command authority.
2. **Traditional conformist organizations ("Army")**
   Highly formalised roles within a hierarchical pyramid, instructions and control from top to bottom (what and how), stability is the highest value and is secured by precise processes, the future is the repetition of the past. Important breakthroughs are formal roles and processes.
3. **Modern performance-oriented organizations ("Machine")**
   The goal is to be better than the competition, to make profits and to expand. Innovation keeps you at the top, management by setting goals (instruction and control in what is done; freedom in how it is done). Important breakthroughs are innovation, reliability and the performance principle.
4. **Postmodern pluralistic organizations ("Family")**
   Within the classic pyramid structure, focus on culture and empowerment to achieve outstanding motivation. Important breakthroughs are empowerment, value-based culture and consideration of all stakeholders (stakeholder model).

What the fifth stage, the "integral evolutionary organization", looks like and what its characteristics are, Laloux leaves open. However, he gives some ideas of the direction in which it could go: individual and collective unfolding, letting go of the ego, the inner voice as a compass and the search for wholeness. The history of these organizations has yet to be written. It is evolving—and both your work and our work in organizations will contribute to it.

If you look at the four organizational models, you cannot help but wonder which organization you are part of or which organizations you work with most of the time.

If I were to lay a normal distribution over our clients, it would be about 20% traditional conformist organizations, 60% modern performance-oriented organizations and 20% postmodern pluralistic organizations. Organizations of all three types want to evolve through co-creation because they are "stuck" at their level:

Traditional organizations have found that their businesses have turned into gilded cages. Employees do things "by the book", and there is little drive and commitment. There is a lack of new ideas, and the companies feel that the market is passing them by. These organizations want to "do something different" with co-creation. But in doing so, they want to have a firm grip on the handbrake. They will experiment under controlled conditions. If the results are successful, they will consider increasing leadership through goals and giving more responsibility to the employees.

Over the years, **performance-oriented organizations** have optimised themselves to the point of an inability to act: budgets are tight, more is demanded of staff than is healthy and everyone is working themselves "to the bone". It is not fun to work in such an atmosphere, and there is no room for innovation. Optimisation is actually a good thing. So why change it?

Such organizations are on the verge of solidification, and it is a challenging management task to make these companies agile again. This requires numerous changes at the operational management and process level, which can be achieved with the help of co-creation. Co-creation is obviously the appropriate approach here, as its processes and management principles are widely accepted. Acceptance of change must come primarily from the leaders, as their role will change most significantly in organizational development.

The postmodern pluralist organization is successfully on its way. The results and the mood are good. Its challenge is that its dynamism threatens to overheat the organization. Speed and creativity are needed. However, the hierarchies that still exist are rather a hindrance. If they could be overcome, nothing would stand in the way of further growth. However, this requires courage and the ability to say goodbye to the classic pyramid structure. Co-creation workshops are used to find the way to structures and processes without hierarchies with the involvement of all employees.

All three organizations have one thing in common: they are (still) hierarchically organised. If further development is to be brought about, the path of change must be compatible with the current situation. This means that the co-creation initiative must use the existing decision-making channels to enable the organization to change itself. In the most extreme case of the postmodern pluralistic organization, this could mean that the classical line management abolishes itself.

10.2 The Eight Stages of Organizational Development

In organizational development, the metaphor of evolution and revolution is used again and again. Evolution describes the continuous development towards the desired goal, which takes place over a longer period of time. Revolution stands for a big change in one fell swoop.

In principle, companies could decide to revolutionise. In order to do so, they would close the doors for 3 days for an organizational inventory. All the employees would meet in a gym and then work until the new organizational form was in place. Then, the following Monday, they would continue according to the new structure.

In our experience, companies prefer the evolutionary rather than the revolutionary path: "Three divisions instead of five. Siemens plans 'evolution'

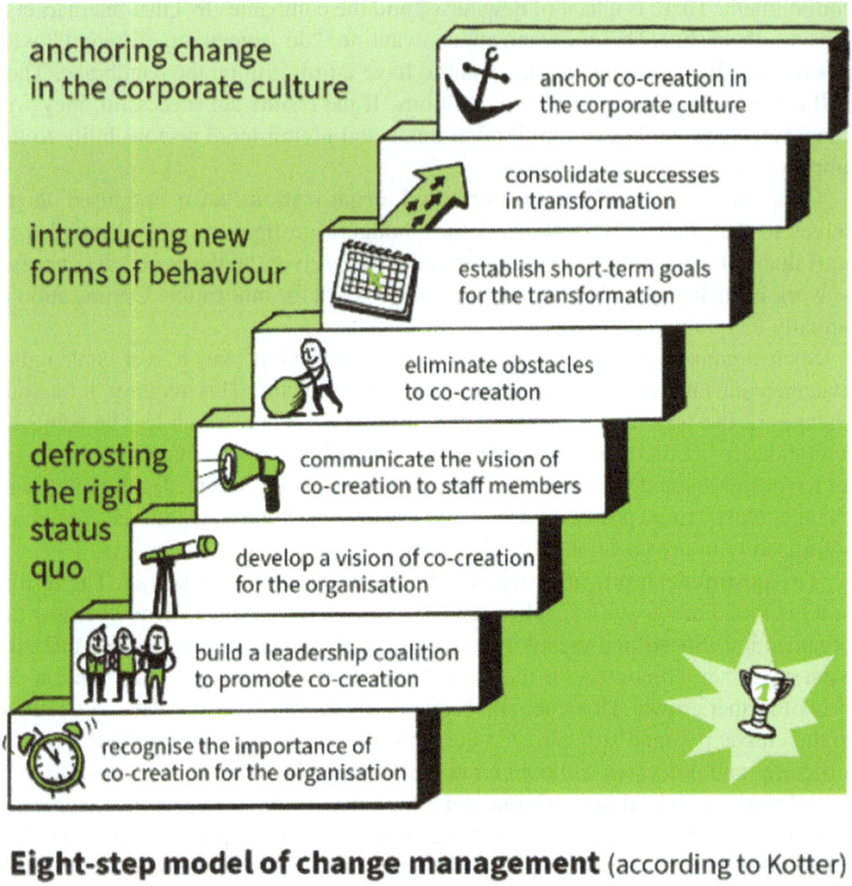

Fig. 10.1 The eight stages of implementing co-creation

instead of 'revolution'. The divisions should be given higher return targets than before, Manager Magazine reported. Siemens wants to present the plans, known under the working title 'Vision 2020+', in August, two insiders said. However, they do not expect major upheavals: 'This will be more of an evolution than a revolution', said one of them" (FAZ, 2018).

One of the best-known models for a step-by-step approach to organizational change is John P. Kotter's eight-step model, described in Leading Change (Kotter, 2011). Our experience in organizational development has shown that we follow a similar process. Therefore, in this section, we will describe organizational development through co-creation following Kotter's logic (Fig. 10.1).

Kotter's eight-stage model is the formulation of K. Lewin's three phases (Lewin, 1947), which have already been explained above. Lewin's phases refer to the micro level. He focuses on change in the individual. Kotter, by contrast, focuses on the macro level and takes into account the numerous interfaces that are affected by a change at the overall company level:

1. Create a sense of urgency: create awareness of the urgency of change among leaders and staff.
2. Build a leadership team: unite direction-giving individuals and develop mutual trust.
3. Developing the vision: the overarching vision for the company serves as a motivator for everyone involved.
4. Communicate the vision widely and convince staff.
5. Empower: broadly motivate and empower staff to act on the vision.
6. Ensure short-term goals and achievements: they must be visible and clear.
7. Secure achieved goals and successes and ensure further changes.
8. Anchor achieved changes in the corporate culture.

Kotter's model has been partially confirmed empirically (Alas & Sharifi, 2002). Critically, Kotter's model fails to point out the crucial importance of shared vision. However, this is an essential component of co-creation, and is thus not lost. Fundamentally, Kotter's cascading approach can also be faulted for not taking into account movements that start "from the bottom". Based on the considerations above, however, it can be said that especially in organizations that are traditional, performance-oriented or postmodern, change strategically emanating from management is an essential factor for success.

Kotter's "eight phases of change" (Kotter, 2011) provide a suitable flowchart to systematically describe the introduction of a co-creation culture into a company.

How can co-creation be fundamentally introduced as an attitude and as a method of working together in companies?

There are two ways of doing this: one way is to develop solutions through co-creation. The goals can be very different, for example, to create a leadership culture that promotes self-responsibility, to become an agile company, to achieve certain critical success factors such as high employee engagement, customer centricity or a flatter organizational structure and much more. If the organization does this consistently on the path of co-creation, the culture changes automatically and co-creation quickly becomes a component of working together.

It is even more targeted, if the organization deliberately sets out to introduce co-creation and makes co-creation itself a theme. Like with other change projects, hierarchically managed institutions need to follow a specific process led by senior management, as described at the beginning of this chapter.

Taking Kotter's model, the question is then: What would such a path along the eight phases of change look like in the case of co-creation?

In order to describe the organizational development process, "the introduction of co-creation" should be taken as the goal. In the following, the eight organizational phases of development are described, as well as what needs to be considered in each of them if co-creation is to be introduced as a way of working together in an organization.

What needs to be taken into account in the respective phases of organizational development when using co-creation naturally applies not only to the introduction of co-creation itself but also to the introduction of other issues (see above) that are to be solved with the help of co-creation in the organization.

The following phases of organizational development, as envisaged by Kotter, are reformulated to fit the introduction of co-creation.

10.2.1 Phase 1: With the Leadership Team, Recognise the Importance of Co-creation for the Organization

Kotter himself writes that three-quarters of the leadership must have recognised the need for change—only then is the importance of change sufficiently anchored at a broad leadership level. In order to win over the leadership to this extent, it is necessary to provoke an open and dynamic discussion on the topic. Leaders are required who stand up for change with conviction.

In the three organizational models mentioned above, this kind of fundamental change starts at the top. Often it is the CEO or the executive board itself that initiates the change. If the realignment starts with the CEO, the next step is for him to discuss his ideas with the other members of the board/management and to try to convince them.

Often this is the moment when we are called in, either as a sparring partner for the CEO or as a facilitator of the discussion at board/executive level. The start of such a process can take place through coaching or through an invitation to a management meeting or board retreat.

If co-creation is introduced in a company, the culture has to change fundamentally in traditional or performance-oriented forms of organization; in postmodern pluralistic organizations, a big step in this direction has already been taken. In each case, the leadership must be clear that there will be a significant change in the way things are done in the company.

If this were merely a vision of the chairperson and not of the entire board, the desired co-creation initiative would soon peter out. It is of the utmost importance that an intensive discussion on the "why" and the "how" of co-creation takes place at this level.

The leadership coalition described in phase 2 already starts here. The company's top team must stand united behind the change, otherwise further steps cannot be implemented. At issue is a fundamental reorientation with strategic scope. One can also speak of strategy development and its implementation.

In large companies or groups, some divisions are very independent in terms of operational management. They are themselves companies within the company. Then the initiator is not the CEO, but the business unit manager, and his team is not the board, but the division managers.

A possible alternative is if co-creation is to be applied to a very specific issue without company-wide strategic relevance. In this case, co-creation can also be started at other levels of the organization. Affected interfaces can be clearly defined and can be specifically included in the development process. In this case, it is not a question of creating a co-creation culture, but simply of using co-creation as an effective tool that involves people and company interfaces at the local level.

If co-creation is to become the way of working together in the future, it is a company-wide issue with strategic relevance. Its introduction should be driven by the top independent decision-maker and his or her team.

To forge this first coalition of leaders, it takes time and space to do two things:

1. The organizational diagnosis: creating a map via Potentialum
2. The first co-creation workshop: determining the "why, how and what" of introducing co-creation

The first co-creation workshop with the board lasts 2 days and, in principle, has the following format:

- **A half-day assessment of the potential re-analysis**: Before the results of the analysis are made clear, the management should agree on which of the 10 fields of action they would like to focus on in the short and medium term. The greatest negative deviations between the short/medium-term desired state and the current situation determine the focus fields to which particular attention should be paid in the further course of the co-creation process.
- **A half-day of team building:** In the second half of the first day, the "Connect" phase of co-creation is run through. Here, clarity emerges about the different personality types and their preferences, about different values and about the dynamics in the leadership team. This should be understood by everyone, so that the team can refer to it in the further course of the process and shape their collaboration according to the dynamics and preferences.

For the "Connect" phase, besides the connection between the various personalities, connection in view of the common goal is also important. Therefore, a common goal should be formulated in a meaningful and succinct way. This goal explains the "why" of introducing co-creation and will be the guiding star for all subsequent co-creation workshops. Therefore, it is imperative that the discussion is extensive and open, until the point that all the board members can give their unqualified approval to it. This should be achieved on the first day, so that the participants can sleep on it and say "yes" to it again on the second day.

- **One day of co-creation:** On the second day, the "Connect" phase is completed and the rest of the co-creation process is run through. In the end, there are project assignments with responsibilities divided among the participants. These must now be taken to the second management level in the next round of co-creation. This corresponds to Kotter's second phase: "building a leadership coalition".

10.2.2 Phase 2: Let a Leadership Coalition Become the Promoter of Co-creation

Growing as an organization by growing connection.

If the company is to become stronger, then the connections in the organization must become stronger. It is not only the strong divisions that make an organization successful, but the art of connecting the individual parts in such a way that they give the whole a positive vibe.

A positive vibe requires harmonious staff members and teams. But this is not enough, and in extreme cases, it can even hinder the development of the desired corporate culture. If first- or second-line managers want good evaluations for their employees, then it makes sense for them to put these employees at the centre of their actions. They need to look after them carefully and ensure that they get what they need to work. They could form a powerful team with them. They could do this by taking a day to go out into nature twice a year or more and working on their team strategy and how to implement it. They could set team goals and see how best to achieve them. They could set themselves the goal of becoming the most successful team in the company. They could build bridges together and cross raging streams, in order to become even stronger as a team. They could learn to challenge and encourage each other.

That all sounds fantastic. It is certainly desirable for more teams to take a look at how they work together and how they can become even better together. Strong teams are desirable, but ultimately it is not about creating strong teams, but a strong company. So what if teams lose sight of overall optimisation in their self-optimisation?

Imagine an organization where teams focus on their own optimal performance. Sooner or later they would create a culture of team competition, and the company has to ask itself if it wants that.

One could counter that competition understood in sporting terms promotes growth. The danger, however, is that teams and departments quickly forget that they are all in the same boat and turn in circles when one side rows faster than the other.

How can co-creation at the level of the whole organization help everyone to get more water under their oar blades? It would be perfect if everyone rowed towards the goal in a coordinated way. The boat should always remain manoeuvrable enough to avoid eddies and use currents to move itself forward.

What must the crew pay attention to if they want to achieve this? In order to act in a coordinated manner, it is important that the different forces support each other. For this, teams need the smoothest possible access to information, resources, coordination and decision-making. If we see this as the energy source of value creation, the energy should be able to flow through the organization. For this to happen, the remaining levels of leadership need to get involved in co-creation and to be held accountable. Subsequently, special attention should also be paid to the interfaces in the organization that the leaders preside over. They must not become blockages to the flow of energy. We will say more about this in phase 5 "Removing obstacles".

Leadership at all levels should become the promoter of co-creation, and it should do so cohesively. In order to do this, it should itself lead the way and work co-creatively at the interfaces. How can this be achieved?

This second phase can either become the key to the success of the introduction of co-creation or, if only half-heartedly pursued, it can also lead to co-creation never really taking off.

How can the entire leadership be involved step by step and what are the success factors for this?

Initially, the introduction of co-creation is above all a task whose foundations must be laid by the leadership itself. In co-creation, the role of the leadership changes more clearly than that of the employees, so it is especially important to take the concerns and questions of the leaders seriously if the implementation is to be successful with the employees. Managers often ask themselves how their employees will react to this and whether they want it at all: "It's not as if all our employees want to take on responsibility. We have many valuable colleagues who come and do their work. But they don't want to stand out in front and take the initiative either—you can't overburden them with that". This is a statement we often hear in these or similar terms.

At this point, it could be countered to the managers that this reaction from the employees can make perfect sense from a systemic point of view and that it says less about their attitude and more about the conditions under which they are supposed to perform. These conditions, in turn, result to a large extent from how they experience leadership. So the attitude of employees says more about the leadership in the company than about the employees.

Managers are not independent but are themselves influenced by the system. Therefore, such a discussion would only potentially lead to a solution at the highest level.

When employees are invited to give feedback and express their attitudes and expectations about co-creation, managers are often surprised to discover they are charging into open doors. The expectations go beyond what the leadership could have imagined, even in its wildest dreams.

The step-by-step roll-out of co-creation in the organization was explained and illustrated in Sect. 7.1.1.5. The inclusion of further management levels is done by making the results of the co-creation into the goals of the next round of co-creation. In this second round of co-creation, the next level or levels of leadership are then involved. In order for this to happen as quickly as possible, it is advisable to follow the 80:20 rule:

Managers in the first round take responsibility for a project topic and carry that to the next level of leadership in a ratio of 4:1. If the co-creation in the first round results in a maximum of five projects, then two or three managers from this first round take on the sponsorship of a topic and thus initiate a second-round co-creation with four times as many managers. So if there are two of them, they could add eight new managers in the second round. With five projects, this would give the same number of co-creation workshops with 5 × 8 additional managers. After the second round, 40 + 10 managers would be involved, making a total of 50. If the company has even more managers to integrate, this round can take place again, bringing the total to a maximum of 20 × 8 new managers, plus 50 existing managers, i.e. a total of 210 managers.

All the managers should be involved in building the leadership coalition. Co-creation is only lived when it is exemplified and demanded by the whole leadership:

- If the employees or other managers have the impression that the co-creation initiative is just a fashion, they will not participate.
- If the classic friction losses at the interfaces do not dissipate over time, the effectiveness of co-creation will be doubted.
- If failures—as well as successes—are not addressed openly when dealing with co-creation, the seriousness will diminish.

Therefore, it is imperative that all levels of leadership participate and that the spirit of possibility is felt.

10.2.3 Phase 3: Develop a Vision of Co-creation for the Organization

The leadership has a central task: the development of the co-creation vision and of a co-creation strategy. The staff need a guiding star to orient themselves by. A vision paints a clear picture for people of what the future should look like and why that would represent progress. The vision of the future through co-creation should be broadly developed by the coalition of leaders. As a result, a plausible co-creation strategy must be formulated and documented.

This third phase takes place together with the second: "Let the leadership coalition become the promoter of co-creation". The leadership coalition is created through rounds of co-creation workshops, where the vision and strategy for co-creation for the organization is worked on. This also creates the goal, vision and strategy for more co-creation through the journey.

In the first phase of change, "With the leadership team, recognise the importance of co-creation for the organization", a vision was created, which served as a working basis for the second phase, "Let the leadership coalition become the promoter of co-creation".

In phases two and three, this vision must now be put to the test and checked with the leaders.

From the vision, clear ideas for implementation projects develop in the co-creation sessions. At this stage, these are spread across different co-creation sessions, and it is likely that certain themes will be repeated or interdependent and need to be integrated.

It is therefore necessary for representatives of the co-creation sessions to meet at the end of phase three and coordinate the results. For large organizations, this should happen earlier on, in an intermediate step.

For this purpose, the leaders meet and present the results of their co-creation workshops to each other. What goals did they have and what conclusions did they come to? What project proposals resulted from this? There are then numerous pieces of the puzzle in the room, which must now be connected with each other in such a way that a coherent overall picture of the co-creation vision and the co-creation strategy emerges.

From this coordination, clarity emerges about how to proceed, what the next steps of communication are, which projects will be launched in which order and in which timeframe, and who is responsible for which projects. Above all, there must be agreement about when the milestones will be set, how the results will be measured and how the projects will be coordinated and integrated, if necessary. The OKR method (Objectives and Key Results) described above is a good tool and process for this.

Not only do the projects recommended for the micro level need to be integrated, but the link to the macro level, with its overarching, recurring themes, also needs to be established.

The diagnosis at the macro level through the Potentialum analysis addresses the overarching themes that recur in all areas of the organization. Micro-level and macro-level actions need to be aligned. This requires co-creation to take place in iterative circles, both between the micro and macro levels and between co-creation projects that are interdependent or interact with each other.

This connection can be illustrated by an example.

The macro level is the overall perspective on the whole company as it can be represented and measured by the Potentialum model. If you look at the model again, you will find themes such as leadership, cooperation, expertise, etc., that are measured at the following levels: customer, employees and processes.

If the Potentialum organizational diagnosis shows that, for example, the quality of leadership across the organization is not yet considered good and that there is a need for action there, then it is very likely that at the meso level and the micro level of the co-creation workshops, "leadership" will also repeatedly come up.

For example, there could be a co-creation workshop with the aim of increasing employee engagement. The analysis shows that it is partly due to hierarchical leadership that the employees feel less motivated. This co-creation workshop suggests, for example, offering training for managers on situational leadership as a project.

Another co-creation workshop may aim to increase commitment and obligation in the company, as deadlines are often not met and somehow "everyone does what they want". This co-creation group—at this point, all the managers—comes to the conclusion that they themselves are not so good at making binding agreements with their employees and demanding results from them. They suggest communication training for managers.

This example shows why the integration of co-creation between the macro level, on the one hand, and the meso and micro levels, on the other, is so important. Similarly important is the lateral integration and alignment between co-creation workshops at the meso and micro levels. In the example, one can see that leadership was identified as an area for action at three points in the co-creation process:

- Macro level: Potentialum company diagnosis; leadership in general
- Micro level: two independently run co-creation workshops

The measures elaborated on this basis concern the same target group and go in the same direction in terms of their content: leadership development. They must therefore be coordinated with each other. Those responsible at both the macro and micro levels need to know from each other who else is working on this issue.

When the opinion-forming process has been completed, projects have been agreed on at all levels and the majority of managers have the desire to become "promoters" of change, then it is time to communicate the processes and structures and to involve the employees. Now the employees can also become part of the co-creation movement in their daily work.

10.2.4 Phase 4: Communicate the Co-creation Vision to the Staff

In the fourth step, after the leadership, all the other employees get involved. Selected managers share the vision and strategy for co-creation that has been formulated with individuals, groups and teams.

If you want to reach all the employees in the organization, you need a good story and a convincing pitch from the beginning. It is important that the understanding of the urgency can be communicated and experienced by the staff. If the "spark catches" and the leadership is fully behind it and exemplifies the change, then the conditions are in place for co-creation to take hold.

In which phases can the communication with the employees be staggered?

At the latest, when co-creation is transferred from the innermost management circle to the next level of leadership, word gets around that there is something going on. Communication should already begin at this point. This creates the best conditions for the initiative to be perceived positively. The transparency that one wants to instil by means of co-creation should be exemplified in communication.

Be open about what it is going on:

> We have concluded that in order to continue to be successful in the market, we should take how we work together to the next level. We need to get to the point faster and more directly in the future, and we need to work more closely with each other to provide the best solutions to our customers. In order to do so, we as leaders have started to put our heads together. However, it will take all of you. We are going to set off a wave that we want to surf together with you. Our timetable is as follows...

This sort of communication at the beginning of the initiative avoids rumours and arouses curiosity. From then on, there should be regular communication about where things stand and what has happened in the meantime. Images and short videos are particularly suitable for this.

The longer the leadership has been working on laying the foundation for the initiative, the more necessary it is to get feedback on the interim results from the staff. Employees should be included in communication, so that they can describe their impressions, give feedback and thus begin to help shape the process. Experience has shown us that in these meetings, the energy that is felt by the leadership is transferred to the employees involved, who return to their colleagues as positive messengers. They may then say to their colleagues: "I didn't really understand what they were trying to do. But the topic—how to lead in the future—was exciting and the atmosphere was great".

Finally, at the end of the preparations and at the start of the implementation, it is strongly recommended to invite all employees to participate in an information event or a large workshop with many other employees and supervisors.

We have had very good experiences using the following procedure:

Example

At the end of the preparatory work with the managers, after completing the third stage "Develop a vision of co-creation for the organization", the employees, 160 in total, were invited to a townhall meeting in the company auditorium. Such townhall meetings had also taken place before. Twice a year, staff members were invited and given a presentation on how the last 6 months had gone and what was coming up next. Direct exchanges did not take place until then.

In this town hall, however, everything looked different. At the front were numerous pin boards with flipcharts covered in writing. They were the results of the management's final workshop, into which the results of the co-creation workshops had been integrated. The projects were presented directly on the flipcharts by the managers. There were microphones so that the audience could ask questions. Staff were also asked to come forward and write their names on the projects they would like to work on.

Afterwards, a date was announced when all the employees would be able to experience co-creation together over a whole day. The topic was at the macro level: "Co-creation lives from the values governing how we want to work together. In the course of the journey so far, three core values have been defined. In the large group co-creation workshop, we want to work out together how these values can now be lived out in a very practical way".

This large group event was held 2 months later. Enthusiasm was huge, despite extreme heat and deafening noise. The day ended with a staff party.

(continued)

This was the official start of co-creation, which then became the way in which complex challenges were solved.

Clarity about the goals, but also the timely and unconventional inclusion of everyone, created the best conditions for this initiative to receive broad support. This reduced frictional losses at the interfaces and unnecessary detours. Moreover, everyone could now participate in co-creation, because they all knew what was coming. People were in the loop and were not caught off-guard. As the example makes clear, the channels of inclusion were chosen very carefully, because how co-creation is transmitted is at least as important as how it is later lived.

10.2.5 Phase 5: Remove Obstacles to Co-creation

By the time the fifth phase of the introduction of co-creation has been reached, much has been said about the vision and the need for engagement from all staff members and managers, and numerous co-creation workshops have been held. Co-creation is now basically accepted, and everyone is looking forward to using it with their colleagues when complex situations arise.

10.2.5.1 Interfaces in Organizations

What can still stand in the way of the success of co-creation? What obstacles can there be in the implementation of co-creation if the first four phases have been mastered consistently and successfully? Which processes and structures can account for the fact that, despite co-creation, the hoped-for suppleness in the organization cannot yet be realised?

At this point, the functioning of hierarchical organizations should be considered once again:

In a hierarchical organizational structure, each unit in the organization is subordinate to another unit. In a company, the hierarchy usually consists of a single peak with successive levels of power below. This is the dominant organizational mode in companies. We talked at the beginning of this chapter about the three organizational models identified by Laloux: "traditional", "meritocratic" and "pluralistic".

Members of hierarchical organizational structures communicate mainly with their immediate superiors and subordinates. Structuring organizations in this way makes sense in part because it can reduce the amount of communication, by limiting the flow of information. This makes the organization faster on the vertical axis, but communication slows down and becomes more complicated when units with a certain degree of autonomy meet and have to solve complex challenges together.

We call these points in the organization "interfaces". Interfaces are areas where personal encounters occur between individuals or units representing their own interests and supported by different resources. Friction may be experienced that interrupts the flow of cooperation.

Blockages to cooperation flows arise mainly at the interfaces between units. They can, of course, also arise in the units themselves, but organizations have introduced numerous measures to promote cooperation within the individual units. The situation is different at the interfaces between units. If one wants to take the organization to the next level, the company must enliven cooperation at the interfaces.

How can it do this? The best prerequisite for this is a culture in which all employees feel the responsibility to make "energies flow". If one wants to achieve this through co-creation, then the parties involved should connect with each other, work out a common goal and work to implement it in a binding way.

10.2.5.2 Overcoming Silo Thinking Through Co-creation

In the first chapter, we saw the challenges that arise when the company works in silos. In silos, the direction of coordination is clear, it runs vertically from the top to the bottom and then from the bottom back up to the top. If there is any ambiguity, one looks "up" at where the next node is and requests a decision from there. This system has worked extremely well for centuries in armies, churches and absolutist states (hierarchical forms of organization).

The more conspicuously a company is organised into silos, the more difficult it becomes to manage the interfaces between the silos. Because then the principle of going up to the common node also applies. The nodes are occupied by the "silo heads". To resolve an issue, they have to agree.

Here, the system slows itself down. Since there is a decision backlog, the nodes are less efficient. As a result, they have less time and are constantly busy doing "urgent" things instead of "important" things. This turns them into bottlenecks, and the decision backlog continues to grow.

How do the staff deal with this? They learn that they can work most effectively within their units. Therefore, they concentrate on their own departments. What lies outside seems to be unsolvable, or at least it would have to be solved by a higher-level unit. At some point, the employees have come to terms with the fact that it is better not to worry about the things that happen outside their silo.

How could the decision-making backlog between units be resolved and the organization made more pliable, even if the hierarchical form of organization is retained?

Instead of climbing all the way up the ladder and then climbing back down again, it would be convenient to take a shortcut to the destination. Imagine a green strip in a public space that has paths laid out at right angles. If people see an ice cream stand in the park at a 45° angle in front of them, only a few of them will follow the path until the end and only then turn off at a 90° angle. Most people will simply cut across the lawn (Fig. 10.2).

To go a step further, imagine that you are the park's head gardener. How do you deal with the unsightly path trampled in the grass?

Fig. 10.2 The direct path to the goal

1. Do nothing and just leave it like that.
2. Fence in the lawn to keep pedestrians on the designated path.
3. Make the existing path a green space and develop the shortcut into an "official" path.

If organizations are aware of the human tendency to prefer the direct route, then the same question arises here: What would now be a sensible response?

Management could simply do nothing and be quite content for staff to disregard the rules. Alternatively, it could insist on compliance with the prescribed silo routes. Finally, if it is on the path of renewal, it could be happy that there is a shorter path, even encouraging staff to find the shortest route.

Now, one might counter that corporate dinosaurs which still follow the "ladder principle" are rather rare. But does the interface problem only exist in extremely hierarchical companies? It is possible that companies organised in a modern way without explicit silos also face this problem. Even if the company is very flatly organised and consists only of teams, the interface between the teams still has to function.

Hence, the interface problem exists regardless of how traditional the organization is. With silos it becomes more obvious and the need for action becomes greater, because here the informal ways of solving it are more complex than in flat hierarchies.

"Growing as an organization by growing connections". This statement refers not only to the connection between people within their teams, but above all to the connection that employees have beyond their teams to the organization. Yes, it is a matter of connecting business units so that there is a seamless integration of interfaces into the organization.

How can co-creation help companies to turn organizational interfaces into seams where the threads run into each other and weave together perfectly?

The solution to this is quite simple: by co-creating precisely at these seams. Co-creation at the seams asks:

- Where do we have the greatest interface losses?
- Which frictions are the strongest and most unproductive?
- Who are the most important protagonists on both sides of the interface?

The company finds out which interfaces work the worst and gets the cooperation flowing there through co-creation. Which interfaces these are can be different in every company, depending on its processes, its organizational form and, of course, the people responsible.

Some interface losses can be worse for an organization than others. If the interface between production and sales is not vibrant, the impact is more serious than if it affects the interface between HR and IT. The latter is annoying and demotivates staff, which is bad enough in itself, but it does not have a direct impact on turnover, as in the case of production and sales.

Next, one should ask oneself: What frictions arise at the interfaces? Where are the different divisions struggling? Deriving a goal from this, understanding the background better and then entering into the solution would teach the organization how to deal with it in principle. Co-creation workshops could potentially help to eliminate friction losses at several interfaces.

The question then remains: Who are the key protagonists in the interaction? They must be part of the co-creation. Those who have the knowledge and the responsibility should connect with each other and let the future emerge together with their interface partners.

10.2.5.3 What If the Interface Creates a Vacuum?

Even though this approach sounds obvious and can be carried out in this way, there is a catch. If there are regulated processes that run vertically or horizontally through the company, there should be little or no decision backlog. Beyond that, however, there are countless interfaces that do not run in a linear fashion. At these interfaces, there often exists a rule-free space, which brings cooperation to a standstill (Fig. 10.3).

When responsibilities in communication, decision-making and action are not clear, a vacuum in decision-making and action occurs. A vacuum is a situation in which something is not filled, and is therefore open to various influences (Wikipedia, n.d.). Why is it that vacuums act as a brake on energy and not the opposite? Why does the open space not make things go even more smoothly?

Vacuums have a certain quality, emptiness, which reflects to individuals both their fears and their possibilities. People who value their influence fear meaninglessness. Others who value structures and processes fear disorientation. People who care about other people fear losing connection with each other. And people who like to move things forward fear stagnation. That is why the vacuum creates a pull to act. In

Fig. 10.3 The dynamics of the vacuum

the rule-free space, it is mainly the quick and the influential who will fill the space. Seen in this light, a vacuum actually invites quick action. However, since this action is not coordinated, what ensues is not necessarily in the overall interest of the organization.

The remedy is a meta-process that prevents the vacuum from being filled by individual interests and needs. It would be better for the organization if decisions were made that take a sustainable overall perspective. To accomplish this, the most important protagonists should be able to work out the connecting solutions with each other through co-creation. The obvious challenge here is to get the process going and to reach a consensus about who the "most-important protagonists" are in a given situation.

Who is responsible for getting the process started and inviting the right people? Who takes on the overall perspective and interest of the whole organization? Who addresses the interface losses and gets the co-creation going at the interfaces?

If the organization does not find a standardised procedure for this, a negative spiral results at the interfaces. In the beginning, there is the rule-free space, which creates a vacuum that invites the assertion of individual interests. This weakens the organization, which in turn increases the probability of rule-free spaces.

If the organization wants to be successful in the long run, it should find a way to deal with unregulated interfaces and thus break the negative spiral.

There are different ways in which such a path can be designed. Only three components need to be mentioned here:

- An independent team of co-creation coaches who can be called in on request. They take control of the process of getting rid of the vacuum and finding solutions.
- A very low-threshold approach to getting the coaches involved. Anyone in the organization who is affected should have the opportunity to call in the coaches. The more independent such a request is from formal authority and resource requirements, the greater the likelihood that the vacuum can be eliminated.
- An experience platform for knowledge exchange: What experiences exist within the organization for resolving interface problems? What has worked and what has not? What successes have been achieved? Who are the contact people who are able to give information about this?

10.2.6 Phase 6: Set Short-Term Goals to Be Achieved in the Transformation

Nothing is more motivating than success. Therefore, setting short-term goals supports the introduction of co-creation. This gives employees a clear idea of what is going on. In addition, short-term goals are achieved more quickly. Once the goals have been accomplished, the employees are motivated to refine and build on the change. By recognising and rewarding employees who are closely involved in the change process, it becomes clear across the board that the company is changing course.

The introduction of co-creation aims at long-term cultural change. At the same time, the change should be supported by short-term successes. How can these two levels be combined?

The knowledge of how successes promote culture change lies in the basic understanding of how goals are interconnected in co-creation. For this purpose, the level concept was introduced in Sect. 4.1 and the alignment of goals between the macro and the micro levels, as well as between micro levels, was explained in Sect. 10.2.3.

At the micro level, short-term goals can be set and implemented in co-creation. Co-creation as a tool is therefore designed for immediate success. Quick wins are thus not something that needs to be additionally planned or taken into account. They are in the nature of co-creation.

However, it was also explained that micro-level goals often point to an overarching issue to be improved in the organization. In the example, we saw both how the need for action in the area of leadership development was identified at the macro level with the help of the Potentialum organizational diagnosis and how it was addressed at the micro level in various projects.

The challenge is that actions taken at the micro level will not necessarily address the fundamental problem identified at the macro level. More resilience is needed here. Successes in addressing overarching deficits must be consolidated, and their development must be measured and promoted with action at the global level. This brings us to the seventh phase: consolidating successes.

10.2.7 Phase 7: Consolidate Transformation Successes

According to John Kotter, many change projects fail because victory is declared too early. However, change is a slow process and needs to be integrated into the whole corporate culture. Quick wins are only the beginning of long-term change. A company must therefore constantly be on the lookout for improvements. Only when repeated successes have been achieved through co-creation can it be determined whether the change is paying off.

If co-creation is to be sustainably anchored in the organization, then it is necessary to lay the groundwork for it, to pace oneself correctly and to repeatedly supply the right sources of energy at the right places during the execution—just like running a marathon.

Andreas Butz, a marathon coach and book author, describes in his blog (Butz, 2012) 12 reasons why so many marathon runners collapse and fail to reach the finish line. There are remarkable parallels. The most important ones are listed here:

1. **Too little preparation time:** "Running a marathon in the fastest possible time requires at least six months of training and competition planning geared towards this goal". If we look at the first steps of the eight phases of implementing co-creation, it becomes clear how thorough the preparation has to be:
   - Work out a clear vision.
   - Have a close management circle on board.
   - Convince the whole leadership.
   - Use co-creation from the beginning and gain experience with it yourself.
   - Communication, communication, communication.

2. **Too few long endurance runs:** "The more long endurance runs a runner has under his belt in the last three to four months before the marathon, the better prepared he will be". When adopting co-creation, it takes persistence and staying power. Keeping at it means starting again and again, not giving up and training seriously.
3. **Running too fast for too long:** "Another classic training mistake is too high an intensity during long runs. Many runners make their long runs too fast". Co-creation is fuelled by attitude. In this respect, marathon preparation is primarily aimed at switching from sugar to fat burning: "Only if the long runs are slow enough can the fat metabolism training reach its full effectiveness". The change in the way we run corresponds to the change in attitude in co-creation. Taking time, connecting with others, listening, absorbing, letting the process work, arriving at the result, and then running and persevering with plenty of energy reserves.
4. **Too many races:** "In marathon preparation, concentrate on those races that are absolutely necessary. Prioritise the long endurance runs". Co-creation is not the panacea that should be applied to every situation. Co-creation should be used in a targeted fashion for complex challenges. Non-complex challenges can also be resolved with sprints.
5. **Too little recovery:** "If you train too much or too hard in the last three weeks before the marathon, you can't reach full strength on race day". Co-creation requires our full concentration; the participants must be rested and have a desire to participate in the workshop and feel good. Co-creation cannot be forced, and it should not lead to cramping. Therefore, it should be used carefully.
6. **Mistakes planning the race**: These include aiming to reach goals too quickly, tackling the first kilometres too fast and using comparative data as a guide instead of finding one's own rhythm. The sustainable implementation of co-creation requires a sufficiently long time horizon—it needs time and space, especially at the beginning—and the people in the organization have to find out for themselves what the best opportunities to work with co-creation are.
7. **Nutritional mistakes:** "Don't rely on so-called sports nutrition, either in training or in competition". In sport, as in co-creation, there is no need for vitamin injections, nor does anything grow without nutrients. The right amount of attention and a reasonable amount of available resources help us to reach our goal even over long distances.

Managers are often performance-driven sprinters looking for quick wins. A long run requires the patience to deal with the planning and then engage in the process. Sprinters do not find this easy. Sprinters see a target, which is at most 100 m away, and run towards it. When introducing co-creation, it can therefore be advisable to include visible intermediate stages.

Likewise, it should be clear to all participants at the beginning of the journey that the "path is forged by walking". This requires stages in which to pause and consider how to proceed. Running blindly will quickly tire out everyone involved.

In other words, the company needs a culture of persistence and positive tenacity. In order to accomplish this, co-creation should become part of the culture that employees identify with and are proud of.

10.2.8 Phase 8: Anchor Co-creation in Corporate Culture

Now comes the final step in the eight-phase model. Co-creation must first become the way in which complex problems are solved, before one can speak of the company having a co-creation culture. Change does not happen by itself. Values and standards need to be aligned with the new vision and staff behaviour should ensure seamless alignment. The employees need to support co-creation. Regular assessments and discussions of the progress being made help to consolidate change.

It is not self-evident that co-creation will be welcomed by managers and employees under all circumstances. Depending on whether the corporate culture is easier or more difficult to co-create, the transformation process may take more or less time.

Essentially, there are two framework conditions. On the one hand, the leadership culture, which manifests itself in processes and structures; on the other hand, the business model with its economic framework conditions.

The greater the degree of economic independence enjoyed by the entire organization and the individual units from external conditions, and the more agile the understanding of leadership with flat hierarchies, the faster the transformation process towards more co-creation can take place.

Why do these factors affect the speed of change (Fig. 10.4)?

10.2.8.1 Leadership (Processes and Structures)

Leadership processes and structures influence the managers' scope for action. The following factors need to be taken into account:

Fig. 10.4 Speed of transformation

To what extent is the understanding of leadership traditionally influenced by self-determination and decentralised responsibility? The longer it has been a tradition for decisions to be made at the very top and then run through the organization until they are executed, the greater the uncertainty among managers as to whether a shift towards co-creation, which inevitably requires decentralised decision-making responsibility, can be realised. Even at the highest level, managers oppose the change, saying things like: "We have always done it this way..." or "It may be like that in other companies, but it won't work here...".

The same consideration applies to the complexity of the hierarchy. With each level of hierarchy, the dependency on decisions increases and the possibility to engage in co-creation decreases. If this is to be changed, then either the number levels in the hierarchy have to be reduced or managers and employees have to be given the freedom to make decisions in co-creation. This transformation takes time.

In general, the question is: What decision-making scope do managers and employees have? Co-creation happens across interfaces. It is oriented towards the challenges to be solved and sometimes calls for unconventional solutions. These cannot be forced into existing vertical decision-making patterns. If they were to be considered in a traditional way, the hands of the participants in the co-creation workshops would be tied. Decisions have to be made and commitments entered into on the ground.

This does not exclude the possibility of consultation with "higher" officials to a certain extent. However, this must not lead to the co-creation of "partially binding solutions", along these lines: "We've realised that we should implement this measure in the organization. We've assigned our best people to the project and will meet again in two months to discuss the results and the way forward... Assuming, of course, that the divisional manager agrees with our approach". In this case, it becomes difficult to conduct motivating and engaging co-creation workshops.

An essential condition for anchoring co-creation in corporate culture is, therefore, the competence of the managers and employees involved in co-creation to make the necessary decisions and implement them in a binding manner. If this is not always possible, there is still the possibility of having the decision-makers themselves take part in the co-creation.

10.2.8.2 Economic Independence

Not only can leadership processes and authority create dependencies that influence co-creation opportunities, but economic factors also have an impact on the successful implementation of co-creation.

Basically, there should be an awareness that time is well invested in co-creation. In his book The Way to the Essential (Covey, 2007), Steven Covey distinguishes activities according to whether they are important or not important and urgent or not urgent.

On the level of important activities, things that are important and urgent can then be distinguished from those that are important but not urgent. Intuitively, one would say: "That's quite simple, always look at the important and urgent things".

The important and urgent things belong to the field of necessities: "This is where we steer, produce and apply our experience and judgement to many needs and challenges. If we ignore it, we will be buried under a mountain of obligations. But we must also recognise that many important matters become urgent only as a result of procrastination or a lack of planning and prevention".

By contrast, the important but not urgent things belong to the field of quality: "This is where we do our long-term planning, prevent foreseeable problems, promote the self-responsibility of others... The more time we spend in this field, the greater our capacity to act".

These two fields stand in an inverse relationship to each other. The more time is spent on quality, the smaller the field of necessities becomes. The less time one takes for the important things that are not yet urgent, the more the number of urgent necessities increases.

Does co-creation belong to the field of necessities or to the field of quality? The answer to this question is not easy and depends on the individual case. What can be said, however, is that the greater the economic pressure, the more difficult it becomes to find time for what is important.

When only what is necessary has priority, the organization begins to go round in circles. It becomes a fire brigade: always trying to put out the fires that are currently burning. Co-creation should help to make a breakthrough here, taking control, instead of merely reacting to external constraints. When this is accomplished, managers and employees regain their self-efficacy. They realise that they can influence things and are not only driven by external forces. This is motivating and can be the beginning of an upward spiral.

But what if there are no resources to even start? What if the organization is stretched so thin that breaking out seems impossible? Resources are usually understood in terms of time and money. These are limited and often seem to be given and can hardly be influenced. However, one important resource often gets pushed into the background: the motivation and enthusiasm of the people in the company.

If people can be made enthusiastic about the change, they will make it happen and, some way or another, find the time to start. Just like that, the spell is broken. If people then invest in the important things with serious dedication, if there is commitment and trust grows, then the economic figures can also soon improve.

The more difficult the framework conditions are, the more important it is that people in the organizations develop confidence in co-creation. This is nothing other than giving them the opportunity to develop trust in their colleagues, the leadership and the whole organization.

Example

Some time ago, I helped guide a department with a total of 30 employees through a one-and-a-half-day co-creation workshop. The initial situation was judged critically by the head of department. He perceived little togetherness,

(continued)

and there were many complaints about all kinds of things. This is exactly how the workshop felt at the beginning: people standing around in groups with their arms folded. But the longer the workshop went on, the more the participants opened up. Already by the evening of the first half-day, the mood was pretty good, and there was something like hope that maybe everything would turn out for the better after all.

At the end of the workshop, after many open and direct discussions, there were substantive results posted on the walls. The projects were clearly defined, responsibilities assigned and the head of department gave a clear commitment to wholeheartedly support the process that had been started. The mood at this point was in no way comparable to the mood at the start.

In the final round, I asked the participants how they would feel on the drive home. All of them found the session very good: they got to know their colleagues anew and felt that the measures adopted went in the right direction. The fly in the ointment was some of the closing words, which said more or less the same thing: "I thought it was very good here and I'm enthusiastic about the results, but I don't know if we will really implement it". Even though everything was in their hands, they were still doubting themselves.

Overcoming doubt in one's own team is the key to success in co-creation. Co-creation is something very valuable, requiring attention, seriousness, protection and every available means of support. Especially at the beginning, it is important to make sure that it is handled with the appropriate care. However, once co-creation starts to take off, it has the potential to transform a company.

The Co-creation Coach and Process Facilitator

11

Abstract

The aim of co-creation is to connect people to a shared consciousness so that they can let the future emerge. Mindset, values and principles are the basic attitudes and assumptions upon which co-creation is based. A co-creation coach is a professional who helps guide the co-creation process. Co-creation coaches can be independent consultants or, if the requisite knowledge has already been brought into the company, an employee of the organization. Whether in collectively solving concrete problems or in corporate transformation, co-creation requires support. The typical stumbling blocks are listed and some ideas are given of how to overcome them.

Keywords

Coach · Consultant · Facilitator · Moderator · Problem-solving

Whether in collectively solving concrete problems or in corporate transformation, co-creation requires support. A co-creation coach is a professional who helps guide the co-creation process. Co-creation coaches can be independent consultants or, if the requisite knowledge has already been brought into the company, an employee of the organization.

The final chapter describes their role in the co-creation process. Furthermore the typical stumbling blocks are listed and some ideas are given of how to overcome them.

G. Michalik, *Co-Creation Mindset*, Management for Professionals,
https://doi.org/10.1007/978-3-031-21191-1_11

11.1 The Role and Attitude of the Co-creation Coach

Co-creation coaches accompany both micro- and macro-level processes. At the micro level, they lead co-creation workshops; at the macro level, they accompany the organization in developing a co-creation culture.

In order to be able to carry out this task professionally, the co-creation coach should have a sound training in and sufficient experience with co-creation. Ideally, the coach is certified by "cocreation" (www.cocreation.com). The certification ensures that the necessary knowledge has been acquired, that sufficient practical experience has been gained and that the coach is constantly keeping his knowledge up to date.

At the beginning of this chapter, the different transformation formats were introduced: the one-day co-creation workshop, the one-hour quick format "CC sixty", virtual co-creation, co-creation in coaching and co-creation leadership.

In the different formats in which co-creation is carried out, the coach needs to master both the methodological knowledge specific to these formats—coaching knowledge, virtual working, management conversations—and knowledge of the specifics of co-creation facilitation. The importance of the role of facilitation is discussed in this section.

Can the co-creation process be self-directed, or does it need guidance? If the conclusion is that it needs guidance, the next question is then whether it should be internal or external and what form the role of the coach should take.

How can the importance of coaching be assessed? The importance of guidance depends on what is to be achieved. Co-creation thrives on people connecting to create a shared consciousness from which the future can emerge. This means that in order to achieve the content-related goals of co-creation, the participants need a certain inner attitude.

The coach's role could therefore be primarily understood as providing support to the inner attitude of the participants. He can achieve this by exemplifying it himself, representing the mindset, attitude and principles described at the beginning. In this case, the coach takes on the role of a role model. His task is to make sure that the participants are connected to each other.

How can the coach tell that the participants are connected?

- The participants bring in issues to serve the bigger picture. They have been sensitised not to take up too much space with their own issues.
- For the duration of the co-creation, the participants agree to be part of a whole, to put their own needs aside and to pay attention to what serves the common goal.
- The participants make sure to be an active part of the group. Withdrawal and passivity create insecurity and do not improve the overall result.
- The participants develop an increasing identification with success and feel responsible for the co-creation producing a result.
- The participants themselves increasingly take on the role of a facilitator. They begin to summarise results independently, bring the process to life and address disturbances.

At the beginning, the coach is responsible for ensuring this. He is allowed to question partial results and directly address disturbances. However, the coach's goal is to increasingly leave these tasks to the group.

This also answers the question of whether or not a coach is needed. For a group that is inexperienced in co-creation, it is advisable to work with a coach. With time, however, they should be able to adopt the coach's attitude and thus replace him.

The same applies when a group meets for the first time in a new configuration, if they have not yet gone through the "Connect" process with each other. Even then, it is advisable to have a coach present. His role is to be neutral, and he enables all the participants to fully engage in their role as participants, without having to reflect on the process at the same time.

What attitude should the facilitator adopt? This point can be illustrated by the following dialogue between a strategy consultant (Steffen) and a co-creation coach (Clemens). Steffen is very experienced in helping senior executives with the strategic realignment of companies. Steffen learned about co-creation and invited Clemens to work on a commission. The group is to be led through co-creation to a joint plan of action.

Example

Steffen is enthusiastic about the mindset and method of co-creation and wants to learn co-creation himself. Together with Clemens, he conducts the workshops and thus gets his thoughts in order. The client is Michael, the CEO of a consumer goods company. The participants in the co-creation workshops are the extended management circle, which is working on six different topics in groups of four to six people. During the break in the third co-creation workshop, the following dialogue takes place between the two coaches:

Clemens: Well, what did you think of the morning of our third session?

Steffen: Brilliant! I now see how things connect with each other.

Clemens: Is that what you just wrote down there?

Steffen: Yes, exactly. Look, in the first session, the issue was how the company is perceived externally, which has a lot to do with how they present themselves. In the second session, the main topic was what role the leadership plays in this. And today we see that in the third session, the employees themselves are the main focus of the analysis.

Clemens: Interesting. What are you going to do with this knowledge?

Steffen: I suspect that a pattern is emerging here of how, starting with the leadership, internal and external interface issues are not dealt with and are carried through this extended leadership circle to the stakeholders.

Clemens: That may well be. So now that you have realised this, how do you plan to deal with it?

(continued)

Steffen: I think we should show this to Michael before the big final workshop with all the participants.

Clemens: Hmm, I see your point. What do you think would happen next?

Steffen: Well, Michael would think about how we could address the problem in the final workshop.

Clemens: Knowing him, he would certainly do that. But then what about the participants?

Steffen: Hmm... What do you mean?

Clemens: What I am getting at is that Michael has given his people the task of finding co-creative solutions for five topics. They will have come up with these solutions by then and will present them. Michael would then introduce his own findings from the overall process and suggest the next steps in a more or less binding way. If you were one of the participants, what would that make you think?

Steffen: Good question! I would probably think: "Aha! Up until this point, I was being asked my opinion, but now that it is time to take a decision, the boss intervenes and says how things will go".

Clemens: How would you feel about it on the emotional level?

Steffen: Probably not so great. I guess I would be disappointed, because I thought things would be different from now on...

Clemens: I suspect so too. At the same time, your observation is very valuable. What else could we do with it?

Steffen: We could certainly share our observation with Michael and suggest that we share it with the whole group, to see what they think.

Clemens: I think that is a good idea. What would our role be then, in contrast to the other approach?

Steffen: We would focus entirely on the process and leave the responsibility with the group.

Clemens: Yes, and at the same time we would not close our eyes to the facts like blind moderating robots. We would address them. What do you think that would mean for the overall dynamics?

Steffen: The participants would probably realise exactly that. They would realise the responsibility that they are expected to take on. Hence, they would also see themselves as having even more responsibility and then consider together how they could break through this collective pattern of action.

Clemens: And how would Michael feel about that?

Steffen: Well, I think he would be very happy, after some initial reluctance, because that was his original idea: to mobilise his extended leadership circle and get them to take responsibility.

Coaches have very different talents. Some are very good at building rapport with the participants and keeping the group together. Others have a talent for keeping the process going and thus providing security. My own strength is paying attention to the inner logic of what is happening in the moment. But there are other important areas, such as the overall goal. How does what is happening in the moment and what should be achieved in principle fit together? Unfortunately, it is not always possible to pay attention to all the levels at the same time. Therefore, it can be helpful to conduct the facilitation along with a partner, especially when the skills of the facilitators complement each other well, as in the example of Steffen and Clemens.

What does the coach have to pay attention to during co-creation? This is explained below using the example of the co-creation workshop.

The coaching of co-creation workshops is oriented towards the co-creation mindset and the situational requirements of the co-creation process. The following section is not intended to be a manual for co-creation coaches. The training of a co-creation coach is more comprehensive and diverse than could be presented in this brief account. Rather, the aim here is to give an impression of what the critical phases are that require special attention from someone providing guidance.

11.1.1 Establish Connection

At the beginning of the collaboration, the participants connect in the "Connect" phase. The coach's task is to help guide this process with empathy. This phase calls for special attention. The connection between the participants is one of the central success factors for the rest of the process. The coach leads the group in establishing a connection. At the same time, the team must also realise very quickly that it is they who are responsible for maintaining this connection. In other words, the coach has to take the lead at the beginning and, at the same time, start to let go in order to hold the group accountable.

As a rule, the participants have not yet taken part in a co-creation workshop and are now waiting with anticipation. The coach should use this knowledge as an opportunity to shape his opening accordingly. For example, he could start like this: "As far as I know, this is the first time that you are participating in a co-creation workshop. I can imagine that you are wondering what will be different here as compared to other workshops".

With this opening, the coach grabs the participants' attention and can then explain the process and specifics of co-creation. He should point out that it is best for the participants to make their own judgement. In this way, he can keep things short. Nevertheless, he should give sufficient orientation concerning the subsequent course of the workshop.

The coach now acts as a role model. At the beginning of the workshop, the participants look for clues as to what the "modus operandi" is. They need signals that they can use to orient their own behaviour. The coach can provide these signals by responding to the participants and addressing what they perceive. He should make his own feelings transparent, and thus exercise a significant influence on the openness and receptiveness of the group.

Example

The following experience illustrates how the coach can contribute to a stronger connection within the group by setting an example. A few years ago I was invited to facilitate a client's team workshop. I knew from previous coaching that it was a group of technically trained men with quite a macho demeanour. This was not surprising, as their supervisor cultivated exactly this culture. At the same time, he had to realise that it was quite difficult to accomplish the tasks at hand together.

The team workshop took place in the rustic back room of an inn. When I arrived, I found the head of department reading a newspaper at the regulars' table. This did not change with the arrival of his staff. While I was setting up the room, the men gradually congregated with their newspapers at the large oval table.

My question at that moment was: "How do I break the ice?" Acting mainly on instinct, I sat down at the table with them and suggested that although they had been working together for some time, it would be helpful at the beginning of this important day if they got to know each other a little better. Perhaps they could also present the sides of themselves that the others knew less about: their values, where they get support from, their life goals, etc.

To give them an idea of what I meant, I started with myself and told them about the things that are important to me. I took my time and spoke honestly about myself.

The participants followed suit. They had been given the space by the coach to share something about themselves with their colleagues, which was simply not possible in the macho culture that had been in place so far. This round with seven people lasted 90 min. It was not planned this way, but at the same time, it was the key to success. The people in the team had connected with each other and had laid the foundation for solving the really difficult issues constructively with each other over the course of the day.

In co-creation, this space between people does not arise by chance. It is part of the process. The coach has to be aware of the importance of this start for the participants and of the fact that, at this point, it shapes the way in which people will work together.

11.1.2 Goal Definition

The common goal is part of the connection established in "Connect" (Fig. 11.1). In co-creation, people do not connect for the sake of connecting; they connect to achieve something together. The coach therefore knows how important it is for success that the team be able to define a goal by means of which they can briefly and clearly express what they are aiming for. There are two types of goals: goals that are

Fig. 11.1 Reaching connection through the goal

set by the group and goals that are given. The goals to be set are addressed at the beginning of the first round of co-creation, while the given goals are derived from the first round of co-creation and worked on in the second round.

For the coach, this results in two different tasks. In the first round of co-creation, the coach helps the group to define and formulate a goal. In the second round of co-creation, he helps the group to understand and accept a given goal.

11.1.2.1 First Round of Co-creation: Determining the Common Goal

What are the challenges for the coach in helping the group to set a goal in the first round of co-creation?

Imagine the following situation: the board decides to work on three strategic topics using the co-creation method. For this purpose, the members of the board assign themselves to the three topics. In addition, they invite the responsible individuals and specialists from the relevant areas to co-creation workshops. One day is planned for each workshop. Dates are set and electronic invitations are sent out. The workshops will begin in 2 months. They should start the day before in the late afternoon, so that the "Connect" phase can begin then. The invitation reads: "Co-Creation Workshop: Employee Engagement. Start: Thursday, 4 p.m. End: Friday, 5 p.m. Lead: Dr Georg Michalik from CoCreative. Seven participants".

Like this, everything is organised, and everyone has an idea of what it is all about when the invitation is issued. The situation is completely different on the day of the workshop. Two months have passed, and we no longer remember exactly what the background to the topic "employee engagement" actually was. Moreover, the invited specialists were not present at the original discussion.

How do the workshop participants now prepare for the event? They will think about the topic again. They will think about why the topic of employee engagement is important and what should be achieved with co-creation.

The perspectives of the participants are quite different. The situation is reminiscent of the parable of the blind men and the elephant. A group of blind men—or men in complete darkness—examine an elephant to understand what kind of an animal it is. Each of them feels a different part of the elephant, and so for one person the elephant is a pillar (leg), for the one who feels the trunk it is a branch, the one who feels the ear thinks it is a fan, and so on.

The diversity of perspectives on the topic is reflected in the diversity of ideas about what the goal should be on the day of the workshop. The sales director would like to see more dynamism and conviction among the employees. The quality manager is interested in employees who stick to processes. The human resources manager and her employee engagement officer can prove that the leadership performance measured in the last employee survey is below the benchmark for comparable companies. She sees management as being primarily responsible for this. At the beginning of the workshop, the participants' ideas about what should be achieved with co-creation are still completely different.

Something else stands out: when the participants think about possible goals, they are guided by the deficits that they perceive in the organization. Since there are numerous deficits, the proposed goals are very different.

The task for the coach is to create transparency among the participants as to how they arrived at their various goals. This transparency is the prerequisite for finding a common goal that goes beyond mere deficits.

Confronted by the coach with their similar thought processes and different results, the participants may react with surprise. This can be the beginning of a learning process that is important for the effectiveness of the group. The participants have the opportunity to realise how their professionally shaped views can stand in the way of finding a common, holistic solution. They can also recognise that deriving goals from individual perceptions of deficits can lead to very different approaches to solutions. It may even lead to goals that contradict each other. Finally, they can also recognise how a conflict could have arisen if they had not been aware of the process.

It is the coach's task to help guide the processes on the content level, as well as on the team level, and to lead them to joint reflection. In order to do so, the coach needs a sure instinct and the ability to take a stand at the right moment. At the same time, he must sense when it is time to take himself out of the process again, in order to give the group the opportunity to develop its self-efficacy.

11.1.2.2 Second Round of Co-creation: Bringing About Identification with the Goal

To put this in perspective, in Sect. 7.1.1.5, we showed how the different levels of co-creation are interlinked. There, we explained that the basic strategic goals from the first round, which are set by the leadership, become operational goals in the second round, which are to be worked on by the next group. This can be configured in such a way that it follows the 80:20 rule. New people are brought into the co-creation in a ratio of 4:1 (see Sect. 10.2.2).

The new participants now have to find their way around co-creation for the first time. They also go through the complete eight-step process. In the beginning, they have to adopt an already-given goal as their own goal for co-creation and identify with it.

In order for the participants in the second round to be able to do this, they must first of all understand the background and the history so far. The two or three representatives present from the first round are responsible for the transfer of knowledge to the second round. The coach should ensure that the transfer of knowledge, mission and responsibility to the second round is done in such a way that the participants are ready to work and motivated to take on the task.

The process that the coach helps guide is the same as in the first round. The participants should network and get to know each other on a personal level. They should also be able to make plausible why the goal that has been given is important to them as a group. This includes arriving at inner clarity about what added value everyone sees for themselves if they pursue this goal together.

If adjustments are necessary from the point of view of the second group, these are negotiated with the participants from the first round. They must be authorised to make such adjustments. If there is doubt, this may mean that they have to consult the first-round group.

11.1.3 Formulations

Naming things in a way that everyone agrees with is a prerequisite for completing the steps of co-creation. Often the participants agree about how something is and yet find it difficult to articulate this insight in terms of a shared vocabulary. The goal formulation, the description of the situation or a field of action can lead to disproportionately long discussions. Then, there is a struggle over the wording, even though there is no disagreement about the content.

Now, one could argue that these discussions are important for arriving at real clarity. Up to a point, this is true. Especially at the beginning of this process of clarification, views become obvious that otherwise would not have been clear. Experience shows, however, that over time the groups start to go round in circles and to doubt themselves. The coach has to sense very carefully where the group stands and what it still needs. He is responsible for time and energy management, and he knows that time and energy are limited. A result should be achieved by the evening of the day of the workshop. To achieve this, it is indispensable that a certain pace be maintained despite all the joys of reflection.

If the team reaches an impasse, it is the coach's task to lead the group out of it. How can he do this?

One possibility is to leave the result as a "working title" and come back to it later. If a co-creation workshop begins the day before and the goal formulation can still be completed in the evening, then this procedure is recommended. The participants can sleep on the formulation and look at it again the next morning. In all other cases, postponing the decision until later is not recommended. In co-creation, each step builds on the previous one. If a step has not been completed, it is difficult to work on the next steps.

Instead, a rather unorthodox intervention is recommended. We have had good experiences with putting the discussion at hand into words and coming up with a proposal ourselves. In doing so, we may or may not hit the nail on the head, but whether the proposal was a hit or a miss is not important. For the group, the formulation from a "neutral" perspective is an opportunity for reflection. They hear their ideas presented in other words. This gives the participants a new perspective on the formulation, and they can judge more accurately from a distance what they like or do not like about it.

If the coach notices that there is a position that appears again and again, but has no chance of gaining a majority, then he can formulate this position precisely, in the form of a "paradoxical intervention". In this way, he leads the group to a decision. Through the coach's formulation, it becomes clear to the participants what this would mean, and the group can now decide whether they want it or not.

For the coach, intervening with his own formulation is not always easy. First of all, he must understand the content at issue—otherwise he will lose credibility. Moreover, coaches who see themselves entirely as process facilitators are reluctant to formulate their own proposals. Finally, if a coach's proposal bombs, this can damage his self-esteem. Therefore, the coach must be very aware of when and for what reason he himself resorts to this means of facilitation.

11.1.4 Energy and Time Management

In order for a group to successfully conduct and complete a co-creation workshop, it must have sufficient time and energy. The role of the coach as process facilitator is to manage the available energy and time well.

One could also call a coach an "energy manager". In the energy field, the individuals brought together into a whole develop energy. What do individuals need in order to engage in this and to remain in this "fusion"? They need to trust that they are in a field that is safe for them, that they can fully engage in the team dynamic without being hurt emotionally or reputationally. The role of the energy manager is to create an energy field in which such a connection is possible. There will always be situations where the sensitivities of individual group members will cause them or others to want to leave the group. The task of the energy manager is to intervene in a supportive way for as long as the group is not yet able to regulate this on its own.

Here are some situations that we encounter again and again in our co-creation workshops and how our energy management reacts to them.

11.1.4.1 Distraction Through Examples

Examples help us to understand. They illustrate—they are pictorial and activate different brain regions. Examples given by the participants can help us to understand the situation better. The content loses its abstractness and become more tangible. Describing an emotionally experienced event helps to deepen the bond within the group.

At the same time, great attention and tact is needed from the coach when examples are brought in, because there is a danger that they can interrupt the flow of collective thinking. This can be useful, but it is not necessarily so. In any case, it entails an investment of energy. The coach as energy manager has to decide at that moment whether the group is still fresh enough and whether there is still enough time to engage in a brief excursion into an individual's experiential world.

It is also important to remember that examples reveal the character of the person giving the example. Self-revelation can be useful to strengthen the shared emotional experience. However, it should not be used for the mental hygiene of individuals. This is because co-creation is about the common journey and not about processing historical events experienced by individuals.

Examples, through their visual strength, have the power to lead the group on a different path than the one taken. However, this should be a group decision and not the decision of strong individuals. Here, the facilitator must question whether the group is ready for this and considers it purposeful to embark on this journey.

Finally, the challenge to the coach is to prevent the group from being "kidnapped" to solve partial problems on an ad hoc basis: "Since everyone is in the room right now and this should have been discussed a long time ago anyway, I would like to give the following example..." Such statements are generally considered positive. After all, in the perception of the participants it is about something important. The workshop is being used for something productive. You can solve an old problem that should have been discussed a long time ago. However, the group also strays from the main issue. The facilitator should intervene here and lead the team back to the topic at hand.

It can also be helpful to set some rules for the open discussion from the beginning. One could be: "We keep practical examples to a minimum, keep them short and concise, and come back to the topic at hand immediately".

11.1.4.2 Dwelling Too Long in Discussions

In the final rounds of the co-creation workshops, we often receive the feedback that the quality of the discussion was exceptional: "We should discuss at such a high level much more often". The participants feel that this is something different than usual. It does them good to talk openly like this and have valuable conversations.

Fig. 11.2 Managing time with the time-timer

This is very understandable and also feels good for the coach. After all, we coaches want to encourage the participants to have an open exchange. Once we have achieved this, it can be difficult for us to interrupt it again. And yet one of our most important tasks is to do just that, because of our role as energy managers.

Each of the eight steps of the co-creation process is demanding in itself and requires the full attention of the participants. Nothing is more demotivating than when the "air goes out" in the decisive phase. Imagine that thanks to your support the group has ingenious ideas for implementation. However, it took all their energy to get to that point. Then, in the "Do" phase, when it comes to distributing the implementation roles and laying out the next steps, there is neither time nor energy left. This should not happen, because even the last step requires the full concentration and willpower of all those involved, in order to commit themselves and make sustainable agreements.

The same applies to all upstream process steps. It is therefore the coach's task to follow the discussions, in order to be able to judge at any given time whether the group is still focused on the current phase or is about to drift away. In the latter case, it is important to interrupt with understanding and appreciation, in order to bring the goal back into focus. This may not always be easy for a relationship-oriented coach, but in the end the participants are often thankful. A helpful tool for this is the time-timer (Fig. 11.2).

You set the available time budget and the time-timer beeps when the time is up. In this way, the coach himself does not interrupt, but only makes the time-timer heard.

Summary

This book sought to provide clarity about what is meant by co-creation and how it is applied. It described an eight-step process for implementing co-creation and showed how the whole organization can move towards a culture and practice of co-creation. It outlined how co-creation is different from other forms of collaboration, as a different way of looking at how people work together.

In this summary, we want to bring together the main insights of each chapter.

Chapter 1: Introduction

The introduction of this book highlights the importance of co-creation and what is so different in co-creation compared to other collaboration forms.

Chapter 2: Co-creation

People feel connected to each other in virtue of the degree of commonality they feel. If emotional closeness develops between actors, cross-sectoral thinking, feeling and acting become possible.

The cognitive abilities and sensations of the participants network with each other. This opens up another dimension of mental possibilities for coping with complexity. People then begin to think relationally, in terms of relationships. We call this state "co-creation".

Co-creation can be consciously brought about and used to enable the future-oriented transformation of organizations. The involvement of employees is a necessary condition for shaping the future. Only by connecting the minds, hearts and wills of people in organizations will it be possible to identify or find forward-looking solutions.

While co-creation seeks to establish a connection between the participants and the goals right at the beginning and makes it a prerequisite of the process, traditional methods are mostly defined by the definition of an abstract goal. It remains unclear what connection each of the participants has to this goal, how the participants relate to each other and what connects them on a human level.

Chapter 3: The Basic Assumptions of Co-creation

Chapter 3 describes the basic assumptions underlying co-creation. This is its mindset, the values of co-creation and its principles. Mindset, values and principles create the common denominator of how co-creation should be lived. They can be

G. Michalik, *Co-Creation Mindset*, Management for Professionals,
https://doi.org/10.1007/978-3-031-21191-1

referred to and thus create clarity as to what belongs to co-creation and what does not. The chapter also creates an understanding of the spirit of co-creation.

Chapter 4: The Potentialum Organizational Model

Potentialum is an organizational model that enables a shared perspective on the company. The reason for this is that the involvement of all the employees in the transformation of the company makes a common language about the future viability of their organization necessary.

Chapter 5: Structure of the Potentialum Model

As an analytical tool, Potentialum can help an organization to hold a mirror up to itself. If improvements are to be achieved, then this can only succeed if the underlying patterns are recognised, addressed and solved throughout the company.

The results of the analysis can be used to agree on the way forward. In the process of co-creation, the resulting map is an important point of orientation for the choice and implementation of the fields of action.

With the help of Potentialum, the organization can take action in many places at the same time and in a coordinated way: (1) co-creation at the macro level, using the Potentialum map to identify fields of action, and (2) co-creation at many different micro levels, using root-cause analysis in co-creation workshops. The success achieved can be continuously checked through the Potentialum measurement and possibly corrected by means of additional measures.

Chapters 6 and 7: The Co-creation Process: Phases and Steps

The co-creation process is structured systematically. It consists of four phases with a total of eight steps. It describes a structured procedure for successfully conducting co-creation workshops.

Phase 1: Connecting

- Step 1—"Connect" at the start of the process: connect people and ideas in relation to the goal
- Step 8—"Connect" at the end of the process: connect people for implementation

Phase 2: Understanding

- Step 2—"Discover": discover the facts
- Step 3—"Explore": understand the background
- Step 4—"Share": share the conclusions

Phase 3: Deciding

- Step 5—"Agree": decide

Phase 4: Implementing

- Step 6—"Create": create solutions
- Step 7—"Do": implement solutions
- Step 8—"Connect": reflecting collaboration

Co-creation puts "connection" before the result. This is because the results are the goal of the connection, the connection is not the goal of the results. Moreover, when working together, connection takes place through a shared process: the inner process that people experience for themselves when solving problems can now be experienced by everyone on the outside. The participants thus feel familiar with the process from the beginning, and everyone can engage in the process together.

Chapter 8: Transformation of the Organization

Transformation begins with the basic framework conditions. This refers to the application-oriented aspects of co-creation, which are primarily: space, available time and the possible forms of co-creation.

Co-creation creates space in which people can move. This means not only the physical environment, but also the space between people. In co-creation, three-dimensional thinking takes place. Within space, CREATE is the projection surface for the group members' thoughts. CREATE is a terminal that connects three elements: space, time and thinking together.

There are different forms of co-creation, depending on how much time is available. From a single hour to a two-day workshop, co-creation offers a range of different formats.

Another distinguishing feature is the roles of the participants. Co-creation can be used as a workshop among employees, as a leadership tool, as a coaching tool or even virtually.

With a focus on organizational development, co-creation can even make it possible to transform the company towards greater sustainability.

Chapter 9: Co-creation and the Role of Leadership

Transformation requires the people in the organization. They have to take the initiative. First and foremost, senior management (as the client) and the HR department (as the project leader), but also managers, employees and internal and external experts (as project collaborators) are jointly responsible for shaping the co-creation transformation.

Employees and managers make up by far the largest group in the company. Their commitment makes the difference between successful and unsuccessful transformation projects.

For the transformation to succeed, there should be a joint "co-creation" initiative involving all employees. Managers have an essential role to play as role models. But today the question still arises whether leadership really wants to involve employees in the transformation via an eye-to-eye engagement.

This is also evident in leadership development as it is practised today. As a rule, it does not encourage the transformation to a culture of co-creation, but rather creates a "two-tier society" between management and staff.

When linear processes in organizational development reach their limits, co-creation can be the next step. Co-creation is broad, works at interfaces and connects people completely independently of hierarchies. Results emerge from the spontaneously created connection, not from rigid processes. In order to do this, individuals learn to trust each other and to function as a whole. People have to be prepared for this and guided in the process.

Chapter 10: Co-creation and Organizational Development

The evolution of companies is a joint learning process in which people want to be picked up and taken along. As a path of transformation, co-creation is mostly chosen by hierarchically structured companies. Their aim is to develop their organization in such a way that they can cope more safely with the challenges of the VUCA world. This book describes an eight-step path of organizational development for this purpose. Co-creation in organizational design uses Kotter's "leading change" model and translates the eight-step process to transformation through co-creation:

1. With the leadership team, recognise the importance of co-creation for the organization.
2. Let a leadership coalition become the promoter of co-creation.
3. Develop a vision of co-creation for the organization.
4. Communicate the co-creation vision to staff.
5. Remove obstacles to co-creation.
6. Set short-term goals to be achieved in the transformation.
7. Consolidate transformation successes.
8. Anchor co-creation in the corporate culture.

Chapter 11: The Co-creation Coach and Process Facilitator

Whether in the collective solving of concrete problems or in corporate transformation: co-creation needs support. The co-creation coach is the professional guide for the co-creation process. The role of the coach is primarily to represent the mindset, the attitude and the principles of co-creation. In addition to his practical task as a facilitator, he is a role model for the participants.

In the process, the coach takes on another role, he is the "energy manager" of the group process. He asks himself what the individuals need, so that they can engage in the closeness of co-creation. They need the confidence to fully engage in the team dynamic, without being emotionally or reputationally harmed. The role of the coach is to create a space where such connection is possible.

Epilogue: Caught in the Dilemma

In closing, I would like to offer a personal assessment, which I have so far refrained from doing in the service of readability.

Co-creation is one possible answer to the dilemma we face at the beginning of the new millennium: Should we meet as friends or as enemies? Against all reason, we are observing a development in which the majority opts to perceive their fellow human beings as "enemies".

Hostility begins when we assert our own needs at the expense of others.

Unfortunately, we do not sufficiently recognise that the "enemy" is not to be found in other countries, in other worldviews, in capitalism or in communism. The "enemy" is neither the power-plant operator nor the environmentalist. Neither refugees, nor my boss, nor my neighbour are my "enemies".

I say "against all reason", because we do not sufficiently appreciate the fragility of the construct "life". If anything is hostile to us, it is the vastness in which our habitat has asserted itself for millions of years. The only life we know of exists on a thin film between boiling magma and the infinite, ice-cold expanse of space.

Why do we not recognise this to an extent that would move us to appropriate action?

My simple answer is: "We didn't have enough time". We are destroying our habitat faster than we can learn from the consequences. Our "social gene" has not had time to become sufficiently influential.

If you are now understandably wondering why I am working as a co-creative coach with this view of things and even writing a book on collaborative problem-solving, it is because I think we need to brave the seemingly inevitable. We should do things because they need to be done. Only then will we rise above the narrow-mindedness of cost-benefit thinking. "If I knew that the world would end tomorrow, I would plant a little apple tree today", Martin Luther is reported to have once said.

G. Michalik, *Co-Creation Mindset*, Management for Professionals,
https://doi.org/10.1007/978-3-031-21191-1

Do You Know the Prisoner's Dilemma?

"The prisoner's dilemma is a psychological experiment which, especially in the 1950s and 1960s, provided methodological access to issues of trust: two people are instructed to put themselves in the position of prisoners in a court case who are being questioned independently of each other about a crime they have presumably committed together and whose sentences mutually depend on whether they decide to confess or deny.[...] If they both deny it, they will receive comparatively light penalties. If only one confesses, he will go unpunished as a state witness and the other will receive the maximum penalty. If both confess, they receive a somewhat reduced sentence compared to the maximum penalty". (Spektrum, 2000).

The conclusion to be drawn from the prisoner's dilemma is: if I don't know that I can trust the other person, then I play it safe and ruthlessly do my own thing.

But there is hope, one that is immediate and immediately realisable:

> We have to cut the Gordian knot of the prisoner's dilemma.
> (Tchaikovsky, 2018)

The prisoner's dilemma experiment is based on one condition: "Prisoners [...] who are questioned independently of each other about an act that was presumably committed together". In the experiment, the prisoners are not allowed to communicate with each other, because if they did, the construct would collapse like a house of cards.

What we need to do is simple and obvious: let us communicate with each other across borders in such a way that we connect, that we accept each other's goals and that we then develop our common goal from this. This is why I wrote this book (Fig. B1).

Fig. B1 Cutting the Gordian Knot

The Author

Dr. Georg Michalik has set himself the goal of showing organizations ways in which they can develop their potential.

An organizational psychologist who studied in Mannheim and Zurich, he was a co-creator of change as head of "Learning and Development" in various global companies. Today, he helps guide companies in their transformation processes with the co-creation method he developed. His clients include multinationals, as well as SMEs and non-profit companies.

Born in Germany, he has lived near Zurich for many years.

www.cocreation.com
team@cocreation.com

G. Michalik, *Co-Creation Mindset*, Management for Professionals,
https://doi.org/10.1007/978-3-031-21191-1

References

Alas, R., & Sharifi, S. (2002). Organizational learning and resistance to change in Estonian companies. *Human Resource Development International, 5*(3), 313–331.

Barczynski, D. (2014). Interview with Gerhard Neumann, in: Coaching Magazin, 1/2014. https://www.coaching-magazin.de/portrait/interview-gerhard-neumann. Retrieved 6 May 2020.

Bass, B. M., & Aviolo, B. (1993). *Improving organizational effectiveness through transformational leadership*. Sage.

Behnsen, S. (n.d.) Problem-oriented or solution-oriented? In Psychoanalytische supervision. https://psychoanalytische-supervision.de/problemorientiert-oder-loesungsorientiert/. Accessed 6 May 2020.

Bendel, O. (2019). Industrie 4.0. In Gabler Wirtschaftslexikon. https://wirtschaftslexikon.gabler.de/definition/industrie-40-54032/version-368841. Accessed 6 May 2020.

Butz, A. (2012). Why do so many marathon runners collapse? In Trailrunning. 12.12.2012. www.trailrunning.de: https://www.trailrunning.de/magazin/andreas-butz/warum-brechen-so-viele-marathonlaeufer-ein/328. Retrieved 6 May 2020.

Covey, S. R. (2007). *The way to the essential*. Campus.

Covey, S. R. (2018). *The 7 ways to effectiveness: principles for personal and professional success*. Gabal.

think-new.com (17 January 2019). The megatrends of the world of work—what's in store for you in 2019. In www.denk-neu.com. https://www.denk-neu.com/megatrends-arbeitswelt-2019/. Retrieved 6 May 2020.

Donges, P. (2008). *Medialisation of political organizations*. VS Verlag.

Kooperation. (n.d.) In Duden. https://www.duden.de/rechtschreibung/Kooperation. Retrieved 6 May 2020.

Evsan, I. (n.d.) What is New Work? In newworkblog.de. From https://newworkblog.de/new-work/. Retrieved 6 May 2020.

FAZ. (2018). Siemens plans "evolution instead of revolution". 21.06.2018. In www.faz.net. https://www.faz.net/aktuell/wirtschaft/unternehmen/siemens-strukturiert-sich-um-evolution-statt-revolution-15652400.html. Accessed 6 May 2020.

Fleig, J. (2019). Was ist Change-Management oder Veränderungsmanagement, 09.07.2019. In Business Wissen. www.business-wissen.de. https://www.business-wissen.de/hb/was-ist-change-management-oder-veraenderungsmanagement/. Retrieved 6 May 2020.

Fokken, S. (2017). German companies get by with far fewer bosses, 04.04.2017. In Spiegel Job & Karriere. From https://www.spiegel.de/karriere/hans-boeckler-studie-deutschland-hat-weniger-chefs-pro-mitarbeiter-a-1141618.html. Retrieved 6 May 2020.

Franzen, G. (2018). *Relationality. Festschrift on the occasion of the 70th birthday of Matthias Sell*. Inita Verlag.

Geropp, B. (2019).FPG165—leadership span: How many employees can you lead? In www.mehr-fuehren.de. https://www.mehr-fuehren.de/fuehrungsspanne/. Retrieved 6 May 2020.

Godin, S. (2005). *The Big Moo* (p. 144). Penguin.

G. Michalik, *Co-Creation Mindset*, Management for Professionals,
https://doi.org/10.1007/978-3-031-21191-1

Grove, A. (1983). *High output management*. Random House.

Harari, Y. N. (2015). *A brief history of humanity*. Pantheon Verlag.

Hüther, G. (May 2016). School of the future. Kongresshaus Zurich.

Jork, M. (2019). Species-appropriate husbandry of humans. 99 ed. BoD—Books on Demand.

Kaplan, R. S., & Norton, D. P. (2008). *Balanced scorecard: Implementing strategies successfully*. Schäffer Poeschel.

Kaplan, R. S., & Norton, D. P. (2018). *Balanced scorecard: Implementing strategies successfully* (Special ed.). Schäffer Poeschel.

Kotter, J. P. (2011). *Leading change: How to successfully transform your organization in eight steps*. Verlag Franz Vahlen.

Kruse, P. (16 September 2013). Zukunft von Führung: kompetent, kollektiv oder katastrophal?. https://www.youtube.com/watch?v=cp_wts8DSl4. Retrieved 6 May 2020.

Kübler-Ross, E. (1972). *Interviews with dying people*. Kreuz-Verlag.

Laloux, F. (2015). *Reinventing Organizations. A guide to designing meaningful forms of collaboration*. Verlag Franz Vahlen.

Lewin, K. (1947). Frontiers in group dynamics. Concept, method and reality in social science. Social equilibria and social change. *Human Relations, 1*, 5–41.

Luhmann, N. (2000). *Organization and decision*. Westdeutscher Verlag.

Mautz, S. (2019). Google tried to prove managers don't matter. Instead, it discovered 10 traits of the very best ones, 05 Jun. 2019. In www.inc.com. https://www.inc.com/scott-mautz/google-tried-to-prove-managers-dont-matter-instead-they-discovered-10-traits-of-very-best-ones.html. Retrieved 6 May 2020.

McGregor, D. (2006). *The human side of enterprise*. McGraw-Hill.

McKinsey (2017). The people power of transformations, 10.02.2017. In www.mckinsey.com. From https://www.mckinsey.com/business-functions/organization/our-insights/the-people-power-of-transformations. Retrieved 6 May 2020.

Michalik, G. (2020). Potentialum. 22.02.2020, www.potentialum.ch. Retrieved 6 May 2020.

Oestereich, B. (2019). Workshop for collegial leadership. https://kollegiale-fuehrung.de/portfolio-item/taylorwanne/. Retrieved 6 May 2020.

Peffer, J. (1982). *Organizations and organization theory*. Pitman Publishing.

Pelz, W. (2016). Transformational leadership—state of research and implementation in practice. In C. V. Au (Ed.), *Effective and sustainable leadership approaches* (pp. 93–112). Springer Fachmedien.

Pelz, W. (2017). Implementation competence as a key competence for entrepreneurial personalities: A theoretical and empirical analysis. In C. V. Au (Ed.), *Leadership in the age of change and diversity* (pp. 103–123). Springer Fachmedien.

Pfläging, N. (2015). *Organising for complexity. How work comes alive again and high performance emerges*. Redline Verlag.

Pfläging, N. (2016). Don't panic: 7 thoughts on digital transformation. 16.04.2016. https://www.linkedin.com/pulse/dont-panic-7-thesen-zur-digitalen-transformation-niels-pflaeging/. Retrieved 6 May 2020.

Playroom. (n.d.) Playroom. https://playroom.rocks/de/. Accessed 6 May 2020.

Quality Services & Knowledge. (n.d.) 5 x Why | 5W Method | 5 Why | 5W Method. https://www.quality.de/lexikon/5xwarum/. Retrieved 6 May 2020.

Richter, I. (2016). Microsoft Germany moves into new corporate headquarters in Munich-Schwabing, 20.9.2016. In news.microsoft. https://news.microsoft.com/de-de/microsoft-deutschland-bezieht-neue-unternehmenszentrale-in-munchen-schwabing/. Accessed 6 May 2020.

Scharmer, C. O. (2009). *Theory U, leading from the future*. Carl-Auer-Systeme Verlag.

Scharmer, C. O. (n.d.) Bio. https://www.ottoscharmer.com/bio. Retrieved 6 May 2020.

Sinek, S. (2009). *Start with why*. Penguin Books.

Spectrum. (2000). *Encyclopaedia of psychology* (Keyword prisoner's dilemma and cooperation). Akademischer Verlag. https://www.spektrum.de/lexikon/psychologie/kooperation/8201. Retrieved 6 May 2020

Sullivan, W. (1972). The Einstein papers. A man of many parts. In New York Times, 29.03.1972. www.nytimes.com. https://www.nytimes.com/1972/03/29/archives/the-einstein-papers-a-man-of-many-parts-the-einstein-papers-man-of.html. Accessed 6 May 2020.

Taleb, N. N. (2014). *Antifragility: Guidance for a world we do not understand.* btb Verlag.

Tchaikovsky, A. (2018). *Children of time.* Heyne Verlag.

Ulrich, D. (2012). *HR from the outside in.* McGraw-Hill.

University of Exeter. (n.d.) The change curve. https://www.exeter.ac.uk/media/universityofexeter/humanresources/documents/learningdevelopment/the_change_curve.pdf. Accessed 6 May 2020.

Weerth, C. & Mecke, I.(2018). Kooperation. In Gabler Wirtschaftslexikon. https://wirtschaftslexikon.gabler.de/definition/kooperation-39490/version-262897. Retrieved 6 May 2020.

Wikipedia. (n.d.-a) Balanced scorecard. https://de.wikipedia.org/wiki/Balanced_Scorecard, as of 22.01.2020. Accessed 6 May 2020.

Wikipedia. (n.d.-b) Design thinking. https://de.wikipedia.org/wiki/Design_Thinking, as of 28.04.2020. Accessed 6 May 2020.

Wikipedia. (n.d.-c) Elisabeth Kübler-Ross. https://de.wikipedia.org/wiki/Elisabeth_Kübler-Ross, as of 15.03.2020. Accessed 6 May 2020.

Wikipedia. (n.d.-d) Scientific management. https://de.wikipedia.org/wiki/Scientific_Management, Accessed 19 Sept 2019, 6 May 2020.

Wikipedia. (n.d.-e) Silo. https://de.m.wikipedia.org/wiki/Silo, as at 01.02.2020. Accessed 6 May 2020.

Wikipedia. (n.d.-f) Spatial awareness. https://de.wikipedia.org/wiki/Räumliches_Vorstellungsvermögen. Accessed 13 Feb 2019, 6 May 2020.

Wikipedia. (n.d.-g) VUCA. https://de.wikipedia.org/wiki/VUCA, as of 06.01.2020. Accessed 6 May 2020.

Wirtschaftslexikon24. (n.d.) Decision theory. In Wirtschaftslexion24.com. http://www.wirtschaftslexikon24.com/d/entscheidungstheorie/entscheidungstheorie.htm. Retrieved 6 May 2020.

Withmore, S. J. (1992). *Coaching for performance: The principles and practice of coaching and leadership.* Nicholas Brealey.

www.welt.de. (n.d.) Malaysia airlines topic. https://www.welt.de/themen/malaysia-airlines/. Accessed 6 May 2020.

Index

G. Michalik, *Co-Creation Mindset*, Management for Professionals,
https://doi.org/10.1007/978-3-031-21191-1

The manufacturer's authorised representative in the EU is Springer Nature Customer Service Centre GmbH, Europaplatz 3, 69115 Heidelberg, Germany. If you have any concerns regarding our products, please contact ProductSafety@springernature.com

Printed and bound by CPI Group (UK) Ltd, Croydon, CR0 4YY
30/09/2026
02225244-0002